W9-BWQ-417

HARE AND CRITICS

HARE
AND CRITICS

–

Essays on
Moral Thinking

–

EDITED BY
Douglas Seanor & N. Fotion

WITH COMMENTS BY
R. M. Hare

CLARENDON PRESS · OXFORD
1988

Oxford University Press, Walton Street, Oxford OX2 6DP
Oxford New York Toronto
Delhi Bombay Calcutta Madras Karachi
Petaling Jaya Singapore Hong Kong Tokyo
Nairobi Dar es Salaam Cape Town
Melbourne Auckland
and associated companies in
Berlin Ibadan

Oxford is a trade mark of Oxford University Press

Published in the United States
by Oxford University Press, New York

British Library Cataloguing in Publication Data
Hare and critics: essays on moral thinking.
1. Ethics. Hare, R. M. (Richard Mervyn),
1919–. Critical studies
I. Seanor, Douglas   II. Fotion, N.
(Nicholas) III. Hare, R. M. (Richard
Mervyn), 1919–
170'.92'4
ISBN 0–19–824780–X

Library of Congress Cataloging in Publication Data
Data available

Set by Cambrian Typesetters, Frimley, Surrey
Printed and bound in Great Britain by
Biddles Ltd, Guildford and King's Lynn

PREFACE

THESE essay discuss the ideas of R. M. Hare as they are presented in *Moral Thinking*.[1] Because the volume is intended to be about *Moral Thinking*, the contributions are from writers whose main interest is in the topics there discussed, and not in Hare's metaethical views as set out in his earlier books.

The essays are, and were invited to be, critical of Hare's work. They have been divided into two parts. Along with a general introduction to the volume, W. D. Hudson's survey of the development of Hare's views constitutes Part I. Part II consists of twelve essays which come from diverse perspectives to focus on Hare's account of normative moral thinking. In Part III, Professor Hare has tried, within the text space available, to answer all the important criticisms one by one; his comments still, after pruning, number about 200. This characteristic thoroughness led him to cast his response in two forms. The first is an essay in which he clarifies some preliminary points about which there has been widespread misunderstanding. The second is Hare's comments on the critics' essays. Here, the section numbers correspond to each previous essay's number, and the page/line numbers identify the precise location of the point to which Hare is responding. The precise location of these points is cross-referenced in the contributors' texts with marginal asterisks. While Hare's page/line references are to the contributors' texts, references of the form 'on author page/line' direct the reader to another of Hare's comments. At least one contributor would have preferred that Professor Hare adopt a different style of response. Another thought the very unconventionality of Hare's style 'strikes home some sparks of the spirit of his mind and personality; it will bring to readers a lively sense of his

[1] *Moral Thinking: Its Levels, Method, and Point*, Oxford: Clarendon Press, 1981.

engaged philosophical style.' The careful reader will find the style pays a handsome return for the investment of close attention.

This volume could not have been completed without the help and co-operation of a large number of people. Gratitude is due to Mrs Patricia Redford and Mrs Rose Bode for secretarial assistance. The thirteen contributors deserve considerable thanks for setting aside their own projects in order to turn their attention to this one. Mrs Angela Blackburn, the editor of this volume at Oxford University Press, merits a medal for the patience she has shown with countless queries, proposals, and counter-proposals. And, of course, Professor Hare deserves the utmost appreciation for his support, which has been both enthusiastic and constant; for his generosity with his time and counsel; and for the honesty and integrity which he and his writings exemplify.

CONTENTS

PART III. HARE

NOTES ON THE CONTRIBUTORS

R. B. BRANDT is Roy Wood Sellars Collegiate Professor of Philosophy, Emeritus, at The University of Michigan.

WILLIAM K. FRANKENA is Roy Wood Sellars Professor of Philosophy, Emeritus, at The University of Michigan.

ALLAN GIBBARD is Professor of Philosophy at The University of Michigan.

JAMES GRIFFIN is Fellow and Tutor in Philosophy at Keble College, Oxford.

JOHN C. HARSANYI is Flood Research Professor in Business Administration and Professor of Economics at the University of California, Berkeley.

W. D. HUDSON is Reader in Moral Philosophy at the University of Exeter.

THOMAS NAGEL is Professor of Philosophy at New York University.

DAVID A. J. RICHARDS is Professor of Law at the New York University School of Law.

T. M. SCANLON is Professor of Philosophy at Harvard University.

PETER SINGER is Professor of Philosophy at Monash University.

J. O. URMSON is Emeritus Fellow at Corpus Christi College, Oxford, and Professor of Philosophy, Emeritus, at Stanford University.

ZENO VENDLER is Professor of Philosophy at the University of California, San Diego.

BERNARD WILLIAMS is Professor of Philosophy at the University of California, Berkeley.

Part I

Introduction

Nothing is so difficult in philosophical writing as to get people to be sympathetic enough to what one is saying to understand what it is. Perhaps nobody will ever understand a philosophical book of any depth without, initially, believing it, or at least suspending disbelief.

Moral Thinking, p. 65

1. The Levels, Methods, and Points
Douglas Seanor & N. Fotion

1.1 ONE could imagine a philosopher reacting with disbelief on being told, in 1981, that a colleague had written a book on moral philosophy in which the logical features of moral discourse were identified by means of painstaking analysis of ordinary language, and that from these logical features, the writer had determined that the only soundly based normative theory is utilitarianism, which he defended against the most familiar criticisms by adopting both the act and the rule forms. 'Normative theory based on logic and the facts? Dowdy old utilitarianism? Act-utilitarianism *and* rule-utilitarianism?'

But a healthy scepticism in moral philosophy should not be restricted to utilitarianism. In the past fifteen years, numerous authors have eschewed utilitarianism after marshalling their considerable argumentative skills against the formulations of Bentham, Mill, or Sidgwick. Thus, a contemporary utilitarian seeking an honest hearing might understandably develop an indignation to match the non-utilitarian's disbelief.

1.2 In this volume, both disbelief and indignation have been set aside long enough for utilitarians and non-utilitarians to examine the ideas R. M. Hare presents in *Moral Thinking*. In that book Professor Hare builds on his earlier metaethical work in order to develop a normative position. The position is utilitarian in character, although it differs from other formulations of utilitarianism in two important respects. First is the way in which Hare argues to his utilitarianism from his analysis of moral language. Second is the importance he attaches to the distinction (which he claims to have learned from Plato, Aristotle, and Mill) between two levels of normative moral thinking.

This volume's contributors address, most generally, the three levels of Hare's position: the metaethical, the critically normative, and the intuitively normative. On the first of these levels, both universalizability and prescriptivity are questioned. It is argued that universalizability cannot do nearly the work Hare would like it to, because universalizability permits different interpretations. This is discussed in most detail by Peter Singer who takes up the late John Mackie's argument about the three stages of universalizability. Allan Gibbard also asks Hare for clarification as to whether Hare embraces a strong version of universalizability, or a weak one. And Thomas Nagel thinks that Hare's account of universalizability is not merely a formal principle, but, in fact, a substantive account of impartiality.

Prescriptivity receives less attention, although W. D. Hudson discusses several of the criticisms that have been made elsewhere. One is that moral language develops a wholly descriptive usage in a stable community. Following Wittgenstein, the claim is that for language to be an effective means of communication there must be agreement in judgements as well as in definitions. Hudson also presents the arguments that Hare, like his long-standing critic, Philippa Foot, is a naturalist. After all these years of championing non-descriptivism, non-cognitivism, and prescriptivism, it has been thought by some people that, for Hare now, facts about desires do entail conclusions about what one morally ought to do.

1.3 The contributors have much more to say about Hare's utilitarian critical level. James Griffin, Zeno Vendler, and R. B. Brandt are concerned with how critical thinking is to be conducted. Griffin wants to know the basis of our interpersonal comparisons. What is it, in fact, that we are comparing? Is it subjective preference intensities or an objective list of primary goods? Vendler is more interested in how we can intelligibly bridge the gap to 'other minds' in order to make those kinds of comparisons. He is generally sympathetic with Hare's account of the process of representing other minds, their experiences, and their preferences. However, Vendler argues that Hare's interpretation of 'I' as purely indexical will not account for the possibility of representing other minds. But even if Hare's interpretation is admitted, Vendler finds Hare's model for the representation of other minds (and for all of critical thinking), the Archangel, to be an incoherent idea. And even if the Archangel is made coherent, Vendler is suspicious of various Cartesian-sounding expressions in Hare's descriptions of critical thinking. For Vendler, these expressions serve only to point Hare in the wrong direction for a solution to the representation problem.

Brandt is concerned that an important claim of Hare's moral psychology is wrong. This is the claim that it is a conceptual truth that each party in a moral situation will desire, in the present, with the same intensity, the same course of action for the logically possible cases in which he is 'in the others' shoes'. Brandt finds this conceptual truth neither conceptual nor true. Brandt argues that there are different causal processes involved for the different parties, and the vagaries of imagination raise doubts about claims of preferring now, in an imagined situation, what one would prefer in the actual situation. Furthermore, even if Hare's claims were correct, for Brandt they would be insufficient to establish the acquisition of a preference which corresponds to the ideal preference of someone else, which Hare needs if the conclusion of critical thinking is to be act-utilitarian as he claims.

The normative acceptability of the moral judgements which Hare's critical level would justify is taken up most extensively by David Richards and John Harsanyi. Richards raises the problems associated with the purported failure of utilitarianism to take seriously the distinctness of persons. The claim is that this failure leads Hare to ignore the difference between moral reasoning and prudential reasoning, a point also made by Nagel. In other words, Richards contends, Hare confuses treating preferences equally with treating people equally. Richards suggests that many reasonable people would reject a policy which would jeopardize guarantees of certain primary goods in return for better utilitarian aggregates.

Harsanyi makes an even stronger claim. He says that act-utilitarianism, even if confined to a critical level of moral thinking, will produce decisions that are not only socially undesirable but also irrational. Harsanyi has several arguments for both of these claims based on the idea that act-utilitarianism cannot account for expectation effects. Thus, under act-utiltiarianism, no one could be expected to honour beneficial institutions such as promise-keeping and private property, or special obligations such as familial duties. Similarly, act-utilitarianism could not recognize a socially useful network of individual rights. This inability then leads to a recasting of Hare's problem with 'the fanatic'. Now the problem seems to be that if the number of Nazis is large enough, then genocide becomes the morally justified social policy. Harsanyi finds the choice of such an undesirable moral system irrational.

One route out of these difficulties, for Harsanyi at least, is to exclude from moral consideration the external preferences people might have, i.e. their preferences for how others ought to be treated. The problem of external preferences also receives considerable attention from Gibbard, who discusses the analogous problems of external preferences and the fanatic.

1.4 The distinction between two levels of normative thought, and the accompanying discussion of the intuitive level, are examined from a number of different perspectives. Bernard Williams reads Hare as having two aims with his two-level distinction. The first aim is to provide a theoretical procedure for moral decision-making. The second aim is to explain people's ordinary intuitive reactions. Williams asks if these are necessarily compatible aims. When the critical level is understood as resulting from a hypothetico-deductive process which begins with the logic of moral discourse, the ordinary intuitions begin to lose significance. However, when the intuitions are taken as primary, it becomes possible to imagine various other theories which provide a coherent explanation of the intuitions.

T. M. Scanlon is also dissatisfied with the way Hare draws the distinction between levels. He argues that Hare's approach misrepresents how our moral thinking is actually done. For Scanlon, when we are making use of our common-sense principles, we are not simply applying firmly implanted precepts. Rather, we are trying to decide what is actually right. This suggests that the intuitive level and the critical level are really part of the same process.

Scanlon also fears that the way Hare draws the two-level distinction leaves him vulnerable to the charge of 'Government House utilitarianism', in which a utilitarian, archangelic ruling class governs a majority population of proles. Richards shares this suspicion, though Williams, who invented the phrase, exonerates Hare. But, perhaps most seriously, Scanlon thinks Hare's two-level distinction does not do what, at least in part, it was designed to do. That is, it does not satisfactorily answer the many cases developed to show utilitarianism's divergence from our ordinary moral intuitions. Scanlon finds Hare's two-level solutions especially problematic in 'free-rider' cases in which someone takes advantage of the co-operative good will of others.

William Frankena wonders about the process that determines when we are to do intuitive thinking and when we are to do critical thinking. How are we to know when to do one rather than the other? And is the methodological principle that makes this determination itself the result of critical or intuitive thinking? In addition, Frankena asks for some clarification as to how critical thinking is to proceed when its purpose is to select prima-facie principles for future intuitive application.

J. O. Urmson is concerned that Hare, the ordinary language philosopher, is misusing 'principle', the central term of his intuitive level. Urmson finds Hare's use much too broad. As a result, Hare treats many intuitive-level difficulties as 'conflicts of principle', a label which Urmson understands as applying to a much narrower range of perplexities.

1.5 Whether Hare succeeds in defending his theory against these critics is, of course, for the reader to decide. But, whether the criticisms or the defences are more successful, there are some interesting questions only obliquely dealt with by the contributors. Has Hare modified or changed his position? If so, how and why? That is, is his position different from the time of *The Language of Morals*, or *Freedom and Reason*, or in the light of the following essays, since the writing of *Moral Thinking*? A related question is whether Hare has any justification for the ordinary-language methodology by which he developed his position? That is, does he have a justification that is external to the methodology itself? This is particularly relevant in the present-day absence of any methodological consensus in moral philosophy, or in philosophy generally.

These two inquiries, dealing with the development and the

methodology of Hare's theory, lead naturally to a third and final one. Where in the theory does Hare see room for further development and refinement? This does not suppose that Hare has left considerable unfinished business. Rather, it merely concurs with Hare's own observation that 'nobody can hope to write the last word on a philosophical subject; the most he can do is to advance the discussion of it by making at least some things clearer'. Few philosophers, if any, doubt Hare's achievements in this regard.

2. The Development of Hare's Moral Philosophy

W. D. Hudson

2.1 A few years ago, after I had remarked in conversation with Richard Hare on the fact that more than 200 American graduate students were said to be writing doctoral dissertations on his moral philosophy, he jocularly replied that this came as no surprise since he had long thought of himself as 'one of the favourite Aunt Sallies[1] on the philosophical fairground'. This remark came back to me when I was invited to contribute a piece under the above title. It must be true that few living philosophers have attracted more critical comment than he. For a generation, analytical moral philosophers in Britain and America have tended to formulate their own opinions, by action and reaction, in relation to his. In response to all this, the development of Hare's philosophy has been not so much a story of change or accretion, as of definition and defence. To have defined a single position with as much clarity, adhered to it with as much consistency, and defended it against all comers with as much skill and agility as Hare has done, seems to me a remarkable achievement by any standards. So far as my severely restricted space will allow, I shall try to convey * some impression of that achievement.

When Hare came into moral philosophy emotivism was in the ascendant. He adopted its central tenet that moral language is at bottom nondescriptive in meaning. Stevenson, emotivism's most painstaking exponent, said that he derived

[1] Having just discovered that only one member of a class of third-year undergraduates knew what an 'Aunt Sally' is—or was—I had better quote Brewer's definition of this expression: 'A game in which sticks or cudgels are thrown at a wooden (woman's) head mounted on a pole, the object being to hit the nose of the figure, or break the pipe stuck in its mouth.'

it from observation of ethical discussions in daily life
(1944:13; on emotivism see Hudson, 1983:107–54 and
Hudson, 1980:105–24), and Hare likewise looked to the way
ordinary people talk about what they ought to do (H 1968:
436–7) as the source and test of his moral philosophy. Two
features of ordinary moral discourse interested him, as they
had interested the emotivists, namely the connection moral
judgements have respectively with the *actions* they are normally
intended to direct and the *reasons* that are normally given for
them. But Hare was dissatisfied with the emotivists' account
of these connections. Those (Stevenson, 1944:31) who subscribed to a psychological theory of meaning explicitly
confused the reasons given for moral judgements with the
causes of subsequent activity; and those (e.g. A. J. Ayer and
Rudolf Carnap) who assented to the verificationist theory of
meaning eliminated, rather than explained, the need for
reasons by likening moral judgements to ejaculations or
imperatives. Hare (1968:437; cf. Hudson, 1983:54–63, 160–4)
saw the basic mistake of emotivism as that of identifying the
meaning of moral language with its perlocutionary, rather
than its illocutionary, force. He set himself to provide a more
adequate account of how moral judgements are connected
with actions and reasons by working out 'a rationalist kind of
* nondescriptivism'.[2]

2.2 Hare's explanation of the connection between moral
judgements and *actions* is briefly as follows: moral judgements
in their central and typical uses are prescriptive, and if a
judgement is prescriptive, then, in assenting to it with
understanding and sincerity, we will necessarily be assenting
also to an entailed imperative (*LM* 171–2). This is what he
meant by prescriptivity. Critics have raised two kinds of
objection which immediately come to mind. One is simply
that moral language sometimes has descriptive meaning (cf.
any descriptivist). In a community, for instance, where there
was general agreement that people are good in so far as they
tell the truth, etc., one could, in appropriate circumstances,
predict that somebody would tell the truth simply by saying
that he was a good man—and that whether one approved

[2] Hare in introductory lectures gave this description. On his prescriptivism see
Hudson, 1983: 155–248, 399–430, and Hudson, 1980: 125–52, 185–98.

oneself of truth-telling or not. Hare (*LM* 111–26) concedes as much from the first, but insists that the prescriptive, or evaluative, meaning of words like 'good' is logically primary in that it remains constant and can be used to change whatever descriptive meanings such words may have acquired.

The other objection (Warnock, 1974:457 and 1971*a*:282) calls attention to the wide variety of uses to which moral language may be put—advising, exhorting, imploring, commending, condemning, deploring, resolving, confessing, undertaking, etc. Hare's critics think it implausible to suppose that, in every single instance of all these different uses, there must be an entailed imperative. If Wittgenstein was correct in his opinion that the boundaries of our concepts cannot be strictly circumscribed (1958:25), there must be some truth in this; but he himself recognized that, in order to avoid philosophical confusion, it is sometimes necesary to draw the boundaries of language more tightly than they are drawn in ordinary use (Wittgenstein, 1974*a*: Part II, §35). If that is allowed, Hare (1968:438) is entitled—in the absence of compelling evidence to the contrary—to maintain, as he does, that all the uses listed above are, in 'typical and central' cases, species of the genus prescribing. In normal circumstances, it would indeed * sound unnatural to say, 'I advise you to do X but don't do it!', 'I deplore doing X but do it!', etc.

Hare's explanation of the connection between moral judgements and *reasons* is briefly as follows: in offering any such statement of nonmoral fact as a reason for a moral judgement * we are implying a universal moral principle (*FR* 21ff). For example, if we give as our reason why X ought to be done the fact that X is the fulfilment of a promise, we thereby imply that all acts which fulfil promises ought *ceteris paribus* to be done. From the ordinary meaning of 'reason', it undoubtedly follows that a reason must be adhered to consistently. But, according to Hare (H 1955*a*:302), there is more to a moral reason than that. From the ordinary meaning of 'moral' it follows that a moral reason must not contain any reference to a particular individual. That is what he means by universalizability. The fact, for example, that she is the particular individual Mary Smith cannot be a moral reason why John Smith ought to help his mother, however consistently he is required to do so; but the fact that John's relationship to Mary Smith is an instance of the relationship between an agent and the person who gave him birth and brought him up could conceivably be a moral reason why he ought to help Mary Smith. Here again, two criticisms that have been levelled at Hare on this score, come quickly to mind.

One (MacIntyre, 1957:332–3) is that he has imported a *moral* principle—viz. that we ought to be impartial in our moral judgements—into what is supposed to be a *logical* analysis of the meaning of moral language. But this criticism is groundless. Hare (*FR* 30) is quite clearly pointing out the
* indisputable fact that we would not normally take someone's being a particular individual called Mary Smith (or whatever)—in the absence of any description in more general terms—as a moral reason why anyone ought to help that individual. The other criticism (MacIntyre, 1957:332–3 and Winch, 1965:196–214) is that Hare has overlooked the particularity of some of the situations in which moral judgements have to be made. It is maintained—to take familiar examples—that if we were in the shoes of Sartre's famous pupil who was torn between looking after his mother or going off to war, or in those of Melville's Captain Vere who had to decide whether or not to condemn Billy Budd to death, we might well make a judgement which we did not want to see universalized but which no one could deny was a moral one. I think Hare (*FR* 38–9) disposes of this criticism successfully by
* differentiating the distinction between 'universal' and 'particular' from that between 'general' and 'specific.' He points out that a moral reason for action in a given situation could conceivably be so specific that it would not only be improbable, but even false, that any other actual situation instantiated it; and yet that reason could be universalizable in a hypothetical sense—it would apply to any other relevantly similar situation, if such there were.

Bringing together these two defining characteristics, prescriptivity and universalizability, Hare (*FR* 123) arrives at the following elucidation of the kind of question which ordinary people are asking when, in a sense that would normally be called moral, they wonder what ought to be done. Any acceptable answer to this question will have to be such that

they are prepared to act in accordance with it (prescriptivity) *
in all similar circumstances whoever occupies the different
roles in the situation (universalizability). Universalizability
requires us to go 'the round of all the affected parties . . .
giving equal weight to the interests of all . . .'; and prescriptivity, to ask ourselves, 'How much (as I imagine myself in the
place of each man in turn) do I want to have this, or to avoid
that?', where 'this' and 'that' refer to what is involved in
acting accordingly. Through this exercise of imagination we
are able to weigh the cumulative satisfaction of affected
parties if we perform any given action, as against their
cumulative satisfaction if we performed any of the conceivable
alternative actions. These remarks bring out the other three
'necessary ingredients' (*FR* 92–3, 97) in moral thinking, *
which are according to Hare an exercise of imagination, an
appeal to interest or inclination, and an investigation of
relevant and available matters of fact. In so far as universalizability calls for a consideration of *all affected parties*, and
prescriptivity, of what *each wants*, we can see why Hare claims
that his analysis of moral thinking provides 'a formal
foundation of utilitarianism' (*FR* 123). He is not, so to speak,
proposing utilitarianism as a version of the moral language
game, which ordinary people should take up, but simply
clarifying the rules which he takes to be implicit in the game
which, in his opinion, they are already playing—presumably,
in order to help them to play it more effectively.

In addition to the criticisms of prescriptivity and universalizability which I have already mentioned, at least two others
have been brought to bear upon Hare's account of moral
thinking. One (Williams, 1973:99, 116–17; cf. Hudson,
1983:392–9) accuses him of assuming falsely that all satisfactions are of the same kind. Is it not clear that the satisfaction to *
be found, for example, in affectionate family relationships is
different from that to be gained by the indulgence of animal
appetites; or, that to be felt in doing what one sincerely
believes to be one's duty, from that which material prosperity
may bring? If the answer is affirmative, how can all these
satisfactions be accumulated and weighed against one another?
In effect, Hare's (*MT* 179, cf. Hudson, 1983:413–15) reply is
twofold. One thing he says is that, despite such differences, it is

possible to *prefer* a given amount of any kind of satisfaction to a given amount of any other kind. Having gone the round of all the affected parties the only question we have to answer is: how much do we *prefer*—i.e., how ready are we to *prescribe*— the cumulative satisfaction of the preferences of certain people to those of others, having placed ourselves imaginatively in all their shoes? The criticism we are considering can be pressed most forcefully when the satisfaction concerned is that to be found in doing what one believes to be one's duty. Can this be weighed against any other kind of satisfaction? Suppose a doctor, who believes it morally wrong to perform abortions, has to decide whether or not to perform one for a woman who is worried because her standard of living will decline if she has a child. In going the round of the affected parties, is the doctor supposed to throw the satisfaction which he finds in refraining from doing what he believes to be morally wrong into the scales along with that which the woman finds in being relieved from materialistic anxiety, as if they were the same kind of commodity? To say he is, so the criticism goes, is to require
* him to ignore the significance of moral considerations in the very act of trying to make a moral decision—and surely that is an incoherent, if not a self-contradictory, requirement! Hare's reply, if I understand him correctly, is that it is this criticism itself which is incoherent or self-contradictory. For a method of deciding what ought to be done, which proceeds on the assumption that what ought to be done is already known, is, to say the least, self-stultifying. On the face of it this reply may appear to ignore the fact that we often have to make moral judgements in situations where our minds are already made up about the rightness or wrongness of certain courses of action. Hare[3] can only make his defence at this point effective by invoking a distinction between what he calls 'critical' and 'intuitive' moral thinking, and to this distinction we shall return in a moment or two.

The other criticism (Robinson, 1982; cf. Hudson, 1983: 415–9) I have in mind is that Hare's elucidation of moral thinking shows him to be himself a naturalist or descriptivist. According to someone like Mrs Foot, who is indisputably a naturalist or descriptivist, to say that an act X ought to be

[3] Cf. *MT* 179: '. . . to arrive at a moral conviction by *critical* thought' (italics mine).

done means, or implies, that it will satisfy certain wants (i.e. desires). If therefore we (i) understand the logic of the moral concepts (i.e. what 'ought' means) and (ii) assent to the statement that X will satisfy the said wants, we must (logically) deduce that X ought to be done. Well, is not Hare in the same case? Does he not say, in effect, that if we (i) understand the logic of the moral concepts and (ii) assent to the statement that, of all conceivable acts in the given situation, X is the one that will maximize satisfactions among the affected parties, then we cannot (logically) refrain from saying that X ought to be done? As I read him, Hare (*MT* 218–26) defends himself against this criticism by calling attention to what he considers a crucial difference. On Mrs Foot's account of moral thinking, to work out what will satisfy desires that all men have is to arrive at a description; but on his own account of the matter, to work out what will maximize the satisfaction of preferences among the affected parties is— since to prefer something is to be willing to prescribe it—to arrive at a cumulative prescription. That being so, the moral judgement at which we arrive by this route is neither descriptive (in the sense that its meaning determines its truth-conditions) or naturalistic (in the sense that it is derived from a statement of fact).

2.3 According to Hare (*LM* 56–78), we are each one free to make our own decisions of principle. We can propose any non-moral statement of fact as a possible reason for a moral judgement. All we have to do, in order to determine whether or not we can accept it as an actual reason, is to test whether or not we are prepared to accept the implications of prescribing and universalizing it consistently. Some critics (Warnock, 1974:469) have objected that this makes a mockery of moral reasoning. Consistent prescribing and universalizing is not enough; madmen and criminals could conceivably conform to these criteria and come out preferring the fulfilment of their own crazy or wicked intentions rather than the avoidance of the suffering which the latter will cause. Thus Hare is accused of leaving us free in morality, not only to make up our own minds, but also our own evidence; to decide for ourselves not only what ought, or ought not, to be done, but also what constitutes a sufficient reason why. And this, it is said, is not rationality but the denial of it. What then do such critics think Hare has left out of account? There are at least five answers to that. I will say briefly what they are and how Hare defends himself against each of them in turn.

One (Foot, 1958:83–104; cf. Hudson, 1983:314–24 and Hudson, 1980: 154–60) is that he has omitted any reference to
* human wants. The main contention on which this criticism rests is that an agent is given a reason for action, if and only if he is shown that it is the way to something he wants (Foot, 1958:102). Of many wants—so the argument goes—it makes sense to ask why they are wanted; but of some—e.g. those for freedom from boredom, loneliness, physical injury, etc.—it does not. Reasons why we ought, or ought not, to do something are said to be only logically compelling in so far as they are grounded in these ultimate wants. Hare's (1963*b*:
* 115–34) reply to this kind of criticism—if I grasp it correctly— is as follows. Things are wanted, or thought good, because they have what have been called 'desirability characterizations'. Two senses can be given to this expression. A desirability characterization may be (i) something about an object (e.g. the fact that it tastes sweet) which makes one desire it, or (ii) something about it (e.g. its being said to be pleasant) which implies that the speaker desires it. Equivocation on these two senses leads to the fallacious conclusion that because there are only some *words* which are desirability characterizations in sense (ii), there must be only some *things* that can be the subjects of desirability characterizations in sense (i).

A second thing (Anscombe, 1958:18–9 and Geach, 1977:16)
* Hare is sometimes accused of overlooking is human needs. Is there better reason to think that moral judgements are logically grounded in needs than in wants? Needs are certainly different from wants. It makes good sense to say that we want—though not that we need—something for its own sake: the question 'What do you want it for?' can be dismissed with 'Not for anything. I just want it'; but what would we make of somebody who told us that he needed something but did not need it for anything? Can it then be argued against Hare that, just as we have reason to do what our doctor tells us because it will fulfil our need for health, so we have good

reason to abide by moral judgements in so far as they will fulfil our need for 'human flourishing'? Once again, Hare's (1963*b*: 129–32) defence turns on a distinction between what is true of words and of things respectively. In certain contexts it would be odd for me to say that I needed something but did not think it good. The word 'good' is logically tied to the word 'need' in such cases. But from them it does not follow that 'good' is logically tied to certain things that are generally thought to be needs.

A third thing (Geach, 1977:1–19 and MacIntyre, 1981: 19–20) Hare is criticized for leaving out of account is the true end—that is, nature or function (*telos*)—of man. Most fundamentally, this Neo-aristotelian attack rests on the contention that the evaluative terms we use in making moral judgements are, in their primary meaning, attributive rather than predicative (Geach, 1956; Hampshire, 1971; cf. Hudson, 1983:333–71). In other words, what is meant by, for example, a *good* character, a *right* action, a way we *ought* to live, etc. cannot be understood until we know what human agents *are*, or are *for*—just as the meaning of 'a good knife' would not be clear to anyone who did not know that a knife is an instrument for cutting. One obvious reply to this criticism is that language-users are by no means as agreed about what people are for as about what knives are for. However, the criticism may still be presented simply in terms of beliefs about the nature and function of man. Moral judgement, it is said (MacIntyre, 1981:50–1), implies beliefs of three kinds: namely about (i) man as he happens to be, (ii) man as he would be if he realized his *telos*, and (iii) what must be done, if any given agent is to move from what he is (cf.(i)) to what he could be (cf.(ii)). Moral judgements are beliefs of the third kind, but their significance is parasitic upon beliefs of the second kind. If people cease to have any beliefs about man's true nature and function, the bottom drops out of their morality.

In reply, Hare (1957:110–11) says that this criticism confuses what people *can* do with what they *ought* to do. Some beliefs about man's true nature or function—e.g. that it is rational or social—seem compatible with the view that it can be fulfilled in acts which most people would regard as evil no less than in ones they would consider good. Such beliefs are therefore of little use morally. But other teleological beliefs—most obviously religious or political ones—do evidently imply that whatever fulfils their concept of man's true end must be good and not evil. A Christian, for example, would maintain that whatever fulfils man's true end of glorifying God and enjoying him forever must be morally good; just as a Marxist would, that whatever helps to bring about the dictatorship of the proletariat must. Hare is entitled to reply, as in effect he does (H 1957:106–11), that all this proves is that these teleological beliefs, though they may look flatly constative, are in reality also commissive, in their illocutionary force.[4]

* Some Neo-aristotelians (Geach, 1977:16) recommend us to stop thinking about the precise nature of man's *telos* and to concentrate simply on the fact that the cardinal virtues of justice, prudence, self-control, and courage are necessary conditions of success in 'any large-scale, worthy enterprise'. Against this manœuvre two objections seem so self-evident as hardly to need stating. One is that it reduces morality to mere expediency. The other, that it begs the question at issue by its use of the word 'worthy'. In any teleological morality one's beliefs about the particular nature of man's *telos* necessarily determine what is right or wrong; and so it is self-defeating for any Neo-aristotelian to think that we can bypass the question of what this *telos* is.

A fourth thing (Phillips and Mounce, 1965:308–19; Winch, 1972; Beardsmore, 1969; Norman 1971; cf. Hudson, 1983: 371–82 and Hudson, 1980:160–8) Hare is accused of over-
* looking is public norms. By the latter are meant generally accepted judgements of what ought, or ought not, to be done in certain kinds of situations. Those who advance this criticism think of rationality as essentially social (Winch, 1960:241). They contend that a reason for a moral judgement cannot be grounded solely in an individual's decisions of principle, because that would leave unanswered the question as to why he had made these decisions. This reason why—if it is to be intelligible—will have to refer to some generally agreed 'desirability characterizations' which show it to be, so to speak, decision-worthy (Winch, 1960:235). In support of this

---

[4] I use 'constative' and 'commissive' in the same sense as J. L. Austin (1962: 132–52).

line of criticism, Wittgenstein's (1974*b*: Part I, §242) famous dictum—that if language is to be a means of communication there must be not only agreement in definitions, but also in judgements—is widely quoted. In morality, an act is sometimes said to be obligatory because it is courageous, honest, generous, etc. Such expressions are descriptive, but they also encapsulate public approval of acts which conform to the description. As such, it may be said (Norman 1971:67), they are—contrary to Hare's opinion—logically more fundamental in moral judgement than purely evaluative words such as 'good', 'right', 'ought'. The meaning of the latter is taken to be parasitic on these descriptive-evaluative words. Even if such criticism implies that the need for 'desirability characterizations' continues to infinity, these critics do not demur (Norman, 1971:65).

Hare (*MT* 70) in self-defence warns against being misled by Wittgenstein's dictum. He insists that two people can both use words like 'right' in the same sense and yet disagree fundamentally on what properties of actions make them right. It is, he thinks, a mistake to suppose that words have to have commonly agreed criteria of application before they can be used for communication. Anyone who thinks not is advised to test the point with 'Don't do it!', the meaning of which is clearly known prior to any inkling of what—or even what kind of—action is prohibited thereby. It is worth noting that Wittgenstein (Hallett, 1977:304–5) himself evidently did not regard his quoted remark as applying to the words 'beautiful' or 'ugly'—a consideration which suggests that he may not have thought of it as applying to moral terms such as 'right', etc., either.

The fifth thing (Searle, 1964:43–58, 1969:188–98; Gewirth, 1978; cf. Hudson, 1983:265–94) Hare is accused of overlooking is institutional facts. The fact that A promised to do X is said to be an institutional one, whereas the fact that A said 'I promise to do X' is merely a brute fact. Institutional facts do not exist outside systems of constitutive rules which create new forms of behaviour—e.g. checkmating in chess. The rules for the use of 'to promise' are such that 'A promised to do X' implies 'A ought to do X'. This implication makes promising an institutional fact. Therefore we would appear to have here a reason, which is factual, for a judgement that is plainly moral, apart from any intervening decision of principle. Hare (*MT* 10–20) does not dispute the linguistic facts on which this argument is based—namely, that in ordinary use, 'A promised to do X' entails 'A ought to do X'—but he contends that no conclusions of moral substance can be deduced from exclusively linguistic premisses. In other words, it would still make sense for someone to ask whether what has been promised ought to be done. Such a questioner would not be asking what implications the word 'promise' normally has in our language, but whether or not the institution of promising is morally acceptable. And the answer we would give to this question would in the final analysis depend, not on some rule about the use of words, but on some decision of principle about what ought, or ought not, to be done in circumstances of the relevant kind. Hare is here insisting once again on the point which is fundamental to his prescriptivism, namely that moral language may always be used in an evaluative sense in order to revise any descriptive meaning it may have acquired.

2.4 Hare (*FR* 9–12) draws a comparison between his elucidation of moral thinking and Popper's of scientific. Just as Popper said that, in science, empirically falsifiable predictions are deduced from universal hypotheses in conjunction with certain initial conditions (cf. Popper, 1959), so Hare is saying that, in morals, deductions about what ought to be done are derived from universal principles in conjunction with imagined situations. In order to know which moral principles to adopt—just as *mutatis mutandis* which scientific hypotheses— we must abide by the logic of the discourse concerned and the relevant and available facts which our investigation brings to light. In each case we are free to dream up the major premiss, be it hypothesis or principle, but for the rest our freedom is a 'freedom to reason' (*MT* 6–7) in the light of logic and the facts.

Again like Popper, Hare has been criticized for failing to recognize the part played by received opinion in the kind of thinking he is intent upon analysing. We do not work out the answer to every moral—any more than to every scientific— question from scratch. We set the question within a context of accepted conclusions and read off the answer from that, thereby treating the question as a 'puzzle' rather than a 'problem' (see papers by Kuhn and Popper in Lakatos and Musgrave, 1970:1–23, 51–8). True though that may be, Hare would claim—as would Popper—that his philosophy brings to light the possibility of revisionary critical thinking in the field which he is concerned to elucidate. We always can go back and start again from scratch. Rationality—freedom to think and think again in accordance with logic and the facts—both constrains and liberates (cf. Hudson, 1977 and 1983: 399–430).

To accommodate this twofold conception of rationality within his 'rationalist kind of non-descriptivism', Hare in his most recent writings, like many a philosopher before him,[5] distinguishes two 'levels' of moral thinking from each other. He calls them the 'intuitive' and the 'critical' respectively. On the former level, we think in accordance with the hitherto deliverances of logic and the facts; on the latter, we undertake revisionary exposure to them.

The utilitarian confidence that all moral questions can be answered through felicific calculation has come in for fierce criticism recently (Anscombe, 1958:17; Hampshire, 1978; Rescher, 1975; Williams, 1973; cf. Hudson, 1983:383–99). Conviction and conflict are said to characterize the ordinary man's moral thinking and experience much more radically than calculation. Hare wonders if much of this criticism is not over-dramatized, but he is ready to concede that ordinary people may well not be any happier than Miss Anscombe (1958:17) with the idea that the judicial execution of the innocent could conceivably be justified on grounds of utilitarian expediency. To find room for such truth as there may be in these anti-utilitarian criticisms, he (*MT* 44–5) draws his distinction between the moral thinking of 'proles' and 'archangels'. 'Archangels' are completely rational, omniscient, and free from partiality; they have therefore a perfect command of logic and the facts. In consequence, according to Hare, they always get the correct answers to moral questions and—this is more surprising—the same ones to boot (*MT* 46). 'Proles' are the very opposite of archangels. Their only hope of

---

[5] e.g. Plato, Aristotle, Whewell, Sidgwick, Ross, *et al.*, referred to in Hudson, 1983:427.

thinking in accordance with logic and the facts is to go by what others have told them. These two classes of moral thinker are not such that one must be either the one or the other. Each of us is part archangel, part prole. In so far as we rely in our moral thinking upon received opinion, we are on the intuitive level. In so far as we re-examine it as fully as our capacity allows in the light of logic and the facts, we are on the critical level. Our convictions on the intuitive level serve us well enough in most of life's ordinary situations. But where they conflict, where we are uncertain whether or not they apply in a given situation, where we wonder whether they are worth passing on to our children, critical thinking comes to our aid (H 1976a:124). Both levels of thinking are therefore required by the exigencies of daily life.

*   Hare (*MT* 46) accords 'epistemological priority' to critical thinking. It alone has complete overridingness (*MT* 24, 53–62). Intuitive moral thinking has only a derived overridingness, in so far as the convictions which guide it have 'acceptance utility' (*MT* 50ff.)—i.e. in so far as their general acceptance is calculated to achieve the fulfilment of principles which have been adopted at the critical level. Hare's opinion that all who think with complete clarity and honesty at the critical level will arrive at the same moral judgements is evidently grounded, in the last analysis, on a matter of putative empirical fact. What he (*MT* 170–82) calls 'pure fanaticism' he regards as a logical, but not an empirical, possibility. It is logically conceivable that someone could in complete accordance with logic and the facts arrive at conclusions which were justifiable by utilitarian reasoning, provided he was a fanatic with incredibly strong and eccentric desires; he could end up thinking, for example, that all Jews ought to be exterminated, or even adhering to such up-market versions of fanaticism as that a doctor ought to prolong the lives of his patients as long as possible, however great might be the consequent suffering that they had to endure. But Hare (*MT* 182) is quite sure that such cases 'are not going to occur' in real life.

2.5 As this book testifies, Hare is still at the centre of critical attention, defending the twin foundations of his universal prescriptivism, namely that 'the freedom which we have as moral thinkers is a freedom to reason' (*MT* 6–7) and that 'we remain free to prefer what we prefer' (*MT* 225). No doubt there are places less harrowing, perhaps more congenial, in which an academic person can find himself after many years of professional life than the middle of the fairground. But none more worthy. In philosophy, to have been all your days an Aunt Sally is to have served your discipline well, just as it is to have been paid the highest compliment your *confrères* could have conferred upon you.

Part II

Critics

The critical sense is so far from frequent that it is absolutely rare, and the possession of the cluster of qualities that minister to it is one of the highest distinctions . . .

Henry James, *Criticism*

3. Act-Utilitarianism and Metaethics[1]

R. B. Brandt

3.1 PROFESSOR Hare's writings on ethics constitute, in my opinion, the most substantial and sophisticated formulation and defence of utilitarianism since Henry Sidgwick. In what follows, however, I shall criticize a central thesis of his recent book: that anyone who thinks that he ought morally to do something in an important ordinary sense of that phrase, which an informed act-utilitarian would judge he morally ought not, must be making some factual or logical mistake.

What is this 'important ordinary sense' of 'morally ought'? It is the sense in which it appears in 'critical' moral thinking, the kind of thinking, he says, an omniscient archangel would use in deciding about concrete problems, and the use of which is our basis for criticizing our standing moral beliefs and deciding which such beliefs we should teach our children.

How does Hare explain this sense? He says that '*A* ought morally to be done' amounts to 'I hereby prescribe, with overriding force, that *A* be done in *every* situation just like this one.' Since Hare thinks 'hereby prescribe', when sincerely used, is the verbal expression of desire, and a desire is moral only if it has overriding force, his account can be taken to be that '*A* ought morally to be done', in critical thinking, is the verbal expression of a desire, strong enough to overcome any competing desire, that *A* be done in every situation just like this one (in abstract properties).

[1] I wish to acknowledge my indebtedness to my colleagues in philosophy at the University of Michigan, especially W. K. Frankena and Allan Gibbard, for their criticisms and suggestions, and also to Martin Hoffman, of the Department of Psychology.

Hare's main normative claim, then, is that, at least for those cases in which there is conflict of interest, a person can judge rationally (= on the basis of full information and making no logical mistakes) that he ought morally (in the explained sense) to perform a certain action if and only if it is one an informed act-utilitarian would choose. He summarizes this claim in the following words:

The thesis of universalizability requires that if we make any moral judgement about this situation, we must be prepared to make it about any of the other precisely similar situations . . . What critical thinking has to do is to find a moral judgement which the thinker is prepared to make about this conflict-situation and is prepared to make about all the other similar situations. Since these will include situations in which he occupies, respectively, the positions of all the other parties in the actual situation, no judgement will be acceptable to him which does not do the best, all in all, for all the parties. Thus *the logical apparatus of universal prescriptivism* . . . will lead us in critical thinking (without relying on any substantial moral intuitions) to make judgements which are the same as a careful act-utilitarian would make. We see here . . . how the utilitarians and Kant get synthesized (*MT* 42–3; my italics).

How all of this works out needs a good deal of amplification. I shall explain what I take the argument to be, and shall raise questions about its force. I am far from certain that I understand the argument rightly, and am pleased that in this volume Hare will have an opportunity to set me right.

3.2 Let us recall what Hare aims to establish. Given his view of the meaning of moral predicates (in critical thinking), he wants to show that a rational person can say sincerely 'I hereby express my overriding preference that all persons do *A* in situations identical in abstract properties with that in which I am acting, rather than any other available action', if and only if the action will maximize (expectable?) utility. (Since a fully informed person will know what the utilities will be, perhaps we can drop the 'expectable'.)

It is important for Hare's argument that the 'all similar situations' covers not only all actual persons and situations, but hypothetical ones, as long as the abstract properties are the same. In particular this includes cases in which the actual agent is in the position of someone else affected by the action, as long as he has all the properties of the person in the actual situation.

The above account of 'morally ought' (or 'wrong') leaves open what I can say I morally ought to do, since the notion of universal overriding preferences leaves open *what* can be so preferred. If we want to determine what a person can prefer universally and overridingly, it appears we need some psychology. This Hare attempts to provide.

What will a prospective agent need to know in order to decide which action he prefers for all situations like the one at hand? The first thing, as we shall see, is what the *actual patient(s)* of the various possible actions would prefer. What data will he need to identify this (or how strongly the patient would want, or be averse to, the various possible acts)? Certainly he will need to know what impact each act he is considering would have on anyone it affects. So he will need to know at least what each act's effects will be on the *experience* of everyone affected. Moreover, we do not know this fully, Hare thinks, unless we know whether each person affected will *like* or *dislike* the effect on his experience, and how strongly. If one is to know this, there must be some solution for the problem of knowledge of 'other minds', but Hare rightly refuses to be a sceptic about this. Is this *all* one needs to know in order to infer whether the target (patient) of a given act will *want* that act to occur or have occurred, and *how strongly*? Hare opts for such a restriction in this book, excluding the patient's 'external desires' and desires about himself except for ones concerning his experiences (e.g. desires about achievement) (*MT* 104). This restriction, however, is rather dubious if we want to know how strongly a patient will want (be averse to) *acts* that affect him, *unless* this is fixed solely by the effects of acts on experiences. Of course, it may be possible to identify a person's preference for an act directly, not inferring it from how well he likes the experience caused by the act, but then we leave open the possibility that a preference for an act is not a matter solely of how much the resulting experience is liked/disliked. (Hare admits that a person's preferences might be affected by whether desires for events other than his own experiences are satisfied: e.g. a desire that people paper their rooms with some shade of grey, or abstain from homosexual

intercourse.) But let us ignore these possible complications for
now. Hare calls a person's desires at a time t 'prudent' if and
only if they are desires only for events at a time t^1 for which the
person will also have a desire at the time t^1 the event occurs
(and presumably with a corresponding intensity). Thus a
prudent person will want an *experience* to a degree corresponding to how much he will like it when it occurs (= how
pleasant it will be?). It follows from these simplifications that
what we need to know about an act, according to Hare, in
order to know whether its patients would want it, and how
strongly, is whether they will, if *prudent and fully informed*, want
the experiences it will cause, and how strongly (*MT* 106).
This reasoning, he hopes, will help show that universal
prescriptivism coincides, in its recommendations, with act-
utilitarianism.

With these simplifications, Hare next argues that the agent
will know that, were he to be in the position of the patient of
his act, he would, if he were *just like* the actual patient in likes
and dislikes, like/dislike the experiences produced in him by it
just as does the actual patient, and if he shares the patient's
function from this to preferences for actions, he would share
the preferences of the patient for whether the act be
performed. This reasoning is perfectly sound if it means
merely that when the same causes are present, the same effects
will occur.

So far, except (as we shall see) for a minor point, pretty
much so good. But now we come to the meat of the argument,
with which I have major difficulties. There are three basic
moves. (1) Hare says it is true, and indeed a conceptual truth
(*MT* 94 f., 99), that if I represent to myself vividly in
imagination what effect an action would have on a person's
experiences, how much they are liked, and how strongly he
would, if prudent, prefer that the act occur (not occur), I shall
now prefer that it occur (not occur) to just the degree he does
for the hypothetical case that I am in his position. (Actually,
Hare seems to think (*MT* 99) that I shall now share, for the
hypothetical case that I am in another's shoes, the preferences
of another, irrespective of his relation to liked/disliked
experiences.) (2) Since, in a two-person case, I can sincerely
say that I *ought morally* (have an overriding desire which

qualifies as *moral*) to do *A* only if I prefer that an action of that kind be done both when I am in the agent-position and also in the patient-position (as universalizability requires), I can affirm that I morally ought to do *A* if and only if the net happiness (experiences liked at the time) it will cause me as agent is greater than the net unhappiness caused me if I am the patient. (3) Hare infers that, in the case of actions which affect many people, when I represent to myself how an action of mine will affect the experiences of all of them (and how well they are liked), I shall form in myself pro or con attitudes towards it corresponding to what I know will be their prudent rational (= fully informed) reactive attitudes. But, since in order for me to be able to say that I morally ought to perform the action I must be able to want the action done for the whole set of logically possible cases, including those in which I occupy the positions of all the parties affected by my action, I shall be able to do this only if the sum total of my present attitudes towards it being done for all these cases is favourable towards my performing the act. It follows that I shall prescribe that act universally only if the total net impact on the happiness of the affected collection is (expectably?) positive. So I shall correctly (given information and no logical mistakes) say 'I morally ought to do this', only if so acting will maximize (expectable?) utility, just as the act-utilitarian affirms.

It may help to illustrate the argument with an example, one Hare himself uses, with minor modifications. Suppose I come to a parking space in my Mercedes-Benz 450 SL, currently occupied by a bicycle. The space is the only vacant one in sight, near to a grocer's shop in which I wish to shop. Is it wrong for me to move the bike, standing it against a tree, so that I can park my car? Hare says, 'No'—provided my rational and prudent experience-based desire to park my car is greater than the bike-owner's similar desire that his bike not be moved. For I can universally prescribe moving the bike only if, given these packages between which moral language requires me to choose, moving-bike-plus-parking-car and not-moving-bike-and-no-parking for all possible worlds (including one of me having my bike moved if I am the bike-owner), I prefer the former. This is also the conclusion which the act-utilitarian will reach provided the above experience-based preferences are rational and prudent (at least a hedonistic one, if not a 'preference utilitarian'—assuming this view can be made coherent).

3.3 The foregoing is the basic structure of Hare's argument from his metaethics, and other assumptions, to act-utilitarianism. The reasoning is of the first importance, if the argument is valid and the premisses sound. But I believe there are flaws. What are they?

The first difficulty is the one mentioned above as relatively minor, and the removal of which requires only some complications. Remember that Hare says that the preference of the car-owner to move the bike is stronger than that of the bike-owner not to have it moved, and that this is the reason the car-owner can say 'It is not wrong to move the bike'. But just which preference, and *at what time*, is to fix this total preference for moving the bike? Like most experiences caused by an action (inaction), the liked/disliked experiences go on over a period of time. If I do not move the bike, there is first the experience of finding a vacant space somewhere. Then there is walking to the store. Then there is carrying the groceries to the car, on a hot day. Then there is driving home. All these experiences are less happy than others would have been had I moved the bike. How unhappy a given slice of experience is (I think) is a matter of how strongly one would prefer to end it at the time. So there is a succession of liked or disliked experiences in the car-owner, each of them different in intensity, from the start of the episode until the end, and maybe later. Correspondingly, if Hare's restrictions are accepted, there will be a *sequence of preferences* about the action which was responsible for these experiences, presumably differing in intensity. Which intensity of resulting preference, at which time, is the intensity relevant for deciding whether it is wrong to move the bike? Surely not necessarily *any* of those occurring during the sequence of experiences, not even the last one of these, when, relieved to be home, the car-owner may not care.

I think Hare must mean something like this: ideally we make a graph representing the car-owner's experience throughout the whole episode, a point representing, by its distance above or below the x-axis, how intensely the car-owner likes/

dislikes the experience he is having at the time, in so far as this can be attributed to the bike not being moved. We assume that measurement is possible, so that a unique point is determined. Then we calculate the net 'happiness' area under the curve composed of these points. (Notice that this area need not correspond with the *last actual preference* for the *action* by the car-owner, the latter being at least some function of the preceding liked/disliked experiences, the form of which is a matter for empirical psychology.) Identify the *ideal preference or desire* as simply correlated with this net happiness. Do the same for the bike-owner. 'External' preferences are ignored except, perhaps, as these affect how the experiences are liked. All of this is complex, but I believe it is what Hare requires, rather than the coarse notion of comparing the preferences of each party deriving from a given experience, at some point in time. Is this, or is it not, proposing to sum the happiness of a person, as affected by an act, over a period of time? And how would Hare propose to effect this summation?

3.4 Let us assume Hare's statement complicated in this way. *
Now Hare thinks that each party to a transaction will know that if he were in the shoes of the other, with exactly his experiences, his likes and preferences, he would prefer that the bike he moved (not be moved) with the intensity of the actual *
preference of the other. (Not, I believe, necessarily the *ideal* preference, indeed probably somewhat different; whereas ideal preference is what he needs to get his argument to act-utilitarianism, hedonist or 'preference'.) Then each party *now*, according to Hare, will desire, *with this same intensity*, that the bike be moved (not moved) for the *logically possible case* in which he is the other. Hare thinks it is a *conceptual* truth that each will have this desire in these circumstances (*MT* 95–9, 222–3). It is this desire (taken along with his prudent desire for moving, or not moving, the bike in the actual case) which enables each to decide whether he prefers that bikes be moved in this *kind* of situation, and therefore whether each can say sincerely 'It is not wrong to move the bike'. (Hare apparently assumes that if each comes to this conclusion for the actual *
case in which *he* is the hypothetical other, he will be content with the same conclusion for all other cases in which other persons are involved. This is not self-evident. Suppose that in

one case the car is driven by one's hated chairman, and the bike belongs to one's daughter. Since it makes a difference that in one possible case *he* could be the other, might the identity of the persons involved not be relevant to whether each would be willing to generalize the conclusion for the case discussed to the case involving the other individuals? If it is, vast complications arise.)

But it is not a *conceptual* truth that each party will have this desire; indeed, it is probably not true at all. Why? (Remember that the strength of a desire for something is to be measured in terms of the costs/disutility one would accept in order to avoid or produce it, not by its relation to liked/disliked earlier experiences.)

To see why, let us try a different example involving just temporally separated states of one person. Suppose, after four hours of no liquid intake on a hot day, I am thirsty and want a drink. We know something about how this works: the de-hydration of the cells signals to the brain through the blood, with the result that the idea of a drink becomes attractive and I exert myself to get a drink. But suppose I merely consider now, with vivid imagination, that I am forthwith to be deprived of liquid, be dehydrated, and feel as I do when I am. Shall I now want a drink, for this hypothesized near-future situation? Perhaps it is true that I shall want not to be unpleasantly thirsty owing to no liquid intake. But the causal process which brings about the thirst, or wanting a drink, in the real case, is totally different from what it is in the case of the mere belief about being dehydrated (etc.). Maybe, *as a result of conditioning* or some other process, I shall want that I have a drink for the hypothetical case. But whereas we can be sure, on account of known processes, that I shall be thirsty and want a drink in the real case, we may not be at all sure what will happen in the purely cognitive situation, even if the person *believes* that the event will actually happen. Will merely thinking/believing plus imagining how I may feel shortly produce a desire now for a drink then, *of equal strength*, particularly if I know (as I do when I am thinking of the case of hypothetically being in another's shoes) that I am certain not to be deprived of liquid? Surely this is an empirical question, and a complex one, involving measurement of desires. For the case of desires *not* so directly related to experiences, it seems clear that I shall *not* have a desire I know I shall have later: for instance, as Allan Gibbard has pointed out in his essay, if I know that I shall want a big funeral twenty years from now, I shall pretty obviously *not now* have a desire for a big funeral then.

The same distinction must be made in the parking case. There will be a causal process in each party, involving experiences each has, and at least partially as a result of these, a preference that the bike be (not be) moved. It *is* true that if either were in the position of the other, with his likes and dislikes (and the same function from liked experiences to preferences), he would want the bike to be moved (not moved) just as the other does. He does if the causal factors are identical. But will each *now*, as a result of reflection on the other's experiences and preferences, have the same desire he would have if he were actually in the other's shoes? This is far from obvious. At any rate the causal process will be very different. The imagination will play a role. How would Hare go about showing that a person's preference about an action now, in view of its hypothetical impact on him were he in the other's shoes, will be exactly like his conception of what it would be if he were actually in that situation, particularly when he knows he will certainly not be in the other's shoes? Surely it is not an analytic truth but only an inference from Hare's a priori psychology that if I know I *would* have a certain aversion to a certain action, I shall *now* have that very same aversion to that action. (An aversion now is more likely to be a conditioned response to the imagined *experience* of one's self in that situation, than a belief that one would have an aversion to the action, were one in that situation.) Thus Hare's supposition is surely not a conceptual truth, and probably not true at all. Hence a major step in Hare's argument seems to be unsupported.

Even if Hare's conclusion were correct, we must remember, it would not show that either would acquire a preference corresponding with the *ideal* preference of the other, which is necessary if the conclusion is to be the one an act-utilitarian would reach.

Suppose we grant for the sake of the argument, however,

that a person will always have *some* desire that an act be not
performed that would put him in a disliked position if he were
in some logically possible (but not actual) situation. Suppose,
then, I have *some* desire that the bike not be moved for the case
that I am the bike-owner. How does Hare's argument go from
here? Hare's view is that the car-owner cannot sincerely say 'I
ought to move the bike' unless his desire to move the bike is
now stronger than his desire that it not be moved for the
hypothetical case of his being the bike-owner. Why not?
Because to make the moral statement is to issue a universal
prescription which I cannot sincerely issue for *all logically
possible* cases if I really desire, all in all, that the bike not be
moved for this hypothetical case, more strongly than I desire
that it be moved in the actual case. So universalizability
requires rejection of a principle if it would not be *acceptable* to a
person that *he* be in a situation as patient less agreeable than
his actual position as agent. Hare's theory, then, essentially
* appeals to a person's *self-interest*. (Remember that Kant
sometimes does the same, asking if we can consistently *want*
everyone to behave in a certain way, e.g. help others who are
in distress.)

Hare's reliance on self-interested motivation and the
assumed universalizability of moral judgements, then, gets
* him to the same position which an Ideal Observer theory
would reach with the notion of the Observer being perfectly
sympathetic—one who is as interested in the happiness of
others as he is in his own. Hare has sometimes rightly
compared the two theories. But there is something both
theories have to show in order to support act-utilitarianism:
they have to show that a moral judge (Observer) would be
concerned, in his reactive attitude towards an act, by *nothing
else* besides the happiness/well-being of the parties involved. I
shall return to this.

There are two further difficulties with the argument. First,
one person may not be interested in the desires of another if he
thinks them irrational, as I have pointed out elsewhere
(Brandt, 1979:216). Second, even if the argument proves that
one cannot correctly say 'I ought not . . .' in certain circum-
* stances, there is a further problem of showing why anyone
should be interested in whether one ought or ought not in that

sense. The showing that we may not use a certain English phrase correctly in a certain situation is not enough to provide a *reason* for acting in one way or another. It does not provide what I have elsewhere called a 'disalienation' from morality (Brandt, 1979:188 f., 233).

3.5 Act-utilitarianism is not restricted to two-person situations, and if Hare's theory is to be extensionally equivalent to it, it must come to the same conclusions about many-person situations, viz. that that act must morally be done which maximizes (expectable?) utility, everybody affected considered. I believe there are difficulties about this extension.

Let me explain by an example. Suppose four lawyers are partners. Each is allowed to draw on a common treasury for legitimate business expenses. The personal income of the partners is fixed, at the end of each month, by dividing equally the net income from all partners. Now let us suppose that Mr X finds a way to inflate his 'business expense' by \$10,000 during a certain month, with the effect that the personal income of the other partners is reduced by \$2,500 each.

The act-utilitarian, in the absence of other information, will say this act is wrong, partly because of the risk to mutual trust if the theft is discovered, and partly on account of the declining marginal utility of money—since the total benefit in utility to Mr X is less than four times the utility from an income of \$2,500 to each. (There might be special justifying circumstances; the thief may need the extra money to save his marriage.)

It appears that use of the argument from the declining marginal utility of money raises psychological complications for Hare. For the prospective thief, Mr X, will want to take the money with an intensity D_X corresponding to the anticipated benefit to him, U_X. He also knows that in a world in which he is Y, he will have an aversion to the theft to a degree D_Y corresponding to the anticipated loss of the \$2,500 to him, U_Y. So he will *now* have an aversion to the theft the same as Y's aversion, if Hare's psychology is correct. And the same for the world in which he is in the shoes of Z, and also for the world in which he is in the shoes of W. In this situation, then, in order to find what he morally ought to do the agent must not only compare *two* desires with each other; he must compare his

desire for the money in the actual world with the *sum* of his aversive desires for the three other possible worlds. At this
* point Hare owes us an explanation of how this is supposed to be done, and why he thinks that different individuals will come out with the same overall preference.

But there is a more serious difficulty with the argument. So far I have said little about what it means to say, as Hare does, that 'It is wrong for me to do *A* in this situation' entails 'I hereby proscribe doing *A* in circumstances like this *in all possible worlds*'. I take it that what this means is that if I utter the first statement I must be ready to proscribe the act (desire overridingly that it not occur) irrespective of a mere change in the persons involved, so long as the situation is held constant. But more than this is required by Hare's argument extending his view to multi-person cases. For if it is wrong for me to perform an act which will do more harm to the patient than it does good to me, it does not follow that it is wrong for me to do
* the same thing when there are *three* patients—for it seems that this change in the structure of the situation alters the *situation*. At least, if Hare thinks it does not, we need an explanation why not.

If we consider this action as only involving the agent and one of his partners, it appears that the agent is morally in the clear in taking the money, indeed that this is what he ought to do, since the desire of the thief to take the money is stronger (the desire for the benefits of $10,000) than the desire of the patient to have the extra $2,500. What Hare has to do, in order to make his argument work, is to find a justification for summing the disutilities of the patients, taking them all together. By what right does he do this?

A tempting thought, suggested by Hare, is that we might
* think of the agent *X* as occupying simultaneously, in some one possible world, the positions of *all three* of his partners, representing the strengths of their several desires that the act not be done, and then forming in himself a desire of strength equal to the sum of the three desires he would have, that the act not be done, when he is simultaneously in the shoes of the three partners. But I find this an unintelligible notion. So apparently does Hare. For, addressing a somewhat similar problem, he says, 'It is not necessary to imagine myself

occupying the four positions simultaneously: that would be asking too much' (*MT* 128–9). Indeed it would: what does it mean to be simultaneously in the shoes of three different persons? Hare goes on to say, 'We might follow a suggestion of C. I. Lewis . . . and suppose that I have a choice between occupying [each of the four positions each with the extra $2,500, and each of the three positions without the extra and the fourth with $10,000] . . . in random order'. Then, given the assumed strengths of the desires of my three partners and myself, I shall prefer the equal income of $2,500 for all to a split of $10,000 for one and nothing for the others.

But this way of putting matters changes Hare's argument essentially. It is one thing to decide what is right by asking   * whether you desire that the act be done when in the agent-position more than you are averse to it being done to you in the patient-position in a hypothetical world. It is a different thing to ask if you would want to experience a succession of lives, in each of which you occupy one of the several positions affected by your desiderated act in the real world. It may be there is some way to show that the second question is essentially the same as the first, but I do not know how to show this. If there is no such way, then Hare's theory of two-person cases cannot be extended to multi-person cases, and his argument for the extensional equivalence of the prescriptions required by his metaethics with those of act-utilitarianism does not succeed.

3.6 So far Hare's argument has been that self-interest, imagination, information, and the requirement of universal-izability will lead to prescribing the very same acts that an informed act-utilitarian would prescribe. But the argument seems to rest on an implicit assumption: that an intelligent person would not be inclined to prescribe anything except on the basis of the production of happiness/well being for all   * involved. But this requires to be shown. We may recall that Hare has concerned himself throughout with 'prudent' preferences, and ones dependent on liked/disliked experiences. Obviously there are lots of other preferences, but I shall here confine myself to what may be called 'moral' preferences. Suppose the cyclist, of our earlier example, wants equality of welfare for its own sake (or queuing, or retributive punish-

ment, or special recompense for soldiers who are handicapped because of wounds incurred in combat). So, when the car-owner arrives with his Mercedes-Benz 450 SL, the cyclist reflects that if the car-owner has to walk for his groceries more equality will be brought into the world. So he desires strongly
* that, as a means to more equality, his bike not be moved. So, when the car-owner gets a desire not to move the bike equal to that of the bike-owner, he will not be able to prescribe moving the bike. But this will be a conclusion discrepant with that of the act-utilitarian, at any rate as here viewed by Hare, since equality is not a liked *experience*. So, then, Hare's argument to extensional equivalence will not work. Or is there a way out?

Let us take a preference for equality of welfare as typical of this whole class of objections which philosophers have thought conflict with utilitarianism. The objection can take two forms. First, some have thought that persons *ought* to try to bring about equality of welfare, even when so doing would diminish the total amount of welfare in the world. Second, it can be thought that equality of welfare is itself a good, although it is not a good of persons. 'Ideal Utilitarians' have held this.

What might Hare say to this? (1) He might wave aside these proposals on the ground that he has deliberately confined his attention, in this book, to prudent desires for states of experience. But he does seem to think that an agent *will* have *all* the relevant preferences a patient of his act will have, when he vividly represents them to himself (*MT* 99). So it would seem that the cyclist's desire for equality *could* play a role in a decision about what one ought to do. And if it can, then the reasoning may not come out where the act-utilitarian
* would come out. (2) Hare says, however, that even if we admit such preferences, it will make no practical difference (*MT* 182), because we then have to count in the possibly more numerous other persons who prefer inequalities. That is, if the cyclist's preference is moved by his desire for equality, we then have to take into account the external preferences of everyone else, counting the attitudes of all who may be con an act because it introduces more equality, presumably even if they have never heard of this case, since they are con equality and would have preferences about the car parking if they knew of the case. To follow lines Hare has sometimes taken concerning

promise-keeping, we should have to include the attitudes of the dead. I am going to assume that manifestly this is an unsatisfactory reply. (3) So, then, why does not the cyclist's desire for equality of welfare just for its own sake not undermine Hare's thesis? Hare's fullest explanation of why not is in his discussion of 'fanaticism' (*MT* 171 ff.) His view seems to be that when the cyclist counts up all the unhappiness in the car-owner that would be brought about just in order to secure more equality, he will find himself unable to prefer not moving the bicycle (*MT* 176 f.). So Hare thinks. But he offers no proof, although he says that a preference for not moving the bicycle could not exist, in view of his argument in Chapter 5 (*MT* 171)—faults in which we have already examined. Some philosophers who object to utilitarian conclusions apparently come to a conclusion different from Hare's; they have thought about all this and think some sacrifice should be made just for the sake of equality of welfare. While I tend to agree with Hare that equality should be brought about only to the extent that maximizing long-term benefit requires, I must concede that I have no *proof*, and can only appeal to a person to consider how much equality utilitarian considerations require, and whether he prefers a degree of equality which goes beyond this. But Hare purports to have a conceptual *proof*, whereas I see no conclusive reason why Hare should think the cyclist cannot have a strong desire for equality of welfare, or why this desire for equality of welfare should not succeed in moving the decision in this case, using Hare's own line of argument, to an anti-act-utilitarian answer, that is, an answer inconsistent with maximizing the welfare or happiness of sentient creatures. Obviously such a conclusion can be *universalized*. As far as I can see, Hare's argument does not slam a logical door on the egalitarian. I concede that the psychology of a desire for equality of welfare needs more investigation.

Much the same difficulty will arise, I think, whenever * desires that are not 'prudent' enter the picture. Until Hare has an adequate response to this difficulty, I think we have to say his attempt to support act-utilitarianism is unsuccessful.

4. Hare on the Levels of Moral Thinking

William K. Frankena

4.1 No recent moral philosopher has thought harder or more systematically and to better effect than has R. M. Hare. Now, in the latest stage of his thinking culminating in the book *Moral Thinking*, he has added to his earlier universal prescriptivist metaethics a particular theory of 'the separation of levels of moral thinking' (*MT* 65), and makes it 'do a great deal of work . . . first in order to shed light on some disputes in metaethics . . . and secondly in order to defend a version of utilitarianism against an extremely common type of objection' (*MT* 25). In my paper I shall be concerned to clarify and to raise questions about certain aspects of this newish part of Hare's total view.

The basic idea of Hare's doctrine of 'the separation of levels' is * that, beside metaethics or metamorals, there are two kinds of substantive moral thinking. Now, as before, Hare tends to call them *levels*, but the term 'kinds' is more accurate and less question-begging, and I shall prefer it, except when the word 'levels' is clearly appropriate. Earlier he also used the expressions 'one-level', 'two-level', 'level 1', and 'level 2' in somewhat confusing ways, as he here recognizes; in what follows I shall use them in the ways I think they should be used. In any case, the first point in Hare's version of the doctrine of the separation of levels is best put by saying that, in the abstract, there are or might be two *kinds* of normative moral thinking (MT): (*a*) pure uncritical or 'intuitive' moral thinking (IMT), in which moral agents use or would use only relatively simple 'prima facie principles' of 'limited specificity' in directing their actions, as most of us do in our ordinary moral thinking, these principles being acquired somehow but not by the use of any kind of critical thinking or reflection; (*b*) pure critical moral thinking (CMT), in which moral agents make or would make no use of any such principles of limited specificity (PLSs) in directing their actions, but only of the method of universal prescriptivism and/or the act-utilitarianism Hare now takes as its offspring, applying it directly to each particular situation. Such thinking would, in effect, be situational ethics plus universalization, and so would issue in principles of unlimited specificity (PUSs) which would not represent prima-facie duties in Ross's sense but actual ones.

Next we should observe (1) that each of these pure kinds of thinking is a species of one-level, not two-level MT, and neither of them is, as such, a level 1 or level 2 form of thinking, (2) that in each of them the requirements of prescriptivity and universalizability Hare regards as laid down by the 'logic' of moral terms, and perhaps even that of overridingness, is or can be fully met (*MT* 41), (3) that, theoretically at least, MT can as a whole take either form and so need not have a two-level structure; a society of *proles*, as described by Hare, would use only pure IMT, but a society of his *archangels* would or at least might use only pure CMT, and a human society might use both kinds of MT, one for certain questions, and the other for other questions, thus not having any two-level MT but only two kinds of one-level MT, and (4) that there may also be impure forms of IMT and CMT, as we shall see.

According to Hare, however, human beings are neither proles nor archangels; 'we all share the characteristics of both to limited and varying degrees and at different times' (*MT* 45). Therefore our MT need not, as a whole, take either of these pure one-level forms. Nor should it. It should not be wholly intuitive or codal because the PLSs used as premises in such thinking may conflict, be inadequate to new situations, and be vague or just plain mistaken. Some kind of CMT is therefore necessary. Indeed, none of our MT should be of the sort I described as pure IMT; any IMT we do should be preceded or accompanied by some kind of CMT, either our own or someone else's. That is, our IMT, if we do any, should be the lower level in a two-level structure of which some kind of CMT is the upper level; it should be impure in the sense of being critically based and hence not 'uncritical'. Our codal MT, if any, ought to be a *criticized* codal thinking.

Nor, according to Hare, should our human MT as a whole take the form I described as pure CMT. It could do so if we were archangels, but, unlike archangels, we are afflicted with various human weaknesses—ignorance, lack of time, partialities to self and to friends and relatives, etc. We therefore need a code of PLSs, accompanied by strong moral feelings like compunction, and the 'relatively simple reaction patterns' that go with them, and should, in fact, do codal or IMT most of the time. It follows that our MT as a whole should include both CMT and IMT and that the IMT should be based on the CMT, that is, that it should, at least in part, have a two-level structure in which the two kinds of thinking are done 'in tandem' in the sense that the intuitive PLSs are selected or tested by some sort of critical thinking (CT).

I said 'at least in part' because it would be open to Hare at this point to say that *all* of our MT should have this two-level structure. This would mean that none of our CMT should be pure one-level CMT of the sort described above; the whole job of CMT would be to 'select' PLSs for use in our IMT. In other words, as in some forms of rule-utilitarianism, we should use CMT (which for a utilitarian consists of appeals to utility) only to determine what our codal principles should be, not ever to determine directly what action we should take or judge right in a particular situation—*this* should be determined wholly by reference to codal principles, and so only indirectly by CMT. Actually, however, for Hare our MT not only should include the two-level thinking described in my previous paragraph, but also must or at least may include some of the one-level pure CMT described earlier for dealing directly with particular situations in which our intuitive principles conflict, as well as with new ones for which we have as yet no such principles, and perhaps also on occasions when we are up to it, for testing such a principle to see if what it dictates is what the archangel would do. For after all, 'the right or best way for us to live or act either in general or on a particular occasion is what the archangel would pronounce to be so if he addressed himself to the question' (*MT* 46), it being understood that he would use the method of universal prescriptivism or the act utilitarian method this entails. In other words, the rational human universal prescriptivist has three ways of dealing with any particular situation on Hare's view: (1) to apply a PLS if no conflict is involved and an adequate critically selected one is at hand, (2) to use CMT to find a satisfactory new PLS to apply, or (3) to apply CMT directly to the particular case without bringing in any PLS; and he or she may and even should use the third way on occasion.

We now have a general picture of Hare's conception of human MT as ideally including (*a*) no pure IMT, (*b*) some pure one-level CMT, (*c*) some two level MT in which the CMT involved is impure in the sense of issuing in PLSs, and (*d*) much impure IMT, i.e. codal thinking that is critically based. What interests me here is some further questions about the nature of CMT and its relations with IMT as Hare conceives these.

4.2 Having distinguished CMT and IMT in chapter 2, Hare takes up in chapter 3 the question of how they are related. The question is, however, more complex than he seems to realize, given his own position as sketched above, and his answer is not as clear as one would like. For, as we have seen, Hare distinguishes two kinds of moral principles: critical principles proper and prima-facie principles.

Critical thinking consists in making a choice [of principles] under the constraints imposed by the logical properties of the moral concepts and by the non-moral facts, and by nothing else . . . But the principles involved here are of a *different kind* from the prima facie principles [to be used in IMT] . . . a prima facie principle has . . . in order to fulfil its function, to be relatively simple and general (i.e. *unspecific*). But a principle of the kind used in critical thinking (let us call it a critical moral principle) can be of *unlimited specificity* . . . [Critical principles] can be, and for their purposes have to be, highly specific . . . each tailored to a particular detailed situation (*MT* 40 f., 200; my italics).

Moreover, even though the first sentence quoted makes it look as if only critical principles are chosen by CMT, Hare actually holds that principles of *both* kinds are to be selected by or based on CMT. It follows that we must distinguish, at least prima facie, between two kinds of CMT, one issuing in critical principles proper or principles of unlimited specificity (PUSs), the other in intuitive or prima-facie principles of limited specificity (PLSs), for, as we have it on good authority, a tree is known by its fruits. Let us call the first CMT1 and the second CMT2. Then CMT1 is what I earlier called pure CMT and consists in using the universal prescriptivist/act-utilitarian method directly to determine what to do in a particular case, i.e. what PUS to act on, while CMT2, whatever it consists in, is to be used to determine what PLSs we should act on when we are in situations in which we should not use CMT1. And, as I said, CMT1 is like IMT in being one-level thinking applied to a particular case, while CMT2 is a kind of level two thinking because it is to provide principles for use at another level (IMT) and is therefore in a sense impure.

Neither kind of CMT *uses* any substantive PLSs, as IMT does, but CMT1 does not necessarily or as such issue in such principles either, and it does not need to be supplemented by any such principles in order to reach a conclusion (or PUS) about what to do in a particular situation, whereas CMT2 does issue in PLSs and must be supplemented by IMT using such principles in order to yield a judgement about what to do in a particular case. I suppose that Hare would think that the archangel can do either kind of CMT, though he (she, it?) would not need any PLSs but would be guided wholly by CMT1 and its PUSs. So too a pure ('crude' is hardly the word) act-utilitarian hardliner would recommend and use only CTM1. On Hare's own view as sketched, a human agent would and should use CMT1 on some occasions, when he or she is enough like an archangel to use it well, and otherwise should act on a code of PLSs selected by CMT2 (done by oneself or by someone else).

The question then is not just how CMT and IMT are related, but how two prima-facie distinct kinds of CMT are related to one another and to IMT, and I shall discuss the question in this form, which Hare does not do. In a way, the relation of CMT2 to IMT is clear: the former is or should be the basis for the latter, i.e. provide the PLSs to be used in it. So too, in a way, is the relation of CMT1 to IMT clear: the former will be connected with the latter if and only if the former is an element in CMT2, as for Hare it well may be. What is, I think, not clear from Hare's account is the nature of CMT2 and its relation to CMT1. It might be that CMT2 is based on CMT1 or makes some kind of use of it, but it also might be that they have to be very different in order to generate such different kinds of principles, though I suppose that both must somehow make use of the canons of moral reasoning Hare regards as embedded in the meanings and logic of moral terms. I think I see roughly how CMT1 goes or at least how Hare thinks it should go. What I do not see very clearly is how Hare thinks CMT2 is to do its job of selecting, justifying, or testing PLSs for use in IMT.

I shall proceed to deal with my question by indicating some lines of reply that Hare might or does give, and then leave it to him to tell us what he really has in mind. But first it will be well to say a little more about two matters. (*a*) We may take it as a fixed point in Hare's view that the right act to perform in a particular situation is the act that one of archangelic powers would pronounce to be so if he addressed himself to the
* question and used CMT1 to answer it. I shall call this thesis A. In holding it Hare is an act-universal-prescriptivist and act-utilitarian (*MT* 46). The right act for him is not defined by any code or set of PLSs, not even by one arrived at by the use of CMT2, as it would be for a Brandtian rule-utilitarian (*MT* 38). However, one can accept thesis A and still hold, as such rule-utilitarians do, that we humans should mostly (or even always) guide ourselves by a code of PLSs, and Hare does hold we should mostly do so. One can also still hold any of various views about the way in which these PLSs are to be selected, justified, tested, or criticized. The question now is: what is Hare's view about this? (*b*) What, according to Hare, is a PLS and what is it to *have* one? I take it that a PLS is a principle of roughly the form, 'In any situation with character-istics ABC, do (or do not do) an action with characteristics DEF', where the characteristics involved are rather limited in number and specificity, e.g. 'If the situation is one to which a promise that has been made is relevant, then the right action is one that will keep the promise' or 'Never kill people except in self-defence or in cases of adultery or judicial execution' (*MT* 41). I also take it that to *have* such a principle is to have a disposition and tendency to do actions with DEF in situations

with ABC and to feel at least compunction (not just regret) if one does not, and also some concern that one's children and others do such actions in such situations, and indignation if they do not (*MT* 39). Thus, our question may be thought of either as one about the way to establish a principle of the sort indicated, or as one of determining what 'relatively simple reaction-patterns (whose expression in words . . . would be relatively simple prescriptive principles)' we should have and foster (*MT* 36, 39).

4.3 (1) One natural view to take is that PLSs are to be established, as 'rules of thumb' would be, on the basis of *previous experience, one's own or another's, i.e. on the basis of a previous use of CMT1 in particular cases. Then CMT2 would be just a kind of inductive extension of CMT1. Having done CMT1 one or more times and having found that in each case it yielded a PUS, and that in each case the situation happened to have ABC and the action dictated by the PUS in question happened to have DEF, one might form the hypothesis, as it were, that when a situation has ABC the thing to do is an action with DEF. Hare alludes to this view and seems to reject it on the ground that 'the breach of [a rule of thumb], unlike the breach of the moral principles we are discussing, excites no compunction'. A 'much better expression' for such moral principles than 'rules of thumb', he then says, is Ross's 'prima facie principles', which he proceeds to adopt with the words,

although formally speaking [such principles] are just universal prescriptions, [they] are associated, owing to our upbringing, with very firm and deep dispositions and feelings. Any attempt to drive a wedge between the principles and the feelings will falsify the facts about our intuitive thinking (*MT* 38 f.; see *LM* 66; H 1979*b*:149.)

This certainly means that he thinks we do and should not treat or feel about our moral PLSs as if they were rules of thumb, but as if they were something stronger. However, this view is compatible with holding that, logically or epistemologically, such PLSs have the same status as rules of thumb and differ only in their psychological accompaniments, and Hare may still be thinking that this is the case. Thus he goes on to write that 'the critical thinker considers cases in an act-utilitarian . . . way, and *on the basis of these* he selects, as I shall shortly be explaining, general prima facie principles for use . . . at the intuitive level' (*MT* 43, my italics; cf. 60). The italicized words suggest the method of selecting PLSs that I have just been describing, even if the explanation he gives in the next chapter does not.

* (2) Perhaps another but somewhat similar possibility, which could be combined with the first, is that Hare believes our PLSs are not normally or even ideally arrived at by any such *previous* use of CMT1; they are and perhaps should be acquired otherwise, e.g. by an uncritical internalizing of a parental or social code, but they can and should be tested on occasion by the use of CMT1 in particular cases covered by them to see if what they dictate is what the archangel would do, and then rejected or at least revised if this is thus found not to be so. Then again CMT2 is or includes a use of CMT1, but a use addressed more to the assessment and criticism of PLSs than to finding or selecting them (let alone to choosing PUSs). That Hare may be thinking along these lines is suggested by his references to Popper in *Freedom and Reason* (*FR* 87–92). On the other hand, here in *MT*, he seems concerned to hold that a PLS sometimes may and perhaps even should continue to be *had* even though it is seen in some particular case to dictate something Archie would not do (*MT* 50, 59, 135), and this view is not easy to square with either of these first two lines of thought, though perhaps it can be done by distinguishing between epistemic status and psychological accompaniments.

Hare's further explanations of the way in which PLSs are to be selected (etc.) are not as clear, unambiguous, or full as one would like; indeed they seem to me not to notice sufficiently the differences between three further accounts that might be given of CMT2, all compatible with thesis A.

* (3) It is possible to espouse thesis A, as Hare does, in opposition to Brandt's kind of rule-utilitarianism, and yet to hold that the PLSs we should use in our IMT or codal thinking are to be determined by precisely the same kind of inquiry that Brandt would use, i.e. by asking what PLSs are such that our having and fostering them will maximize the general utility or such that their 'general acceptance' in a society will be for the greatest good of that society—in other

words by asking, not about the utility of any particular action, as act-utilitarian CMT would do, but about the utility of our having a certain rule, practice, or PLS, as rule-utilitarian CMT would do. This is not the kind of 'specific rule-utilitarian' inquiry that is 'in effect not distinguishable from act-utilitarianism' that Hare takes as part of his own form of utilitarianism (*MT* 43), since it does not allow its rules 'to be of unlimited specificity', and it is also not a kind of inquiry that involves doing CMT1. CMT2, done along such Brandtian lines, would simply be entirely different from CMT1. Yet Hare sometimes seems to me to write as if this were the kind of inquiry to be used in selecting (etc.) PLSs for use in IMT. Thus he often says the PLSs are to be chosen on the basis of their 'acceptance-utility', an expression that is probably due to Brandt and most naturally suggests Brandt's line of thought. This comes out most clearly in the following passage:

the method to be employed is one which will select moral principles . . . on the score of their acceptance-utility, i.e., on the ground that they are the set of principles whose general acceptance in the society in question will do the best, all told, for the interests of the people in the society considered impartially. (*MT* 156; see 62, 137 and 1979*b*:148 f.)

I myself believe that Hare means to be more act-utilitarian or act-universal-prescriptivist than is suggested by this passage (and others), but there it is.

   (4) A more actarian approach is expressed in other some- *
what more official passages in chapter 3. In one Hare writes,

The best set [of PLSs] is that whose acceptance yields actions, dispositions, etc. most nearly approximating to those which would be chosen if we were able to use critical thinking [CMT1] all the time.

Then he adds, 'This answer can be given in terms of acceptance-utility, if one is a utilitarian', which suggests the *
Brandtian line (notice that Hare does not say, 'if one is an act-utilitarian'), but goes on to say:

if one is not a utilitarian but a Kantian, one can . . . [answer] by advocating the adoption of a set of maxims for general use whose acceptance yields actions, etc., most approximating to those which would be chosen if the categorical imperative were applied directly on each occasion by an archangel (*MT* 50).

In another place Hare speaks of a justifiably selected PLS as one 'whose general acceptance would lead to people's actions and dispositions approximating to the greatest extent to the deliverances of a perfectly conducted critical thinking', and a bit farther on he writes that

> well conducted critical thought will justify the selection of prima facie principles on the ground that the general acceptance of them will lead to actions which do as much good, and as little harm, as possible (*MT* 62).

These passages, except for the one that suggests a Brandtian line, describe a way of selecting (etc.) PLSs that is not rule-utilitarian; in fact they give a very different sense to the expression 'acceptance-utility' from that given in the passage previously quoted—an actarian rather than a rule-utilitarian one. That is, they imply that 'this PLS has acceptance-utility' may mean, not that its general acceptance maximizes utility,
* but that it leads us more often to hit the right action as determined by act-utilitarian CMT, i.e. CMT1, than we would otherwise—it ensures 'the greatest possible conformity to what an archangel would pronounce', or tells us what way of acting 'will *most probably* be in accord with the act-utilitarian ideal—i.e., be what the act-utilitarian archangel . . . would choose' (*MT* 46; H 1979*b*:148).

I think that the line in (4) is more nearly what Hare has in mind than that in (3), but am inclined to think that he is not very clearly realizing the difference between them, or seeing that the line in (3) can also be taken by one who is an act-utilitarian in the sense of accepting thesis A. In any case, if he means to take the line in (4), then it looks to me as if he must regard CMT2 as taking the form described in (1) or (2) or perhaps as some kind of combination of the two. Now I should like to point out that there is another line that an actarian might take.

(5) The line indicated in (4) might be called a 'frequency' view of the way in which CMT2 is to select (etc.) PLSs, since it involves rating PLSs by the frequency with which what they dictate turns out to be what the archangel (or well-done

CMT1) would conclude should be done. But a 'total utility' view is also open to the act-utilitarian who insists on thesis A and rejects the rule-utilitarian line in (3).[1] This emphasizes, not the frequency with which following a PLS will lead us to do the act-utilitarianly best act, but the *net* cost *vs.* benefit of the *series* of acts that constitutes following it, based on a * calculation of the cost *vs.* benefit of *each* act in the series, as compared with alternative PLSs. E.g., let E1, E2, E3, E4, and E5 represent all of the acts of conforming to a certain PLS, and suppose that the cost *vs.* benefit scores for them are, respectively, $+10$, -10, -5, $+15$, and $+30$. Then the net cost *vs.* benefit score for the series of acts and thus for that PLS will be $+40$. If we suppose that E1, E4, and E5 are also what the archangel would do, while E2 and E3 are not, then by the frequency test, that PLS will score 3 out of 5 hits. One PLS may score higher than another using the frequency method but lower using the total utility method, or vice versa.

The total utility method just indicated seems to fit the following passage from Hare better than the method described in (4): 'To generalize: if we are criticizing prima facie principles, we have to look at the consequences of inculcating them in ourselves and others . . .' (*MT* 48, 62). It is also different from the rule-utilitarian method described in (3), since it finds the score for a given PLS by adding up the scores for the various particular acts of conforming to it rather than by looking for some more global utility of our having that PLS.

(6) A somewhat different approach to the whole problem I * am raising is suggested by a passage in 'Utilitarianism and the Vicarious Affects' (H 1979*b*:149; cf. *MT* 48). In it Hare writes that, in dealing with the question of what our PLSs or IMPs should be, the act-utilitarian is 'concerned with a particular and very crucial kind of act'; Hare then distinguishes, in effect, between acts of the sort that an IMP instructs us to do or not to do, e.g. killing someone or keeping a promise by taking one's children on a picnic, and acts of adopting or teaching an IMP, or of fostering in oneself or others a * disposition to act on it or to feel compunction if one does not.

[1] This possibility was suggested to me by Peter Railton in conversation and elaborated by him in a letter.

Let us call acts of the first kind A-acts and those of the second, 'particular and very crucial kind', B-acts. Then B-acts will be on a different level from A-acts in the sense that B-acts will be acts involving IMPS about which A-acts to do or not to do. My problem is to find out just how Hare thinks we are to determine what our IMPs about A-acts should be, and so far I have been assuming that, unless he adopts line (3), he must be thinking that our IMPs are to be determined wholly by some sort of application of CMT1 to A-acts, i.e. that what I am calling CMT2 consists entirely of applying CMT1 in some way to the A-acts that constitute conforming to those IMPS, or that we are to ask always whether a certain A-act will maximize utility or not, not whether a certain B-act will. But if we make use of the above distinction, then there are two further possibilities. (6*a*) One is that we are to determine or appraise our IMPs about A-acts by applying act-utilitarian CMT1 not to A-acts, but only to B-acts involving the IMPs, i.e. that CMT2 consists of CMT1 as applied to B-acts rather than to A-acts—in it we are to ask not whether A-acts conforming to an IMP will each maximize utility, but always and only whether each B-act involving it will do so, or perhaps whether the whole series of B-acts that constitutes our *having* that IMP will do so. This is an interesting line of thought, and if it is what Hare has in mind in the sentence containing the words last quoted, as it seems to be, then it would give us a clear answer to my questions about what CMT2 is like, viz., that it would consist entirely of a use of the total utility method described in line (5) but as applied to the B-acts involving a given IMP rather than to the A-acts of conforming to it.

*   Line (6*a*) does, however, seem to me to pose a difficulty. According to Hare, as we saw, we humans need IMPS about A-acts because we are not archangels and are afflicted with such weaknesses as ignorance, lack of time, and partiality to friends and relatives, which often prevent us from doing sound CMT1 of the sort needed to discover critical moral principles to act on in particular cases. But, if this is so, will these weaknesses not also mess up our attempts to apply CMT1 to B-acts in the way required by (6*a*)? Will we not be driven to seek for IMPs about B-acts by the same troubles that drove us to look for IMPs about A-acts in the first place? Hare may reply that we are to seek for or criticize IMPs only if and when we are cool and competent, but we cannot always be so when our IMPS conflict, and yet we must then seek some kind of resolution by the use of critical thinking.

(6*b*) The other possibility is more complex. Let us suppose, as seems plausible in the light of all the things he says, that Hare would not be satisfied with lines (1) to (5) as described above—especially given that, except for (3) which is rule-utilitarian, they include no attention to B-acts—or with (6*a*). Then he might answer my question by saying that what I call CMT2 consists of applying CMT1 to *both* A-acts and B-acts in some kind of tandem, i.e. that the appraisal of a given or proposed IMP is to proceed by applying CMT1 to each of the A-acts that are or would be dictated by that IMP *and* to each of the B-acts that our *having* that IMP would involve. I take it that this would entail using the method described in line (5) to get a total utility score for the A-acts dictated by or conforming to that IMP by using act-utilitarian CMT1 on each of those acts and adding up the scores, plus doing the same for the B-acts relating to that IMP. Doing the latter would in effect be to make a cost-benefit analysis of the business of accepting, teaching, and sanctioning that IMP. Doing both would yield us two total utility scores which we could then add together to get the final score for that IMP. Of course, this would have to be accompanied by a similar study of alternative candidates for adoption as our IMPs to see which is preferable. And presumably all of this should be preceded by a stage of inquiry in which types of situations and actions are distinguished and possible IMPS are formulated, and in which those that would have little likelihood of applying in our actual world would be eliminated from consideration. In any case, it should be noticed that for line (6*b*) what I call CMT2 consists of two things: a use of act-utilitarian CMT1 to get utility scores for individual A-acts and B-acts, plus an adding up of these scores to get a total utility score for each of our IMPs. Clarity requires distinguishing two kinds of CMT, one using CMT1 to arrive at critical moral principles proper, and the other using it only as *part* of the selection and appraisal of IMPs. In neither of them, as described in (6*b*), would CMT be as much of a rule-utilitarian sort as Hare sometimes makes the latter appear, even if the latter does issue in just such IMPs as the rule-utilitarian is seeking.

4.4 My concern has been to get clear about Hare's views of the nature of CMT and its relation to IMT, and my main question has been about the nature of the kind of CMT that he thinks is to be employed in the selection and testing of the PLS or IMPs to be used in our IMT. Hare has been and in *Moral Thinking* still is less clear, unambiguous, or full than I think he should be, and I have tried mainly to formulate the lines of reply he might or sometimes seems to take in answer to my question. Perhaps I can put that question now by asking which of them comes closest to what he has in mind. I have other questions, of course, and I would also like to discuss some of the uses Hare makes of his distinction between levels or kinds of moral thinking, but these concerns must await another occasion.

5. Hare's Analysis of 'Ought' and its Implications

Allan Gibbard

5.1 PERHAPS no philosopher since Kant has developed a theory of moral judgement and moral reasoning so ingenious and so carefully worked through as R. M. Hare. Like Kant, Hare holds moral judgements to be expressible as imperatives of a special kind. Like Kant, Hare thinks that by the nature of moral judgement and moral reasoning, ideally rational judges must all agree in their moral conclusions. Probably unlike Kant, Hare thinks that in an important sense these conclusions will be utilitarian.

In *Freedom and Reason*, subsequent articles, and recently in *Moral Thinking*, Hare has clarified his account of the nature of moral judgement and developed the argument for his utilitarian conclusions. In these notes, I shall expound the theory as I read it and give my own rendition of what follows from it. Hare's own central argument in *Moral Thinking* comes on pages 110–11. Let me simply report, dogmatically and without commentary, that I do not find it clear what the argument on those pages is supposed to be. If the general line of the argument is correct, then there ought to be a theorem to that effect, precisely statable and clearly demonstrable. If not, there should be counter-examples: logically conceivable cases in which Hare's premises hold and his conclusions do not. In these notes, I shall be examining what can be proved from Hare's premises and what those premises leave open.

Whether Hare's premises are true will not concern me; I simply want to ask what follows from them. The chief premises are two: first, there is Hare's analysis of moral language. Moral statements, Hare says, are 'universal, prescriptive, and overriding'. I shall be offering a reading of

these requirements; indeed for universality I shall offer two
readings, one more stringent than the other. Second, there is a
principle I shall call *Conditional Reflection* put forth by Hare as
a conceptual truth. 'I cannot know the extent and quality of
others' sufferings and, in general, motivations and preferences
without having equal motivations with regard to what should
happen to me, were I in their places, with their motivations
and preferences' (*MT* 99). It is a combination of these two
premisses that gives Hare's argument its force.

5.2 Moral statements, Hare says, are (1) prescriptive,
(2) universalizable, and (3) overriding. One way to present
his analysis of moral language is to see what these terms mean
as Hare uses them. I am not confident of the explanations I
give, but they do seem to fit much of what Hare says and so
they seem well worth venturing.

Moral language, according to Hare, is 'prescriptive', and
that means that moral language expresses preferences (*MT*
107). A moral 'ought' statement expresses a speaker's
preferences in much the same way as a factual assertion
expresses the speaker's beliefs. A moral conviction, then, is a
state of preference, and we need to understand preferences.[1]

As Hare uses the term, 'preferences' can weigh against each
other; the resultant of all one's preferences Hare calls one's
'preferences all told'. 'Preferences', then, are tendencies
towards preferences all told. In what follows, I shall sometimes
speak of *preference tendencies* and *tending to prefer*, on the one
hand, and *preferences all told* or *preferring all told* on the other.
When I do speak simply of 'preferences', I shall follow Hare
and mean preference tendencies.

A moral 'ought' statement expresses a state of preference all
told. That is perhaps what Hare means when he says that
moral judgements are 'overriding'.

Sometimes a person will be indifferent between two
alternatives. In consequence, there may be more than one
alternative that, all told, he most prefers. Throughout this
paper, however, I shall ignore this possibility. Everything I

[1] Sometimes Hare speaks of 'motivations and preferences', and sometimes he uses
the term 'desire', but no sharp distinction is drawn between these terms. I shall be
using 'preference' as an all-purpose term for speaking of motivations.

say must be read as applying only to the special case in which no one is indifferent all told between any two alternatives.

We next need to understand *conditional preferences*. A   *
conditional preference is a preference I actually have for a
hypothetical circumstance. It may not be a preference I *would*
have if I *were* in that circumstance. We can construe it as a
straight actual preference between two hypothetical alternatives. To say

I *prefer* all told doing X to doing Y *given* circumstance S

is to say that I prefer all told

being in S and doing X

to

being in S and doing Y.

This account will hold for conditional preference tendencies
as well as for conditional preferences all told. Conditional
preference tendencies will add up to yield conditional preferences all told.

That sets the stage for two readings of universality. Moral
'ought' statements are prescriptions of a special kind: they are
universalizable: 'they entail identical judgements about all cases
identical in their universal properties' (*MT* 108). Given the
rest of what Hare says, this is equivalent to a requirement on
preferences—to a necessary and sufficient condition for a
person's preferences all told to constitute moral judgements. A
moral statement, Hare says, is an overriding prescription that
is universalizable: the prescriber must stand ready to prescribe
the same thing no matter what position he is to occupy. An
overriding prescription expresses one's preferences all told. To
say that moral 'ought' statements 'entail identical judgements
about all cases identical in their universal properties', then,
amounts to saying this: One's preferences all told about a
situation constitute moral judgements only if they favour the
same alternative for each position one might occupy: only if
for each position one might occupy, one's conditional preferences for the hypothetical case of being in that position put the
same alternative on top.

Let me call this the *Requirement of Weak Universality*, and call   *
preferences all told which satisfy it *weakly universal*. Some of

Hare's arguments appear to invoke a stronger requirement of universality. Weak Universality requires only that I prefer all told the same alternative for any position I might occupy. It does not require that my preferences all told be equally strong for each of those positions. I can care what position I occupy, so long as I do not care enough to reverse the direction of my preferences all told. If, on the other hand, a person's preferences all told are position-independent in strength as well as direction, then I shall call them *strongly universal*.

That gives us two possible readings of the universality that preferences all told must have if they are to constitute moral judgements. They might count as moral judgements so long as they were at least weakly universal; I shall call this the *liberal reading*. Alternatively they might count as moral judgements only if they are strongly universal—independent of who is who in strength as well as direction. This I shall call the *stringent reading*. In what follows, I shall take up both readings, and see what follows from each.

5.3 What preferences can a person have and be perfectly rational? Hare's account of rationality is a full-knowledge account: a preference is *rational* if it is formed with full and vivid awareness of everything involved.

Hare writes,

> I cannot know the extent and quality of others' sufferings and, in general, motivations and preferences without having equal motivations with regard to what should happen to me, were I in their places, with their motivations and preferences (*MT* 99).

I shall call this the *Conditional Reflection Principle*. To what 'motivations and preferences' does it apply? On a strict reading, it seems to apply to all, but we should allow for the possibility that it might not. In the first place, it might not apply to preferences that are irrational; indeed in an earlier statement of the principle, Hare did restrict his claim to rational preferences (II 1979c:631). In *Moral Thinking*, Hare gives his derivation in provisional form, restricting the preferences he treats to those that concern the intrinsic qualities of present experience (*MT* 106–7). Perhaps it is to this restricted class of preferences that the Conditional Reflection Principle applies.

I shall not try to settle which preferences fall under the Conditional Reflection Principle, but simply classify possible kinds of preferences. I shall call preferences to which the principle applies 'rationally required', and those to which it does not, 'idiosyncratic'. Hare explicitly applies the Conditional Reflection Principle to preferences not to suffer; thus if Hare is right, tending to prefer not to suffer will count as rationally required. Anyone who really understands what the suffering is like will tend to prefer not to undergo it, and tend as strongly as the person who is actually undergoing it.[2] Certain other preferences might be idiosyncratic. Suppose Cheops is rational and wants a big funeral. I may not care whether, if I am in Cheops's exact circumstances with his preference for a big funeral, I in fact have one. True, I do care whether I pleasantly anticipate the things I want to happen or live without hope. Hold all that constant, though: suppose I am to live a life like that of Cheops, full of well-founded hope for a big funeral. Why should I now care whether, things being equal before I die, I have a big funeral afterwards— even though I am forthwith to be like Cheops, who does care? If I might not care, even fully comprehending what things are like for Cheops, then Cheops's preference tendency for a big funeral is idiosyncratic.

A preference, then, is *rationally required* if anyone who fully and vividly understood its circumstance would have a like conditional preference—one exactly like it in strength and direction—for the hypothetical case of forthwith being in that precise circumstance. Otherwise, the preference is *idiosyncratic*. A preference tendency might, for all I have said, be rational without being rationally required. It is rational so long as the person whose preference it is would retain it if he were ideally knowledgeable. It is rationally required only if every ideally knowledgeable person conditionally reflects it—if every ideally knowledgeable person has a like conditional preference for the like exact circumstances.

Conditional preferences are actual preferences between hypothetical eventualities. A conditional preference may be echoed by a preference regarding the actual situation—but it

[2] Indeed, as I am reading Hare, he thinks that all preferences concerning the intrinsic qualities of one's present experience will be rationally required.

62 A. Gibbard

need not be, even if one is rational. The torturer wants not to be tortured himself, but may lack any preference that others not be tortured. If we, unlike the torturer, do intrinsically want others not to be tortured, I shall call those preferences *sympathetic*. I define sympathetic preferences broadly as follows: where someone tends to prefer A to B, I *sympathetically copy* his preference if I tend to prefer A to B, as strongly as he does or perhaps less strongly, because of what it is like to be in his situation. A *sympathetic preference* for a circumstance is a preference tendency for that circumstance which either (1) sympathetically copies a preference that, as a part of that circumstance, someone else has, or (2) sympathetically copies a conditional preference that one has oneself for the case of being in the position of that other person. Where Conditional Reflection applies, (1) and (2) are equivalent.

Sympathetic preferences must be sharply distinguished
* from conditionally reflected preferences. Conditionally reflected preferences are preferences on one's own behalf, and they pertain to the hypothetical situation of being in the position of someone else. They are governed by the Conditional Reflection Principle, which applies to altruists and egoists alike. Sympathetic preferences, in contrast, may pertain to the actual situation, and they are preferences on behalf of someone else. Egoists lack them, whereas according to Hare, anyone whose preferences constitute moral convictions must have them. Hare's strategy is to let Conditional Reflection interact with a requirement of universalization to yield this result.

Both conditionally reflected preferences and sympathetic preferences are derived, in a sense: having them depends on a realization of what it is like to be in a circumstance one is not presently in. One takes on, at least conditionally, preference tendencies that primarily fit the circumstances of someone else. What are we to say, then, of the preferences from which these are derived? A preference not forthwith to suffer is Hare's prime example of such a non-derived preference tendency. It has two chief properties. In the first place, as I have noted, it is rationally required. In addition, though, it has another important property: it is self-pertinent.

A *universal preference tendency*, I shall say, is a preference for one thing's being true rather than another, where these things are describable in universal terms. A *self-pertinent preference tendency* is one that is not universal, and is in effect a preference for oneself having some property. My preference that I not break my promises is self-pertinent, whereas my preference that knowledge advance is universal.

We can now label various important kinds of preference tendencies. A preference not forthwith to suffer is self-pertinent and rationally required; I shall call such preferences *basic preference tendencies*. Cheops's preference for a big funeral is self-pertinent, but if what I suggested about it is right, it is idiosyncratic, not rationally required. A preference that is self-pertinent and idiosyncratic I shall call a *personal ideal*.

5.4 On the liberal reading, one's preferences all told constitute moral judgements so long as they are at least weakly universal; it is not required that they be strongly universal as well. One must prefer the same alternative for any position one might occupy, but one can do so with varying intensities. Now on the liberal reading, few of Hare's conclusions follow from his premises. The Principle of Conditional Reflection and the Requirement of Weak Universality do not together entail that one must be a utilitarian or anything close. They do not rule out a partial amoralism. Take, for example, a person whose preferences all told are partially altruistic. He will have weakly universal preferences all told for some situations and not for others. On the liberal reading, he will make moral judgements in some cases, and refrain from making any moral judgement whatsoever in other cases: he will be a partial amoralist.

Now even when a person's preferences all told do constitute moral convictions on the liberal reading, those convictions need not be in any way utilitarian. A universal preference tendency—say, an intrinsic preference that promises not be broken—may be strong enough to render my preferences all told for a situation weakly universal even though I lack sympathetic preferences altogether. Suppose it satisfies the greater totality of the basic preference tendencies of the people involved in a situation for me to break a promise rather than keep it. Nevertheless, if I tend to prefer universally that

promises not to be broken, that universal preference tendency
may prevail for each position I might occupy. It may be that
for each person involved, when I form my preferences all told
for the case of being in his circumstances, my own preference
tendency that promises be kept outweighs whatever basic
preference tendencies I acquire from him by Conditional
Reflection. If so, then on the liberal reading I think I ought to
keep my promise. Preferences can be weakly universal and yet
lack all trace of utilitarianism.

On the stringent reading, my preferences regarding a
situation do not constitute a moral judgement unless they are
strongly universal. My preferences for the situation must be
independent of the position I am to occupy, and be so not only
in direction but in strength. For this stringent reading, we can
prove a theorem of the kind Hare seems to need. The
'Sympathy Theorem', as I shall call it, says roughly this:
Suppose I am ideally rational and my preferences all told for a
situation are strongly universal. Then I shall want for another
whatever I want for myself should I be in his exact
circumstance. In addition, I may have universal preference
tendencies that are not generated in this way. How close all
this comes to making me a utilitarian will depend on the
kinds of preference tendencies an ideally rational person can
have.

The Sympathy Theorem is tricky to state and to interpret,
and so I begin with a simple case. Take a motorist who can
park conveniently only by crushing a bicycle. Suppose my
own preferences for the case are strongly universal. Now by
Conditional Reflection I must tend to prefer that if I am the
bicyclist, my bicycle not be crushed. Therefore, we shall see, I
must tend to prefer with equal intensity that if I am the
motorist, the bicycle not be crushed.

*   Begin with basic preference tendencies. Let $B(m)$ be the
strength of the motorist's basic preference that he be able to
park, and let $B(b)$ be the strength of the bicyclist's basic
preference that his bicycle be crushed—a negative quantity.
By Conditional Reflection, I must tend to prefer with strength
$B(m)$ that I be able to park if I am the motorist, and tend to
prefer with negative strength $B(b)$ that my bicycle be crushed
if I am the bicyclist. That holds whether in fact I am the

Table 1. Preference Tendencies for Crushing the Bicycle

Preference tendencies in favour of
crushing the bicycle for the case of:

My being the motorist:	My being the bicyclist:
$B(m)$ basic	$B(b)$ basic
$N(m)$ non-basic	$N(b)$ non-basic
$B(m)+N(m)$ preference all told	$B(b)+N(b)$ preference all told

motorist, the bicyclist, or a third party. These conditional basic preferences are shown in Table 1.

What sympathetic preference tendencies must I have, then, if my preferences are to be strongly universal? Let $N(m)$ be all my preference tendencies apart from the basic ones for the case of my being the motorist. Let $N(b)$ likewise be the non-basic preference tendencies I have for the case of my being the bicyclist. The Requirement of Strong Universality is that my preferences all told be the same, in strength as well as direction, for each position I might occupy.

$$B(m) + N(m) = B(b) + N(b).$$

By algebra, this holds if and only if

$$N(b) - B(m) = N(m) - B(b).$$

Call this quantity K. Then we have

$$N(b) = B(m) + K \text{ and } N(m) = B(b) + K.$$

My non-basic preference tendencies for each circumstance, this says, are equal in strength to the other's basic preference tendency plus a constant K, which is independent of position. They are composed of a sympathetic preference that echoes the other's basic preference at full strength, plus, possibly, a universal preference tendency that is the same for all positions I might occupy.

A simple case illustrated the kind of argument that proves the Sympathy Theorem. To state and prove the theorem itself, we must generalize in two ways. First, we must extend the argument to many-person cases. Second, we must allow for self-pertinent preference tendencies that are idiosyncratic rather than basic.

In the car and bicycle case, we applied Conditional Reflection to the basic preferences of the motorist and the bicyclist. The motorist wants to park; the bicyclist wants his bicycle intact. We treated these as basic preference tendencies, and so derived self-pertinent conditional preference tendencies that anyone must have for the case of being the one and for the case of being the other. For the case of being the motorist, I must tend to prefer being able to park, and for the case of being the bicyclist, I must strongly tend to prefer an intact bicycle.

To prove the theorem in general, we simply take as given the self-pertinent conditional preference tendencies an observer has for each position he might occupy. Let there be n people, and consider two alternatives a and b. Consider an observer who may and may not be one of the people $1 \ldots n$. For each person i, let B_i be the totality of the observer's conditional self-pertinent preference tendencies, positive and negative, for a over b, for the case of his being in i's exact circumstance. Let N_i be the totality of his other conditional preference tendencies for the case of being in i's position. Suppose that his preferences all told are strongly universal. That is to say, the strength P of the observer's preferences all told for a over b is the same for each position he might occupy: for each person i, we have

$$B_i + N_i = P,$$

where P is fixed. Now let

$$K = P - B_1 - \ldots - B_n,$$

so that

$$P = B_1 + \ldots + B_n + K.$$

For each i, we can write $B_1 + \ldots + B_n$ as $B_i + S_i$, where S_i is the total of the B_j's for $j = i$. Thus we have

$$P = B_i + S_i + K.$$

Each B_j, recall, is the observer's conditional self-pertinent preference tendency for a over b, for the case of his being j. S_i, then, is what his total sympathetic preferences would be for the case of his being i, if for that case he sympathetically echoed, at full strength, his conditional self-pertinent preference tendencies for the case of being each other person.

This, then, is the *Sympathy Theorem*. Take an *archangel*: an observer who is ideally rational, and whose preferences all told for a situation are strongly universal. For each position he might occupy, his conditional preferences all told for the case of his occupying that position can be represented as having three components, one of which may be null: (i) his own self-pertinent preferences for the case, (ii) sympathetic preferences that echo all his self-pertinent preference tendencies for the $n - 1$ remaining circumstances he might have occupied in the situation, and (iii) other preferences that are the same, in their total strength and direction, for each of the n circumstances. This constant preference may have strength zero, in which case only components (i) and (ii) are present. The self-pertinent preferences in (i) and (ii) may include both basic and idiosyncratic preference tendencies.

An archangel, then, tends to want for others what he wants for himself if in their exact circumstances. His sympathetic preference tendencies echo at full strength whatever conditional preference tendencies he has for the case of his occupying the position of anyone else. In addition, he may have universal preference tendencies. Strongly universal preferences all told can always be represented as the resultant of these three kinds of elements.

5.5 The Sympathy Theorem is independent of the Principle of Conditional Reflection. The argument for utilitarianism must presumably come from combining the two, and perhaps adding further assumptions about the kinds of preference tendencies archangels can have.

What are we to make of the decomposition the Sympathy Theorem displays? Much depends on what goes into the constant preference K. If we could show that K must be null, then on the stringent reading of universalization, we would have proved an important part of Hare's utilitarian thesis.

On one special assumption, there does seem to be an

argument for thinking K to be zero. Suppose there are only two kinds of preference tendencies an ideally rational person can have: basic and sympathetic. Then, we might say, the constant preference K is ruled out.

A stronger argument is needed, though. The Sympathy Theorem gives a way in which strongly sympathetic preferences can be represented. They can be represented, it says, as having three kinds of components, one of which is K. The theorem does not tell us, however, that these components are psychologically distinct. K might, for all it tells us, be a mere book-keeping device. If it were, then ruling out preference tendencies that are universal in a psychologically genuine sense will not force K to zero.

What we can say is this: if partial sympathy produces strongly universal preferences all told, it must do so by coincidence. If I lack universal preference tendencies in any psychologically real sense, then a non-zero K will be simply the difference between my actual partially sympathetic preferences and what these preferences would be if they were fully sympathetic. Call this my *sympathy differential*. This sympathy differential might have been different for each position I could occupy in a situation. If it is non-zero and yet the same for each such position, that will be by coincidence. Any small change in the basic preferences involved will break the equality.

Suppose, for instance, Eve basically tends to prefer eating the apple with strength B, and for the case of my being Adam I sympathize in proportion $1 - \varepsilon$. That contributes a quantity of εB to my sympathy differential for the case of my being Adam. It contributes nothing to my sympathy differential for the case of my being Eve, since for that case I conditionally reflect her basic preference tendencies at full strength. Now had Eve wanted less strongly to eat the apple, this contribution to my sympathy differential εB for the case of my being Adam would have been less. The change would not affect my sympathy differential for the case of my being Eve, and so the equality of sympathy differentials would be broken. We see, then, that when sympathy differentials are non-zero and equal, the equality is broken by any change in the basic preferences involved; in that sense the equality is a fluke. Partial sympathy can yield strongly universal preferences all told only by fluke.

Moral convictions, Hare could well say, are preferences all told that are not only strongly universal, but strongly universal reliably—strongly universal by more than a fluke. In what follows, I shall assume this stronger requirement on moral convictions.

Return, then, to the main line of the argument. Rational preference tendencies, we are now assuming, are all either basic or sympathetic. It follows, I have argued, that if one's preferences all told are strongly universal by more than a fluke, the *K* of the sympathy theorem is zero. The rest of the argument for utilitarianism is straightforward. On the assumption that rational preference tendencies are all either basic or sympathetic, all self-pertinent preferences are basic. They are all thus subject to Conditional Reflection. Hence for any circumstance the archangel might be in, his self-pertinent conditional preferences will simply be the basic preferences of the person whose circumstance it is. By the Sympathy Theorem emended, the archangel sympathetically echoes these preferences at full strength for the actual situation. His preferences all told, then, are composed of his own basic preferences and the basic preferences of everyone else: he is a utilitarian.

The provisional argument Hare presents in *Moral Thinking* does invoke a special restrictive assumption close to the one here. 'We are to assume, when we come to universalize our prescriptions, as morality demands, that we have to consider only those prescriptions and preferences of others which they would retain if they were always prudent in the sense just defined' (106–7). I shall not try to interpret this restriction precisely. Eventually, after all, Hare wants to dispense with it, and so I am chiefly asking what happens if we do. If, though, we read Hare as assuming that rational preferences are all either basic or sympathetic, then the Sympathy Theorem gives us an argument for his utilitarian conclusion.

Whether in fact rational preferences are always either basic or sympathetic is an empirical question. It is a matter of *
which preference tendencies would survive fully realizing everything involved. We can address a priori not whether the

answer is yes or no, but whether Hare needs an answer of yes as a premiss—and whether, as I have been asking, that premiss is sufficient for Hare's utilitarian conclusion to follow. On the stringent reading, I have argued, the premiss is sufficient; I next show that it is needed.

What happens, we still need to ask, if some non-basic, non-sympathetic preference tendencies are rational? Take first, preference tendencies that are self-pertinent and idiosyncratic. I call such preference tendencies *personal ideals*. Cheops tends to prefer a big funeral, and let us suppose he is rational in doing so. Let us suppose also that I am rational in being indifferent between being like Cheops and having a big funeral and being like Cheops and not having a big funeral. Then Cheops's preference tendency is self-pertinent and idiosyncratic; it constitutes a personal ideal. It is self-pertinent because it is a preference tendency that he himself have a big funeral, not that people like him in general have big funerals. It is idiosyncratic because it is both possible (i) rationally to have that preference tendency for the circumstance of being like Cheops, and possible (ii) rationally to lack that preference tendency for the circumstance of being exactly like Cheops. By assumption, after all, Cheops rationally has that preference tendency and I rationally lack it.

Now since I have no conditional preference tendency for my having a big funeral if I am like Cheops, the Sympathy Theorem does not come into play. My preferences can be strongly universal even though I do not echo Cheops's preference tendency for a big funeral with any sympathetic preference tendency of my own. In this case, then, archangels may disagree. For suppose Cheops and I are both archangels. Cheops's preferences all told will be composed, among other things, of a preference tendency for a big funeral. I, on the other hand, need not tend to prefer in the slightest Cheops's having a big funeral.

Cheops might conditionally tend to prefer having a big funeral not only for the actual case, but even for the case of his being someone who, like me, is indifferent to the size of his funeral. In that case the Sympathy Theorem does apply: it says he must echo these conditional preferences with sympathetic preferences for the actual case. He wants to have a big funeral if he is like me, and so he must want me to have a big funeral. Otherwise his preference for whether I have a big funeral would depend on who is who: on whether he was to be in his position or mine.

In short, then, the preferences all told of an archangel with personal ideals will be somewhat utilitarian, but with a difference. His archangelic preferences all told for a situation will depend, in effect, on the sum of his evaluations of how each person fares in that situation. In evaluating how a person fares, the archangel will weigh in the degree to which that person's own basic preference tendencies are satisfied; in that respect, he will still tend to be utilitarian. If, though, the archangel has personal ideals, he will also include in his evaluation of how the person fares the degree to which the archangel's own personal ideals are satisfied, as they apply to the circumstance of his being exactly like the person in question. The archangel will be a 'welfare plus his own ideals' utilitarian. If different archangels have different personal ideals, then not all archangels will agree.

Finally, we need to look at universal preference tendencies. A preference tendency is universal if its content makes no reference to the person who holds it.[3] Now if my preferences are otherwise strongly universal, adding a universal preference tendency will not make them otherwise. Universal preference tendencies are position-independent: the conditional preference tendencies they generate are the same for every position one might occupy. For suppose otherwise: suppose my preference for A over B depended on what my own position was to be. In other words, suppose that for some pair of circumstances C_1 and C_2 that differed only in the position I occupy, my conditional preference for A over B if I am in C_1 differed, in direction or intensity, from my preference for A over B if I am in C_2. Then as far as that preference tendency goes, either I am not indifferent between $A \& C_1$ and $A \& C_2$, or I am not indifferent between $B \& C_1$ and $B \& C_2$. Since each pair differs only in the position I occupy, the preference tendency in question is not universal.

---

[3] We might instead say that a preference tendency is universal if it contains no reference to particulars. I doubt that much in my argument turns on which characterizations we use, and so I shall ignore the issue.

Now since universal preferences are already position-independent, the Requirement of Strong Universality leaves them undisturbed. It generates no sympathetic preferences on account of them. In particular, I can have strongly universal preferences all told without adding up the strengths of the universal preferences I have for the various positions I might occupy.

Universal preference tendencies, then, may be left as they are by Strong Universalizability. We need to consider universal preference tendencies of two kinds: rationally required and idiosyncratic. A universal preference tendency is rationally required if every rational person shares it; otherwise it is idiosyncratic. Nothing I have said rules out universal preference tendencies of either kind. If a universal preference tendency is rationally required, then all rational people will share it, and it will figure in their preferences all told. It need figure only once, though: an archangel need not echo the universal preferences of anyone else with new sympathetic preference tendencies. If, on the other hand, a universal preference tendency is idiosyncratic, then it can perfectly well figure in the strongly universal preferences of those who rationally have it, and be left out of the strongly universal preferences of those who lack it. Archangels with idiosyncratic
* universal preferences may disagree.

6. Well-being and its Interpersonal Comparability

James Griffin

6.1 TO my mind, the two most important new contributions in Hare's *Moral Thinking*, not to be found in his previous books, are his proposal of a two-level structure for moral thought and his solution to the problem of interpersonal comparability. The first has deservedly received a lot of attention. The second has received less, though it is full of interest, and I should like to take it as my subject now.[1] I am largely sympathetic with Hare's solution. But I see a difficulty with it that seems to me to require amendment. What is at issue here about comparability also has interest for the light it throws on the nature of well-being—the nature, that is, of what we compare. Let me start with a few points about links between conceptions of well-being and problems about comparability.

The link between conceptions of well-being and problems of comparability. On a mental-state conception of well-being, the problem about comparability is largely, though by no means entirely, a problem about knowledge of other minds. Mental-state accounts face well-known difficulties, the main one being lack of scope; they have a hard time accommodating all that it seems right to regard as part of well-being.

We might therefore use instead an actual-desire conception of well-being, say the conception of utility as the subjective value that a person attaches to a gamble. If we do, the problem about comparability is still largely one of knowledge of other minds, though with a different focus. One trouble

[1] The argument in this paper is drawn largely from ch. 7 of Griffin, 1986, applied here to Hare's proposed solution.

with the actual-desire account is that, though it may suit empirical parts of decision theory and of economic theory, it is much less suitable for moral theory (and for welfare economics, and the normative parts of decision theory, and large parts of social choice theory). A person may in fact want what will be bad for him, and the notion of well-being that we, as moral philosophers, are after must be centred on real, not subjectively perceived, benefit. So if we manage to give an adequate account of the comparability of utilities defined on actual preferences over gambles, it is not clear that we should yet have shown how well-being, in the sense that is of interest to normative theories, is to be made comparable.

Were we, therefore, to abandon conceptions of well-being out of the utilitarian tradition and use, say, an objective conception such as John Rawls's index of primary goods (Rawls, 1971, sects. 15, 49), the problem of comparability would obviously be much eased. We should now compare persons in respect of such objective and relatively accessible things as their income and social institutions in which they live. Still, these narrow objective conceptions of well-being have their troubles too. They impose a cut-off on considerations available to moral theory that it may not be able to accept and still answer questions at the centre of its interest.[2]

We ease problems about comparability almost as much, if we adopt what Derek Parfit has called an 'objective-list' account of well-being (Parfit, 1984, App. I). How well off a person is would then turn on the extent to which he realizes the objective prudential values on the list—say such things as autonomy, accomplishment, deep personal relationships, and so on. But objective-list accounts have obvious troubles. They are, at least on simple interpretations of them, too insensitive to variations between individuals to provide a plausible account of well-being, if 'well-being' is understood as an all-encompassing assessment of the quality of a particular person's life.

That brings us to informed-desire conceptions, which can be developed in different ways. Comparability would now, as it was on the actual-desire conception, partly be a matter of knowing how strongly a person wants something (when he is

[2] I argue this in Griffin, 1982, sect. 7.

informed, or would want it if he were informed). But since the informed-desire conception can be developed in ways that bring it at least into the vicinity of an objective-list conception, many interpersonal comparisons might often be made simply in terms of the items on the list. Still, informed-desire accounts have their troubles, chief among them being whether, in the end, they really can explain comparability (Brandt, 1979:146–8; and 1982, sects. 8–10). Can they even explain intrapersonal intertemporal comparisons, when the latter involve radical change in preferences? If not, the informed-desire account will not do even as a theory of prudence.

What these links between comparability and conceptions of well-being show is that we need three things to come together for us at the same time: first, we need the account of well-being that we adopt, whether it is of a broad utilitarian sort or a narrower objective sort, to be a plausible account of the domain of prudential value that it tries to cover; second, it must be what we want to use, for purposes of moral judgement, as the basis for comparison between different persons; and, third, it has to lend itself to the sorts of measurement that moral deliberation needs.

6.2 *Hare's solution.* Hare adopts, I believe correctly, a version of the desire conception of well-being—one, I think, that belongs in the informed-desire category.[3] Later on I shall return to how this might influence his solution to the problem of comparability.

Hare's solution is simple—subtly argued but in outline simple. There is, first, the thesis of Chapter 5. (1) '. . . to have knowledge of somebody else's motivations is *eo ipso* to form the same motivations oneself with regard to hypothetical situations in which one would forthwith be in the others' positions' (*MT* 127–8). Next, Hare simply assumes that (2) we do indeed sometimes have knowledge of other minds (*MT* 118–19, 126–7). In making this assumption, Hare may seem to be helping himself to far too much—in effect, to most of what a solution of the comparison problem needs. But it seems to me

---

[3] See *MT* 103–4. But Hare records there some doubts about where precisely to stand on those issues. The doubts, if I understand them, are connected with the success that a desire account has in accommodating certain kinds of intrapersonal intertemporal comparisons, about which more below.

an entirely reasonable move. As he observes, a way of meeting
extreme scepticism about other minds is 'crucial to almost all
parts of philosophy' (*MT* 119). And there is a practical pay-off
in making the assumption; it allows us to focus our attention
on the remaining moves that comparability also needs. What
exactly is the nature of an interpersonal comparison? Are
comparisons possible on some conceptions of well-being (say,
the sort of desire account Hare holds) but not on others? Are
they possible on the scale that moral and political thinking
needs?

The first is the important question. And it is a difficult
question even with the assumption of knowledge of other
minds. Suppose I know a lot about your experiences. I can
correctly, fully, even vividly, represent them to myself. But my
being able to represent to myself the feel of your experience is,
in a way, too much of a good thing. It leaves me with one
perception of the feel of my own experience and a second
* perception of the feel of yours. There is still a gap. How do I
get the *two* experiences on to *one* scale? Knowledge of other
minds does not take us far enough. But premises (1) and (2)
together, Hare says, enable us to reduce interpersonal
comparisons to the much less problematic intrapersonal ones
(*MT* 128). We can say that (3) '. . . in so far as I fully
represent to myself the strengths of other people's preferences,
I have preferences, myself now, regarding what should
happen to me were I in their positions with their preferences.
If I do this with two other people or more, I can then compare
the strengths of their preferences by comparing the strengths
of my own corresponding ones. Thus, on these assumptions,
the comparison problem would be solved' (*MT* 128).

The central move in this solution—the reduction of
interpersonal comparisons to intrapersonal ones by appeal to
the judger's own preference as to possible states of himself—is,
as Hare acknowledges, now a quite popular one. Though they
develop this basic idea in different ways, John Harsanyi
(1976, ch. 2; 1977, ch. 4), Kenneth Arrow (1977 and 1978),
and Amartya Sen (1973:14–5) have all employed it.

6.3 *A difficulty with the solution.* Could the crucial judger's
preference really be a preference of his at all? I am supposed to
introduce interpersonal measurement for my own use by

forming a preference between possible states of myself. I prefer, I decide, taking on a life like that quiet scholar's, with his risk-aversion and security and contentment, to taking on a life like that mountaineer's, with his taste for adventure and the perils and challenges he faces. Now, usually when I decide whether I should prefer one of these lives to the other, I appeal to my own values or tastes or attitudes. I might, for instance, prefer the scholar's life because I morally disapprove of risking one's life on mountains if one has, as that mountaineer has, children to support. But that would not be a preference that gets us at the well-being of the two lives. To get at that I must strip away my own moral views. But then, stripped of my moral views, I might still prefer living the scholar's life simply because I am, like him, risk-averse. But that would not get us at an interpersonal comparison of well-being, either; it merely shows what I, as I am now, enjoy. So I must strip away my own tastes and inclinations as well. Now, the difficulty that I have in mind is not whether one can ever learn enough about the scholar's and the mountaineer's lives to form a preference between them, or whether one can ever decide that one of them is better off than the other. It seems to me that one can. The problem is, rather, how I, stripped as I have to become in order not to distort the comparison, can form *any* preference of my own between what are supposed to be in some sense states of myself, *me-as-the-scholar* and *me-as-the-mountaineer*. By reference to what can I now form the preference? Disendowed as I have to be, I have only what anyone else has at his disposal, namely general knowledge of human nature and particular knowledge about that scholar and that mountaineer. I can appeal to the human sciences; I can appeal to information about the extent to which that scholar's and that mountaineer's interests are satisfied. But then the reference to *my preference*, to which states *I should choose* to enter, is superfluous. It is not, at least in the first instance, a matter of my personal choice or preference at all, but rather of judgement on grounds available to anyone about two lives. *I* enter only as making the judgement that the one person is better off than the other. My judgement in certain cases may be wrong; it may differ from yours. But these are possibilities with any judgement. And if you and I disagree over the scholar and the mountaineer, our disagreement is not like a disagreement in our personal preferences, which typically arise from our differing tastes and attitudes.

The purified preference that this solution to the comparison problem needs, preference purged of any particular point of
* view, seems to leave too little; it looks like preference purged of what is needed to make sense of preference. Could there be preference in these circumstances? So could preference, after all, be what bridges the gap?

6.4 *Can the difficulty be met?* Hare is well aware of the difficulty (*MT* 125). It is not a difficulty, he rightly remarks, just for *interpersonal* comparisons. Not only may my values, tastes, and attitudes differ from yours, they may also differ from what mine were in the past or will be in the future; *intrapersonal* comparison is also at stake. Hare agrees that I cannot use *my* antecedent values, tastes, and attitudes to form the preference that yields interpersonal comparison (*MT* 128), since they may not be relevant to what things are like for you with your possibly different tastes. But if we get around this difficulty by banning all appeal to our own present values, tastes, and attitudes, Hare sees my difficulty arising: '. . . how can we form a preference at all? For are not all preferences formed on the basis of tastes existing at the time?' (*MT* 125). He replies that to *form* preferences one does not have to have them already. And surely he is right. Tastes and attitudes change; we frequently form new preferences. Anyway, not only do our tastes and attitudes go through changes that we passively observe; we also actively change them. Many preferences—and preferences central to prudence and morality—come about because we go out and gain under-standing of the nature of the options before us with the aim of
* giving shape to our inchoate or unenlightened desires.

However, this does not seem to me to meet the difficulty. Even if I form an entirely new preference it must still be an expression of *my* values or tastes or attitudes—not, of course, necessarily antecedent ones, possibly ones that only now, for the first time, come into existence. Still, they must be *mine*, and not everyone need have them. Without them, I would have no
* preference. Of course, I have—we all have—a general (vacuous) preference to have a more, rather than a less,

valuable life, a life of higher, rather than lower, quality. But this general preference just takes the question about what is going on in comparisons back one stage. If I can form a judgement as to the relative quality of the scholar-state and the mountaineer-state, as no doubt sometimes I can, then I should prefer entering the better state. But how do I decide which is better?

Take this case. Smith's great ambition in life is to become a millionaire. He sees it as life's crowning achievement. Whether or not it is, that is how he sees things. Perhaps he lacks imagination; perhaps his horizons are limited; but he does not even entertain the possibility of another goal in life. In a way the very limits of his vision contribute to the intensity of his desire: being a millionaire gets invested with all the attraction of being what it is to have a valuable life. Jones, on the other hand, attaches no intrinsic value to money; his ends in life are to live autonomously, to love and be loved, to accomplish something important in his life, to enjoy himself, . . . Suppose Smith and Jones both reach their goals. How do I compare their well-being? According to Hare, my knowing Smith's situation and aims would give me now a desire of a certain strength about my landing forthwith in that situation with those aims—and similarly for Jones. But 'strength' in what sense? No doubt, with a million in the bank and seeing things Smith's way, I should want it a lot. And, with Jones's success seen through Jones's eyes, I should want that a lot too. But there is still a gap. How do I get these two strong desires on to one scale? We cannot be after 'strength' in   * the sense of felt intensity, because just how strongly we feel our desires is largely a matter of upbringing (Smith easily gets emotional; Jones has a stiff upper lip), and has no secure correlation with how well off we end up. Nor could it be 'strength' in the sense of motivational force; a person can succumb to desires that are not in his best interest. What we are after must be 'strength' in some such sense as 'place in an informed preference ordering'. The relevant desires here must be desires formed by appreciation of the nature of the objects of the desire. Maybe Smith is sufficiently cushioned by his lack of imagination so that he is not at all disillusioned when he gets his million; but perhaps also, if his horizons were not

so limited, he would want some of the things Jones is after even more. Perhaps some things just do make life more valuable than others; some things may just be more desirable, when we are informed, than others. It seems very likely. But then judgements to that effect have little to do with the judger's own preferences about entering one state or another. It is less a matter of what the judger in fact wants (even of his desires formed on the spot) than of how desirable certain things are. The judger cannot form a preference between entering the total Smith-state or the total Jones-state until he knows the strength of Smith's and Jones's desires, in the relevant sense of 'strength'. Hare gives no clear answer to the question, 'what is the relevant sense of "strength"?' If the answer is, 'strength' in the sense of 'place in an informed preference ordering', then part—not the whole, but part—of
* the ground for interpersonal comparisons are the things that are desirable for persons generally.[4]

This is not to say that individual differences do not much matter. Take a simple case. Lately Smith has eaten so much marzipan that the prospect of a piece now makes him feel sick; I, however, should love one. But I have no trouble making the counterfactual judgement that if I had had a surfeit of marzipan, my stomach would be just as much turned by another piece as Smith's is. And here all I need appeal to is my own values, tastes, and attitudes, applied to counterfactual circumstances; the sense in which it is my personal preference at work is unproblematic. And it is beyond doubt that many interpersonal comparisons turn on differences between people that result from their peculiar circumstances, variations in their upbringing or genes, and so on. Now the solution to the comparison problem would be simplest if we could say that all comparisons are to be seen on the model of the marzipan case—that comparisons may often involve much more radically

---

[4] The question, ' "strength" in what sense?', is a pertinent one for all the many writers who explain interpersonal comparisons as comparisons of strength of desires. A recent example is Donald Davidson (1986). What he offers as the 'basis' of interpersonal comparisons seems to me right as far as it goes (indeed, it seems to me to reorientate discussion of comparability very much in the right direction), but it does not go far enough. One way to see this is to press the question, ' "strength" in what sense?', and to press also the variety of kinds of comparisons (some of which I take up below) that this sense of 'strength' must fit.

counterfactual conditions, but they are always *my*, the *judger's*, preferences (tastes, values, attitudes) that come into play. But take a much less simple case. Take a case where there is no obvious overlap in the values, tastes, and attitudes of the judger and his subject—at least, in the values, tastes, and attitudes relevant to the judgement that has to be made here. The Fool attaches no value to Socrates' life. Socrates attaches * none to the Fool's life. How would each decide how relatively well off they are? Socrates can, of course, decide: if I had the Fool's values, tastes, and attitudes, I should find the Fool's life valuable; I should actually want it a lot. But *finding* it valuable and *actually* wanting it in those circumstances, cannot be what matters. In any case, would this decision of Socrates be a personal preference of his? And is this the sort of decision that leads to comparability? The answer in both cases seems to be, 'No'. What Socrates needs to make is a judgement of a very different sort from what we ordinarily understand by a personal .preference. He needs to know how much persons generally, when informed, would want each life, how desirable they are. This judgement *can* be expressed as a personal preference, but the nature of the judgement is very special: it is a judgement about prudential values that is independent of what any particular individual's desires or preferences happen to be. That is, Socrates should need to know, primarily, what made life valuable. He should have to appeal to his understanding of what humans, or sometimes humans of a certain type, are capable of, and of the various peaks that human life can reach. Then he should have to decide how close he and the Fool came to some peak. What he should not particularly need to consult is the phenomenological 'feel' of their experience, nor their personal tastes and attitudes, nor his own preferences about landing in the one sort of life or the other. The case of Socrates and The Fool is, as I have said, relatively complicated. It represents only one kind of compari-son, and in other kinds a judger would indeed have to consult the personal tastes and attitudes of the parties to the comparison. Still, it is one kind, and it shows something about the grounds of comparisons.

It is true, of course, that Mill's own discussion of Socrates and the Fool gives preference considerable prominence, but I

do not think that the prominence he gives it is at odds with what I am saying. It was not at all implausible of Mill to take as the authoritative comparison of Socrates' life and the Fool's the *preferences* of persons who have experience of both. Still, there is an important sense in which the preferences that
* appear in this comparison are not personal ones; they are not expressions of each individual's tastes or attitudes or concerns. They are desires formed by the perception of the nature of the two lives. The preferences relevant to this comparison are not the ones formed by anything peculiar to the judger.[5] They are formed, in a way, both from scratch and from no particular point of view, simply from an understanding of the objects
* before us. So reference to the *judger's* personal preference between *himself-as-this* or *himself-as-that* drop away as irrelevant. And the judgements relevant to comparisons do not even need to take the form of pair-wise comparisons. Each object can be placed singly on the general profile of values: the values in a Socratic life matter a lot; the Fool's gratifications do not matter much.

These issues about comparability, and the issues about the nature of well-being that they largely turn on, go very deep, and I know that I have just scratched the surface.[6] Let me say a little more about the latter, and then return to the former.

6.5 *Well-being*. All that I can do here is quickly to sketch one way of developing the informed-desire account of well-being.[7] All the terms in the definition of well-being—*fulfilment* of *informed desire*—and the terms central to its theoretical development—e.g. *strength* of desire—become to a fairly large degree technical, and their technical senses would have to be supplied. For instance, 'informed' could not mean 'what one would desire in a state of full knowledge or experience', because clearly many things that would be valuable to me then would not be valuable to me now in my actual state of knowledge or experience. So 'informed' must cover some sort of mix of actual and counterfactual desires, which would have

[5] This is Mill's view too, 'If there be one to which *all or almost all* who have experience of both give a decided preference' (1861, ch. 2, para. 5; my italics).

[6] A full discussion would have to consider, for instance, John Harsanyi's position, which is in important ways like Hare's, and especially his powerful defence of it (1977:58–9).

[7] For fuller discussion see Griffin, 1986, ch. 2.

to be made clear. And the key terms would have to be interpreted in such a way that one most fulfilled the relevant desires not by fulfilling as many as possible, or as large a proportion, as if one's desires were all on a level. Desires form a hierarchy, and a lot of what we should mean by 'aggregation' is already present in the order that our global desires (that is, our desires about the large-scale contours of our life) give to our desires in general.

Now, there is the obvious danger with informed-desire accounts that they become plausible accounts of well-being only by, in effect, ceasing to be in any real sense desire accounts. By qualifying 'desire' with 'informed', we give prominence to the features of the objects of desire, not to the mere existence of desire. Is desire any longer playing a real part? This quickly brings us to the ancient question, are things *
valuable because desired, or desired because valuable? I think that the right answer is 'Neither'. If we take a wide enough range of cases, we shall see that sometimes the explanation runs largely from value to desire and sometimes the other way, but in the end the only adequate explanation has to run both ways. There is no priority.

Admittedly, this way of developing the informed-desire account takes it some distance from the preference accounts common even in the more normative parts of economics and decision theory. It also takes it some distance from the account of utility in much philosophical utilitarianism. For instance, it is compatible with pluralism on prudential values: one can allow, as I think one should, that people value irreducibly different things. 'Well-being', on the more familiar *
monistic account, was the super over-arching substantive value. But on this account it is not seen as the single over-arching value, in fact not as a substantive value at all, but instead as the formal analysis of what it is for something to be prudentially valuable. Is such an account 'subjective' or 'objective'? By 'subjective' I mean an account that makes well-being depend upon an individual's own desires, and by 'objective' one that makes well-being independent of desires (see e.g. Scanlon, 1975:656–8). Well, this account need not make values rest on *one* person's desires; it can allow that some values (enjoyment, accomplishment, autonomy, etc.) are

values for everyone, although there may be persons for whom any value on the list (say, autonomy), though valuable for him as for everybody, conflicts enough with another value (say, freedom from anxiety) for it not, all things considered, to be valuable for *him* to have. The distinction between 'objective' and 'subjective' therefore marks no deep or important
* difference, so the best answer is that the informed-desire account is both 'objective' and 'subjective'. This helps with the comparison problem.

6.6 *Another solution.* Interpersonal comparisons of well-being, we might say, are judgements of the following sort. I, informed as I am, want this thing very much. You, or virtually anyone, would want it, if informed, the same amount. It is, for most persons, roughly that desirable. He, on the other hand, wants it less; he lacks, let us say, certain normal capacities (for instance, he is depressed, so wants nothing very much). The quantitative phrases 'very much', 'same amount', and 'less' that appear in these judgements come from the same scale.
* We can make judgements, based on causal knowledge about human nature and information about particular persons, of how much persons want things, and these judgements place the desires of different persons on the same scale. Perhaps the mistake made by accounts of comparability in terms of judger's preference is to misunderstand the forms that knowledge of other minds can take. If one thinks of it as limited, say, to representations of the texture of experiences, then of course there is a gap which needs bridging, and preference looks a likely bridge. But if we know that you want this only a little and I want that a lot, and these terms are not relative to other things that each of us, in his own case, wants but relative to each other, then there is no gap, so no need for a bridge. This seems to me the best solution to the comparison problem, and I want now to suggest a way of developing it.

We have a picture of normal human desires: virtually all persons, when informed, want to live autonomously, to have deep personal relations, to accomplish something with their lives, to enjoy themselves, . . . and so on. With experience, we build up such a profile of the components of a valuable life, including their relative importance. These values, if our profile is complete, cover the whole domain of prudential

value. They are valuable in any life; individual differences *
matter not to what appears in this profile of general prudential
values, but to how, or how much, a particular person can
realize one or other particular value. Then, we also build up
understanding of how individuals deviate from the norm. For
instance, one person may find autonomy anxiety-making, so
his life is more complex than the normal one: he faces, as a
normal person does not, a hard choice between competing
values. Or you may enjoy things more than most people, while
he is depressed and enjoys nothing very much. Also, there will
be differences in the form that a value takes in different lives:
what you can accomplish, or enjoy, in your life may be
different from what I can in mine. But all this reasoning about
individual differences takes place within the framework of a
set of values that apply to everyone. And these three elements,
a list of universal prudential values, general causal knowledge
of human nature, and the information about particular
persons relevant to these causal generalities, make up our
grounds for judging how well off persons are.

Of course, one prudential value is enjoyment. And that does
seem much less amenable to treatment in terms that apply to
everyone. It is the plainest of facts that different persons enjoy
different things, or the same things to very different degrees.
Enjoyment seems to present special difficulties for interpersonal comparison: namely, the problem of knowing varying,
personal, and even sometimes idiosyncratic tastes, attitudes,
and interests that persons have. But these tastes, attitudes,
and interests are relevant to only a relatively small corner of *
prudential values. And even that corner is misunderstood if
the large common element in enjoyment is overlooked. There
are natural human enjoyments. When I consider ways in
which my tastes and interests might develop, I look at general
issues such as what normal human capacities are and how I
am placed to develop them. For example, you like fine clarets;
I like only plonk. My palate, no doubt, could be trained too.
And faced with that possibility, I should reason something
like this. Is it more enjoyable to have these powers of
discrimination? Well, persons who have them do not, in
general, lose their capacity to enjoy plonk, and most persons
find that they have more to enjoy. So I, and most other

persons, would be better off developing these powers of discrimination. And we decide this not by deciding how strong this or that particular person's desire is but by deciding how strong this kind of desire is compared to that other kind. We enter them on the general profile of human desires.

Of course, interpersonal comparisons cannot be conducted entirely in terms of general profiles and general causal regularities. We often need information about particular persons. When I go to decide whether you enjoy wine more than I, I need to know what your powers of discrimination are and whether your capacities for enjoyment are more or less normal. I do not need to know the texture of your experience or your peculiar tastes. And once I know whether your palate is trained and your capacities normal, I know where in the general profile of desires to place this desire of yours. And even with simple divergence of tastes (you love oysters; I hate
* them), our knowledge of the strength (in the relevant sense) of your wish to have oysters and mine not to will typically include some rough understanding of where they fit in the whole scheme of human desires. The same is true of divergence of interests, inclinations, partialities, and so on. In general, to decide how much someone enjoys life, one does not need to get inside his skin; one needs to know what makes life enjoyable and how he is placed to exploit its possibilities.

This seems to me to give us a much more realistic picture of how we actually deliberate about different persons' well-being. It is not that the general profile of prudential values is the whole ground of interpersonal comparisons. Individual differences of the sort that I have just been discussing are obviously an important type of argument in any plausible utility function that aspires to completeness. The profile of prudential values gives the general framework for comparisons. It forms much of the ground of comparison when we choose between different ways of life. But often we are interested in how good various options are within a single way of life, and often with individual ways of reacting and responding. My stressing the role of the profile of prudential values may make my account sound too objectivist, and so defective in just the way that I said at the start objectivist accounts tend to be. But one defect of objectivist accounts is that they have no place for

individual differences, and my account does. Another defect is *
that it is hard to see where an objectivist's values are coming
from, but there is nothing to prevent our saying that all values
in the general profile must find their place inside informed
desires. In any case, my point about the general profile is that
the ground of interpersonal comparisons is not full without it,
not that it is the full ground.

Not surprisingly, the wrong conception of well-being
distorts the problem of interpersonal comparisons. If well-
being consists in mental states, then interpersonal comparisons
present the daunting task, first, of learning about the texture
of individual experiences and, then, of finding a way of
ranking them. If well-being is fulfilment of desires, but desires
are seen largely as a product of tastes that are personal and
varying, then interpersonal comparisons present the equally
daunting task of learning each individual's desires and their
intensity.[8] But tastes do not take up so much of the ground for
comparisons. The desires that are relevant to well-being are,
for the most part, informed desires. Basic prudential values
provide us with an important standard for judging many
(ordinary) human lives. They let us say, though only roughly,
how good the life is, how it could be better, and how it
compares to other lives. They considerably ease the burden of
comparison. The deepest and most decisive issues about
comparability are ones about the nature of well-being.

This solution to the comparison problem also helps with
intrapersonal intertemporal comparisons. When I think at all
ambitiously about what will enhance my own well-being, I do
not consult my present tastes and desires or even my future
tastes and desires, as if which desires I have at any moment,
and how they change, is something that just happens to me.
In fact, when I am thinking radically, I do not consult any of
my tastes and desires, seen as *mine*. Instead I consult the
profile of prudential values. Would I be better off giving up *
my fool-like gratifications for a more demanding Socratic life?
I should answer that question by deciding what sorts of life
are valuable and what I am capable of. I should reason in

---

[8] This conception of preference is still widespread, probably dominant in
economics and still strong in philosophy. See e.g. Layard and Walters, 1978:124;
Arrow, 1963, esp. section on 'Choice under Static Conditions'.

much the same way even over rather trivial matters. Should I learn to like oysters? Well, if I am full of food fads, then I am missing a lot in life, and it would probably be worth changing. But if it is only oysters that I hate, and if I think that my dislike is pretty stubborn, then it would probably not be worth changing. I do not consult my own particular tastes, attitudes, and concerns; I reason in terms that apply to anyone.

Part of the insight in the wish to reduce interpersonal to intrapersonal comparisons is that the reasoning in the two is virtually the same. Is Socrates dissatisifed better off than the Fool satisfied? Am I better off going down the Socratic path or the Fool's? I often need the same materials to answer either the interpersonal or the intrapersonal question. The problems thought to be connected with our forming desires about these two sorts of life are avoided if we realize that what we need is, not a personal preference of the judger (which, anyway, seems not to be available), but desires—yours, mine, and other persons'—shaped by our understanding of the two options (which are available). In first forming a preference between the options, I give expression to a value. I do not consult a value that is already built into me in the form of a utility function of one sort or other; on the contrary, I create and give shape to part of my utility function. Neither intrapersonal nor interpersonal comparisons are the more fundamental; both rely on the same sort of reasoning.

The solution to the comparison problem that I am proposing is available to Hare within the resources of his own position. Indeed, I am aware that I may be exaggerating the difference between his solution and mine. There are obscurities about what each solution amounts to, and how they are related, that I have tried here to dispel, but I realize that I have by no means completely succeeded. Still, the solutions
* are, I think, in important ways different. If so, we have to decide which is better.[9]

[9] I have benefited from discussions with Richard Hare, Michael McDermott, Derek Parfit, and Amartya Sen.

7. Problems with Act-Utilitarianism and with Malevolent Preferences

John C. Harsanyi

7.1 OVER more than thirty years, Professor Hare has proposed many very interesting and ingenious philosophical ideas both in metaethics and in ethics proper.[1] Even those of us who disagree with him on some important points have found his numerous writings a constant source of intellectual enjoyment and of philosophical stimulation. In his recent publications, Hare has proposed a *two-level* utilitarian theory, under which our moral thinking is rule-utilitarian at the *intuitive* level but is act-utilitarian at the *critical* level. More exactly, he claims that at the critical level act- and rule-utilitarianism collapse into one theory.

It seems to me that Hare's two-level model and, in particular, his conception of *intuitive* moral judgements fairly well capture some important aspects of human morality. But I cannot accept his analysis of *critical* moral thinking. For one thing (though this is a less important point), I feel his 'archangel' *
who can predict the future in every detail (*MT* 177) is the wrong analytical device for studying moral decision-making by humans in the face of real-life risk and uncertainty (see note 3, below). More importantly, I cannot agree with his claim that at the critical level the act-utilitarian and the rule-utilitarian approaches would generate the *same* moral decisions. On the contrary, even at this level, the act-utilitarian approach would tend to generate moral decisions of much *lower* social utility than the rule-utilitarian approach would.

Another disagreement I have with Hare is this. He fully

[1] I want to thank the National Science Foundation for supporting this research through grant SES82–18938 administered by the Center for Research in Management, University of California, Berkeley. I want to thank also Professors Hare and Brandt for helpful comments on an earlier version of this paper.

admits that a utilitarian can legitimately disregard people's *uninformed* preferences,[2] i.e. those based on factual or logical mistakes. But he opposes disregarding people's *anti-social* preferences (he calls them 'evil desires'), such as those based on sadism, envy, resentment, or malice. Though he argues that, under his two-level theory, in practice such anti-social preferences would be given very little weight even if we did not specifically exclude them (*MT* 140–1). In contrast, I will argue that, as a *matter of principle*, anti-social preferences should receive no weight whatever in the utilitarian calculus.

This leads me to the following more general point. Hare argues that, by the very nature of everyday moral language, our moral judgements always possess the two formal properties of prescriptivity and of universalizability; and that, in view of this fact, consistency requires us to assign our moral judge-
* ments a largely utilitarian moral content. Brandt (1979:9, 229–30) has questioned the cogency of this argument by pointing out the considerable vagueness, or at least flexiblity, of everyday moral language.

Yet even if we accepted Hare's argument at its face value, prescriptivity and universalizability would be of very little
* help in deciding the *specific form* our utilitarianism should take. Should it disregard uninformed preferences or anti-social preferences or both (or neither)? To what extent should it be act-utilitarian or rule-utilitarian? How much weight should it give to the interests of unborn (and perhaps even to those of as-yet-unconceived and merely potential) babies? (This list could be made much longer.) This fact clearly demonstrates the very serious limitations of linguistic arguments in moral philosophy.

7.2 As is well known, the basic difference between the act-
* utilitarian and the rule-utilitarian approaches lies in the fact that, according to the former, our basic moral decisions involve choosing specific *individual actions* in specific moral situations in accordance with their expected[3] social utility;

---

[2] I owe the terms 'informed preferences' and 'uninformed preferences' to James Griffin (1986).

[3] The adjective 'expected' is short for 'the mathematical expectation of'. In situations involving risk and uncertainty (as *all* real-life situations do), we are not in a position to maximize social utility; all we can do is try to maximize *expected* social utility in terms of the probabilities we assign to alternative possible outcomes.

whereas, according to the latter, our basic moral decisions involve choosing *general moral rules*—and indeed a general *moral code*—in accordance with their expected social utility.[1]

In assessing the social utility of any particular moral code, a rule-utilitarian would have to consider both its likely *compliance effects*, direct and indirect, and its likely *expectation effects* in case it would become the socially accepted moral code. By its *direct* compliance effects I mean the specific actions people would undertake to comply with it. By its *indirect* compliance effects I mean such things as the guilt feelings people would feel in case of noncompliance as well as the admiration they would feel for *other* people's compliant behaviour and the disapproval they would feel for other people's noncompliant behaviour (cf. Brandt, 1970:291–2).

Finally, by its *expectation* effects I mean people's expectations that other people will display direct and/or indirect compliance with this moral code. These expectations in turn will have important secondary effects: they will be major factors in determining people's *confidence* in the future and in determining their *incentives* to undertake various socially desirable and undesirable activities. For convenience, I will include these confidence effects and these incentive effects under the general heading of expectation effects. It is easy to see that these expectation effects of various types will be no less important than the (direct and indirect) compliance effects will be in determining the social utility of any given moral code.

As I have argued in earlier publications (see e.g. Harsanyi, 1983), the basic advantage of the rule-utilitarian approach over the act-utilitarian approach lies in the fact that the conceptual framework of the former does, while that of the latter does not, permit us to take account of the *expectation effects* of alternative moral codes (or of alternative moral rules). This is so because an act-utilitarian's moral decisions always involve choices between alternative *individual actions*, rather than choices between alternative *moral codes* or alternative *moral rules*. Accordingly, an act-utilitarian will have to

[4] The social utility of any given moral rule will always depend on the *other* moral rules accepted by society. Thus we cannot judge the social utility of a moral rule specifying the parents' obligations to their children without knowing the accepted moral rules defining the other relatives' obligations to them. Therefore, in principle we must always examine the social utility of alternative moral codes in their entirety.

make his moral decisions in terms of the likely effects of these alternative individual actions, rather than in terms of the likely effects of alternative moral codes (or alternative moral rules) being adopted by his society.

For instance, suppose that A made an important promise to B, but now finds it very inconvenient to keep it. Will he be morally free to break his promise? Clearly, both act-utilitarianism and rule-utilitarianism will agree that the answer must depend on three variables:

1. the utility loss B would suffer if A broke his promise;

2. the utility gain A would obtain if he did so; and

3. the total utility loss that many other people would suffer if A were permitted to break his promise and as a result the social credibility of promises were seriously impaired.

Even though act-utilitarians and rule-utilitarians will agree that the answer must depend on these three variables, they will often arrive at very different answers. To be sure, they will presumably assess the utility loss under (1) and the utility gain under (2) in much the same way. But their assessment of the utility loss under (3) will be radically different. This is so because an act-utilitarian will always have to ask how much effect *one act* of promise-breaking will have on people's confidence in promises; and will correctly conclude that in all probability this effect will be negligibly small.

In contrast, a rule-utilitarian will have to consider the expectation effects of a moral code condoning a *general practice* of promise-breaking in *all* similar situations (as well as in all situations where there would be even *stronger* prima-facie reasons for absolving people from their promise-keeping commitments). Even if *one act* of promise-breaking is likely to have negligible effects, the expectation that promises will tend to be broken in a rather *wide range* of social situations cannot fail to have socially very undesirable consequences by weakening people's *confidence* in their ability to predict other people's future behaviour, and by weakening people's *incentives* to act on the expectation that promises will be kept.

Thus a rule-utilitarian society will be much *less permissive* than an act-utilitarian society would be about the breaking of promises, because the rule-utilitarian calculus provides a clearer picture of the undesirable confidence and incentive effects of a more permissive morality; and this less permissive morality will generate a *higher* level of social utility, precisely because it will avoid these undesirable confidence and incentive effects.

It is easy to show that a rule-utilitarian society will have stricter moral standards than an act-utilitarian society would have also in a number of other fields, such as showing gratitude to one's benefactors, being loyal to one's friends, and telling the truth even in cases where this will have somewhat undesirable consequences. It is likewise easy to show that acceptance of these stricter moral standards will have considerable social utility.

7.3 Traditionally, utilitarians have attached little importance to such deontic concepts as moral rights and moral *obligations. In my view this has been a mistake. For the moral code of a society can make a major contribution to social utility by establishing a suitable network of individual rights and of social-role-dependent special obligations which will normally take *precedence* over direct social-utility considerations and which can be overridden only in exceptional cases where fundamental social interests are at stake.

The social utility of individual rights and of special obligations is again largely a result of their very beneficial *expectation effects* (and in particular of their confidence and incentive effects). For this reason they could not survive in an act-utilitarian society, whose moral calculus would be unable to take account of these expectation effects.   *

As an example of individual *rights*, consider a person's property rights over his boat. (Of course, property rights are primarily a legal concept. But I will discuss them solely from a moral point of view.) By the very concept of private property, the owner may use his boat whenever he wants to, whereas other people normally may not use it without his permission. (Though they may do so in some emergency situations, for instance, in order to save a human life.)

Yet a consistent act-utilitarian cannot recognize private-property rights in this sense, because he must hold that any person is always morally free to use another person's property, even without the owner's permission, as long as he thinks he will derive a greater utility than the owner would from its use. But in actual fact, under suitable conditions, private-property rights have great social utility because they are a major incentive to very useful economic activities and because they make economic relationships more predictable and more secure (incentive and confidence effects).

As an example of special obligations, consider a parent's obligations to his or her own children. In our society, parents are expected to establish close social relationships with their children, and to assign very high priority to their needs.

Nevertheless, a consistent act-utilitarian cannot approve of this arrangement. In particular, he cannot approve of the *special priority* the parents may assign to their children's needs. For he must take the position that these parents (as well as all other people) must always assign the highest priority to helping those people who would derive the *greatest utility* from their help—even if this means giving priority most of the time to the needs of complete strangers over the needs of their own children. It is, however, rather obvious that the special relationships often found to exist between the parents and their children, including these parents' willingness to give very special priority to their children's needs, has very high social utility because it gives both the parents and the children a greater feeling of security and gives them many socially desirable incentives (confidence and incentive effects).

One indication of the great social utility of such individual rights and such special obligations is that most of us *would strongly prefer to live* in a society where basic individual rights and special obligations were widely recognized and widely respected rather than in a society where this was not the case.

7.4 In the last two sections I have argued that moral standards based on the rule-utilitarian approach will have much greater social utility than moral standards based on the act-utilitarian approach would have. Now I propose to discuss the extent to which my conclusions apply to Hare's two-level theory, which uses the act-utilitarian approach only at the critical level.

According to Hare's theory we resort to critical moral thinking for two different purposes:

1. to decide what general *moral rules* we should use, and people under our moral guidance should use, at the intuitive level (Hare calls such moral rules *intuitive principles*);
2. to decide what *specific action* to take in a specific situation where our intuitive moral principles fail to give us sufficient guidance because they are too vague or because they conflict or because they are unhelpful for any other reason.

Now, my negative conclusions about the act-utilitarian approach have no application in case (1). In this case it will be quite true that, as Hare in fact claims, the act-utilitarian and the rule-utilitarian approaches will lead to the *same* moral decisions. This is so because choosing between two alternative   * *moral rules* is logically equivalent to choosing between the *act* of adopting the first moral rule and the *act* of adopting the second. To put it differently, when we choose between two alternative moral rules at the critical level, even if we use the act-utilitarian conceptual framework in making our choice, this will in no way prevent us from taking account of the social effects of either moral rule, including its expectation effects.[5]

On the other hand, our negative conclusions about the act-utilitarian approach will fully apply in case (2). Since our task in this case is to choose between alternative individual actions, our choice will have to be based on the social effects of these specific actions rather than on the social effects of any moral rule or moral code permitting, or perhaps even prescribing, these actions. Thus the expectation effects of any such moral rule or moral code will not be a factor in our choice.

This fact will have the following paradoxical implications. If a given person asks himself whether to keep a very inconvenient promise or not, his answer to this question will depend on whether he conducts his deliberations at the intuitive level or at the critical level. In the former case his answer will reflect the rather strict moral standards of intuitive morality, based on the rule-utilitarian approach; whereas in the latter case his answer will reflect the much more permissive, and therefore socially objectionable,

---

[5] A possible objection to Hare's analysis is that he always envisages the choice of individual moral rules without any systematic investigation of how the social utility of any given moral rule depends on the *other* accepted moral rules (cf. note 4, above). But this is a minor point.

standards of act-utilitarian morality, which Hare makes us use at the critical level.

Likewise, a person who follows his intuitive moral principles will fully respect other people's property and will do his best to satisfy his children's needs, as required by the rule-utilitarian approach. In contrast, a person who relies on his critical moral thinking will take considerable liberties with
* other people's property and will assign much lower priority to his children's needs, because this is what the act-utilitarian approach will require him to do. This means that at the critical level, supposedly representing our *most rational* moral thinking, we will follow socially much less desirable, and therefore much *less rational*, moral standards than we will follow at the intuitive level—which is hardly an acceptable conclusion.

7.5 Hare, like most other utilitarians, holds that the utilitarian social-utility function (social-welfare function) should disregard people's *uninformed* preferences but should give full weight to their *anti-social* preferences. I disagree with this view and will argue that anti-social preferences should be given *zero* weight.

Let me illustrate the problem by one of Hare's own
* examples. Suppose that a given society consists of *x* Nazis and *y* Jews, and that the Nazis would strongly prefer all Jews to be killed whereas these Jews, of course, would strongly prefer *not* to be killed. Let us assume, as it is plausible to do, that each Jew's desire to survive is *much stronger* than any Nazi's desire for him and his co-religionists to die. Nevertheless, if we want to give the same weight to anti-social preferences as to other preferences then, if the number *x* is large enough in relation to the number *y*, we will have to conclude that the social-utility maximizing policy will be to kill all Jews!

Clearly, this is an absurd conclusion. A utilitarian is presumably a utilitarian out of benevolence to other people; and, being a *benevolent* person, he can no doubt rationally refuse to co-operate with anybody's *malevolent* preferences. Surely, he will be entitled to the status of 'conscientious objector' when he is asked to co-operate with some people's malevolent attitudes (cf. Harsanyi, 1977:647).

More fundamentally, we can argue as follows. We can make

use of Dworkin's (1977:234) helpful distinction between an individual's *personal* preferences and his *external* preferences. *
The former are his preferences 'for enjoyment of some goods and opportunities', whereas the latter are his preferences 'for assignment of goods and opportunities to others'. It is natural to define his *personal interests* in terms of his—informed—*personal preferences* with complete exclusion of his external preferences. Thus my personal interests include my economic assets and opportunities, the benefit of being alive (if I prefer to live rather than to die), my health, and the rights and opportunities I have as a result of my family relationships, my friendships, my job, my social position, etc. On the other hand, I have no 'personal interest' in my neighbour's joining a particular church, even if I would strongly *prefer* his doing so—unless his doing so would yield me some economic gain or would increase my prestige in the community or would provide other personal benefits for me.

Let me add that if an individual has a preference 'for assignment of goods and opportunities to others', I will go on classifying it as an external preference even if he has developed a strong *personal* involvement in this preference, because, by assumption, this is primarily a preference about what should happen to *other* people, and his own personal involvement in this preference is a secondary result.

Now, my proposal is that our utilitarian social-utility function should be based solely on people's *personal interests* and, therefore, on their *personal preferences*, and should make no use of their external preferences. Utilitarian morality requires us to respect people's preferences about how they *themselves* ought to be treated. But it should not require us to respect their preferences about how *other* people ought to be treated.

This proposal would immediately resolve the problem posed by our Nazi example: the Jews' preferences to stay alive are *personal* preferences and should be given *positive* weights. In contrast, the Nazis' preferences for these Jews to die are *external* preferences (even if some Nazis have developed very strong personal involvements with these preferences) and should be given *zero* weights.

To be sure, not all external preferences are socially undesirable preferences. Of course, *malevolent* preferences, like those of the Nazis, are always socially highly undesirable. Most of the time the same is true of *censorious* preferences, even if they are meant to be benevolent, because they give rise to a temptation to interfere with other people's personal affairs. (Yet, under some conditions, censorious preferences expressing moral disapproval may serve a useful social function because they will help to maintain the moral standards of the community.) On the other hand, *supportive* benevolent preferences, based on a desire that other people should succeed in satisfying their own—informed—personal preferences are socially very beneficial attitudes.

*   Nevertheless, it seems to me that even socially *desirable* external preferences should be *excluded* from our social-utility function. This is so because if they were not excluded then they would defeat the fundamental utilitarian principle that our social-utility function must give the *same weight* to every individual's interests. For if such external preferences were included then the interests of persons with many well-wishers and friends would obtain much *greater weight* than the interests of persons without such supporters. Thus the very nature of utilitarian ethics suggests the exclusion of all external preferences, whether benevolent or malevolent or in between. The exclusion of *malevolent* preferences (anti-social preferences) is a mere corollary of this general principle.[6]

7.6 I have tried to show that use of the act-utilitarian approach, even if restricted to the *critical* level of moral thinking, will give rise to socially undesirable and, therefore, irrational moral decisions; and that a utilitarian should disregard people's anti-social preferences and, indeed, all their external preferences. I have also argued that, even if we accept Hare's contention that the utilitarian content of moral judgements can be established by an analysis of everyday moral language, such linguistic analysis will give us very little

---

[6] If we want to exclude people's external preferences from the social-utility function, the question arises how this proposal can be implemented mathematically, that is to say, how we can construct a cardinal utility function representing an individual's *personal preferences* from his cardinal function representing *all* his preferences, both personal and external. Lack of space prevents me here from discussing this question. But I will be happy to send any interested reader a short note of mine dealing with this problem.

help in deciding the *specific form* that our utilitarianism should take.

Let me add that, even though I concentrated in this paper on those issues on which I disagree with Professor Hare, this should not obscure my great admiration for his philosophical work and for his important contributions to resurrecting substantive moral philosophy as an active and very much alive branch of philosophical investigation.

8. The Foundations of Impartiality

Thomas Nagel

8.1 CAN an ethical theory be too successful? If it proposes a *
foundation for moral argument that lies beyond the reach of
moral disagreement, it may leave the existence and intractability of actual moral disagreements unexplained. If it tries to
appeal only to facts outside morality which all parties must
admit, then the most fundamental disagreements are likely to
resurface, either in the interpretation of what has been proved
or in dispute over moral assumptions hidden in the premises.

I believe that Hare's attempt to ground morality in the logic
of the moral concepts runs into this problem. It is true that
when people disagree about what is right and wrong, and how
they should live, they must mean the same thing by the terms
they use to express their differences. But this common ground
does not by itself provide the materials needed to settle their
disagreements, and the attempt to show that it does inevitably
introduces morally controversial elements into the interpretation of the alleged common ground. This happens elsewhere
in philosophy, when one or another view is criticized for
violating the logic of the terms in which it is stated. The
mistake, if there is one, is usually located in another place.

It may happen sometimes, in the case of specialized, quasi-
legalistic disputes among members of the same moral sect,
that the method of settling a moral disagreement can be
extracted from the meanings of the terms that parties to the
disagreement must use in common. But I believe this is not
possible with respect to those large-scale moral issues that are
of greatest philosophical interest. There we must look beyond
the terminology, and we may find that no shared method is
available at all that is not itself the subject of moral
controversy. The best we can hope for is to discover

arguments and counter-arguments that display the basis of disagreement more clearly within the confines of morality, and perhaps to identify some contributing non-moral differences. This puts us in a better position to continue the search for a method on which wider agreement can be secured, as we gradually emerge from the moral bronze age.

The theory developed in *Moral Thinking* holds that the
* possible content of a morality is more narrowly restricted by the logic of moral language than Hare had thought it was at the time of *The Language of Morals*. That is because he includes in his later account of what moral judgements mean an interpretation of their universality which amounts to a strong substantive requirement of impartiality among all persons. It is this interpretation that I want to discuss, concentrating mostly on its relation to the logic of moral language, rather than on its independent plausibility as a moral assumption.

Hare believes that actual moral disagreements, if they are not based on confusion, can best be accounted for as differences over what follows from such a requirement, in conjunction with the facts—differences due partly to variation in the accuracy of reasoning and partly to variation in belief about the relevant non-moral facts. But I believe that some
* disagreements are at the level of the principle itself—disagreements within morality about the stringency and proper interpretation of moral impartiality.

8.2 What gets us from bare universality to Hare's strong form of impartiality? The bare universality of moral claims is relatively uncontroversial, and might well be called part of their meaning. If I make a judgement about what I or someone else ought to do, I am committed to the view that anyone else in the same circumstances (construed in as finely grained a way as you like) ought to do the same. The particular judgement is a consequence of more general principles, perhaps highly general ones. But this by itself yields nothing like impartiality in the content of moral judgements; indeed it tells us very little about their content at all. Ethical
* egoism, for example, meets the condition of bare universality perfectly. And Hare in his earlier discussion of the 'fanatic' (*FR* ch. 9) recognized that some appalling positions could be embraced as universal prescriptions, in some sense.

We get impartiality only if we give a particular answer to the question, 'What is the attitude I take towards the acts covered by such a universal principle when I judge that they ought (or ought not) to be done?' That is, we need an account of what it is to *prescribe* that they be done—that everyone act in a certain way. Hare's view is that a prescription that something be done is the expression of a desire or preference that it be done. And a universal prescription expresses a desire that the thing be done in all similar cases in the actual world, and also in all similar hypothetical cases which differ from the actual ones only in the identities of the participants.

If we permute the identities of all the people in the world through each position in all the actual cases covered by a given universal prescription, this yields a vast number of cases. But Hare assumes that my preference with regard to this universalization can be taken to depend on what I want to happen to myself, in those cases in which I occupy one of the *
positions. He argues further that what I want to happen to myself in each of those cases will depend directly on what the person actually occupying the position would want, given his preferences and full information. And he claims finally that what I want to be done universally, in all of these cases, will be determined by a balancing out of the preferences I have about each of them, so that total preference-satisfaction is maximized.

With this we have arrived at preference-utilitarianism: the right thing to do is what will maximize the total satisfaction of the preferences of all the parties affected. (I omit complications arising from the distinction between critical and intuitive levels of moral thinking. This discussion has to do entirely *
with what Hare calls the critical level.)

This amounts to a strong substantive moral position, *
involving a number of morally controversial elements which cannot plausibly be assigned to the logic of moral language. Specifically, it embodies a view about how moral judgements should give equal consideration to everyone, how everyone's interests should be understood for moral purposes, and how the conflicting interests of different individuals should be combined to reach moral conclusions.

We can set out the path from universal prescriptivism to utilitarianism in a series of propositions:

* 1. To say that something ought morally to be done is to prescribe that it be done in all similar hypothetical cases with the personnel switched.

2. To prescribe that something be done is to express the desire that it be done.

3. What we desire to be done in a set of hypothetical cases with the personnel switched depends only on what we desire to be done in those cases in which we occupy one of the positions.

4. What we desire to be done in a hypothetical case in which we are in someone else's shoes, with his desires and preferences, depends on what we believe he would desire in those circumstances.

5. What we desire to be done universally in a set of hypothetical cases is a simple additive function of what we desire to be done in each of them.

Propostions (2), (4) and (5) are controversial and in the context morally substantive. I find Hare's claim (*MT* 95–6) that something like (4) is a conceptual truth particularly unconvincing. But I want to concentrate on (2), and to a lesser extent on (5). While (4) ensures that the resulting moral theory will take preference-satisfaction as the basic measure of value, (2) and (5) ensure that it will be a form of agent-neutral, maximizing consequentialism. The rightness of actions will depend on their tendency to increase the quantity

* of a value which is the same for all agents, and is defined independently of the perspective of the agent. If Hare were right that all this is part of the meaning of the moral terms, then the most prominent alternatives to utilitarianism could not even be consistently stated in moral language.

8.3 We can begin to discuss assumption (2) by asking what

* alternative interpretations of what it is to prescribe an act are being ruled out. Hare's answer to the question what we are to prescribe universally derives from his definition of what it is to prescribe universally. To call the answer into question it is necessary to propose an alternative definition—not necessarily one incompatible with Hare's substantive moral view, but one which does not entail it. I believe the place to start is with the idea of what everyone has a reason to do.

Assumption (2) has a peculiar consequence. When I

prescribe universally in the sense defined by that assumption, this does not imply that I believe everyone has a reason to act in accordance with my prescription: at best, it implies that I acknowledge a reason to obey it myself—(though even that follows only if we assume that in using moral language I acknowledge a reason to care about universalizability). But a moral judgement ought to have a connection with practical reason not only for the person who produces it but also for the persons to whom it is addressed. If it is supposed to be correct, it ought to claim that others have a reason to obey it, even if they do not yet happen to recognize that reason.

This claim can be expressed by a moral judgement even if it does not also express the utterer's *desire* that those others act as it says they should. It is only when the judgement is about his own conduct that any such desire need be implied.

This is not meant as a complete account of moral judgement. More would have to be said to differentiate moral prescriptions from the class of judgements of practical rationality in general—moral reasons must have some degree of independence from the particular interests and desires of the agent, for example. But whatever may have to be added, the condition that it imply the existence of reasons for the person to whom it is addressed ensures the connection with motivation that should be preserved by any account of moral prescription. It follows that if I apply a moral prescription to myself, I must recognize a reason to act; this connection with motivation is an essential condition of a judgement's being prescriptive at all. But it is not essential in addition that any motivation or desire on my part be expressed by a prescription about what someone else ought to do—even if particular moral views make this connection.

Hare's position to the contrary is due to his interpreting moral judgements as imperatives in a fairly literal sense, and not in the sense in which Kant thought they were imperatives. In the literal sense, I would not ordinarily tell someone to do something unless I wanted him to do it. But in the Kantian sense, the utterance of either a hypothetical or a categorical imperative has a closer connection with the utterer's conception of the reasons that might motivate the addressee than with the utterer's own desires. This conception would count as

prescriptive a judgement I made about someone else, even if I
had no desire that he conform to it, so long as *he* could not
sincerely assent without accepting a reason to conform.[1] In his
interpretation of the universal prescriptions of morality, Hare
does not allow for this reading. But it seems to me natural and
perfectly intelligible to think of a universal prescription simply
as a claim about how everyone ought to act, such that if
anyone sincerely assents to it, he must acknowledge a reason
to act that way.

This interpretation is quite weak, for it says nothing about
what type of reason it might be. It could be the type
recognized by utilitarianism, but it might not be. The
question is how the interests of all parties affected by the act,
including the agent, enter into the generation of the universal
reasons implied by a moral judgement.

One answer to this question is that the interests of all
affected parties generate reasons on an equal basis, in
proportion to the strengths of their individual preferences.
This is equivalent to Hare's view of the content of morality,
for it corresponds to what you would want, taking up the point
of view of each of the parties in turn, and somehow combining
all those vicarious viewpoints into a collective preference. But
other universal systems of reasons are imaginable which also
give consideration to everyone, in some sense.

Specifically, some moral views can be formulated only in
terms of agent-relative reasons. One fairly common view,
right or wrong, is that an individual may count his own
interests and the interests of those to whom he is personally
attached more heavily than the interests of strangers: there is
not a single, neutral measure of the good that everyone is
morally required exclusively to try to promote (though such a
neutral value may form *part* of the basis of morality). Other
agent-relative principles are involved in the belief in selective
obligations to those to whom we are related in certain ways,
and also in the belief in deontological restrictions of the kind
that limit what we may intentionally do, as opposed to what
we may bring about. To avoid the complications of discussing

[1] I am not referring here to Kant's view of the content of the categorical
imperative, which of course does include a reference to what we can will that everyone
do. I am referring to the *concept* of a categorical imperative.

a moral permission, which is the denial of a moral requirement, let me use the example of an agent-relative requirement to favour the interests of one's children over the interests of strangers—a requirement that many people would accept. I am concerned for the moment not with its truth but with its formal character.

Unless such a moral view is covertly derivative from something more fundamental, it clearly cannot express a   *
universal prescription interpreted in accordance with assumption (2). If someone believes that he ought to favour his own children, he believes that anyone ought to do this, and that this is true of all similar actual and hypothetical cases, including those in which he occupies a different position. But that does not mean that he *desires* that everyone should act that way in all those cases. If he puts himself in each relevant position successively, and considers what he would want to be done, and how strongly, he might get a very different result.

For example, an affluent American or European might refer *
to his obligation to his children to explain why he should not (even if he were inclined) contribute over half of his income to famine relief—because although this would save many African children from starvation, it would seriously lower the standard of living of his own children. But if he puts himself in the position of even one of the starving African children who would be saved from death by his sacrifice, or in the position of one of their parents, his desire for the donation will greatly outweigh the desire he has not to give it as things actually are. He may in fact think that if he were in their position he would be justified in taking the needed resources by force, if he could. So this agent-relative obligation claims that each person has a reason for concern about his own children that can, in cases of conflict, lead him to wish that others would pursue their children's interests as wholeheartedly as they would if they gave that reason its full weight. And the result may be that what one universally prescribes is not what one desires should universally be done.   *

Hare's response would be that such a special obligation appears only at the level of intuitive moral thinking: perhaps it can be justified at the critical level on account of the general utility of people's having a deeply ingrained disposition to take special care of their children—but if it cannot be justified in that way, no such special obligation exists (cf. *MT* 199).

Perhaps Hare is right. But if someone else disagrees, and claims there are special obligations and permissions far in excess of what utilitarianism would allow, he cannot be refuted by an appeal to the logic of the moral concepts that * they both share; because Hare's crucial logical claim, that to prescribe universally is to express a universal desire of a particular kind, embodies the central moral view which is in dispute.

It is hard to know how these disputes can be settled if they cannot be settled by logic. Their real subject-matter is human motivation, specifically practical reason. We are not in possession of a general method of discovering what people have reason to do, and therefore of discovering those universal principles of practical reason, concerning the ways in which we must consider each other, which form the basis of morality.

Derek Parfit has argued that some agent-relative principles like the one I have discussed may be criticized on the ground that they are collectively self-defeating. For example, it might be the case that if we each give priority to our own children, the results will be worse for all our children than if none of us do. It might even be the case that each of us will be able personally to benefit his own children less than if none of us follows this policy (see Parfit, 1984:100–8). But in the actual * world, it is clear that if no one gave priority to his own children, or if everyone radically reduced the degree of this priority, some children would gain and some would lose; the policy would not be collectively self-defeating in this strong sense.

So the criticism of such principles cannot be merely an internal one. It must be a defence of radical impartiality among persons as the motivational foundation of morality. The question is, do I have a reason to regulate my conduct by principles designed to give equal weight to everyone's preferences?

For Hare, that is not a question within morality, since he believes it follows from the logic of the moral concepts that * these are the only kinds of principles that can be correct. Moral argument stops at this point, and if there are any

arguments to be given, they must be of another kind. To some extent he believes it is possible to appeal to prudential reasons in addressing the motivational question (*MT* ch. 11). But to the extent that such reasons recommend utilitarianism, they are likely to work even better, for most of us, in defence of a *
less demanding morality with agent-relative permissions to favour yourself and those close to you.

In the end, we are left with a confrontation between someone who is willing to do only what he can universally prescribe in the strong sense implied by assumption (2), and someone Hare calls the amoralist—who does not prescribe *
anything in this sense, and therefore has to refrain from using the moral vocabulary. Since I believe this to be a dispute within morality, I would describe as an amoralist only someone still farther out, who refuses to produce universal prescriptions even of a much weaker kind: he has no views about how everyone should behave, or what reasons for action everyone should recognize. Someone who does not think he ought to do what he wants done in all similar cases may not be an amoralist at all, but just someone with a different moral position.

The question whether agent-relative principles have a place in morality at the fundamental level is a complex one with many aspects. It includes the analysis of rights and permissions as well as of special obligations. Hare's position on all these apparent exceptions to agent-neutral morality is that they can be explained, in so far as they are valid, as consequences at the intuitive level of utilitarian thinking at the critical level. But the main theoretical question is whether the utilitarian method is correct at the critical level, and this, I believe, depends on whether an impartial consequentialism has overriding weight as the governing principle of practical reason. This is probably the first question of ethical theory. It requires that we consider further the alternative degrees of subordination of our conduct to the review of a detached, external standpoint which abstracts from who we are. I do not think we have ready to hand a general method for thinking about these sorts of questions.

8.4 Let me move briefly to another issue. I shall pass over assumption (4), except to mention that the question of

whether the concern we owe to others should be determined
by their preferences or by something else—a restricted subset
of their preferences, or their interest measured by some
* objective standard—has received extensive discussion recently
(for example by Rawls in his theory of primary goods, and by
Scanlon, 1975). Here again, what Hare assumes is certainly
not a moral tautology. But what I want to discuss next is how
conflicting interests are to be combined in moral deliberation,
once they have been recognized, in whatever form.

The question is answered for Hare by assumption (5). The
right thing to do is determined by balancing the strengths of
the preferences I would have for different courses of action if I
were in the position of each of the affected parties, including
the agent. The course of action with the greatest quantitative
balance of favourable over unfavourable preferences for all
these possibilities taken together is the right one. It is the one I
would prescribe, if I had to prescribe universally.

My question is not whether this is what I *would* want, given
such a choice, but whether this form of balancing is the right
way to accord equal moral consideration to everyone.
Obviously it is *a* way of according equal consideration:
everyone's preferences (or interests, if some other measure of
individual benefit and harm is used) are counted the same
way in the total. But even if we assume that morality requires
us to be impartial, or that at least a component of morality
does, is this the way to do it?

The problem about a maximizing principle is familiar. Can
the relatively weak preferences or minor interests of a large
number of people legitimately outweigh the much stronger
preferences or interests of a small number? This kind of
aggregation is particularly uncomfortable when the majority
is significantly better off than the minority in other respects. It
* seems possible that the straight maximizing answer is wrong
in some cases—that a marginal advantage to the majority or
the better off should not always win.

Hare, like Rawls, finds the model for moral reasoning in a
specially constrained situation of rational individual choice.
Instead of ignorance of who one is and a great deal else, Hare
uses the device of imaginative identification with each person
to guarantee that each person's point of view will be fully

considered. But the question is whether we can combine our concern for the well-being of distinct persons by the same * principles that are appropriate for settling conflicts among the different interests of a single person. Hare's position is clear: 'I can see no reason for not adopting the same solution here as we do in cases where our own preferences conflict with one another' (*MT* 109–10).

This question has been discussed at length and with inconclusive results in recent years. I myself think there is something in the view that compensation across lives cannot take the same form as compensation within lives, and that the same principles should not govern the two kinds of conflict. If we take an equal interest in everyone's interests, our concern for all those people will be as divided as its target, and it just is not obvious how the components can be combined.

I incline to think that we should give priority to those individuals who are most in need of help, because they are objects of a concern that has priority over our concerns for those better off, even if the latter are far more numerous. Where there is no interpersonal compensation for benefits and harms, some kind of priority ranking seems a reasonable device, at least as part of the solution. But no doubt there are other, better alternatives which I have not imagined. Moral theory suffers here from an impoverishment of possibilities. None of the familiar options seems clearly right. Again the situation requires us to search for a method of thinking that we do not yet have, rather than to extract one from the rules that already govern our moral language.

8.5 My limited aim has been to show that the elements of * Hare's logic of the moral concepts which do the crucial work in his argument for utilitarianism are best understood not as part of the logic of those concepts at all, but as moral claims, whose foundation remains to be discovered, and which can be denied without violating the logic of moral language. The foundations of morality have not yet been discovered anywhere else, either. But by making his main moral claims part of the definition of morality, Hare excludes the search for their basis from moral theory, which is where it belongs.

There is another drawback to this method, having to do with moral motivation. Hare sometimes compares his view to that of Kant. But on Hare's reading the imperatives of morality are hypothetical imperatives. Someone has a reason to obey them only if he cares about acting in ways that he could prescribe universally. We may be able to show him that he has reasons of self-interest to care about this—to be the type of person who will be governed by moral principles. But unless some external motive like this is present, he will have no reason to be moral at all. He will have no reason to ask himself whether he could prescribe universally the sort of conduct he is about to engage in, and no reason to be influenced by the answer to the question if he does ask it. (If he concludes that he could not prescribe his form of conduct universally, he can just say: 'So what?') If someone does not have the motives which according to Hare are presupposed by the use of moral language, then Hare's theory implies that moral argument cannot reveal any reasons for action that he does not already recognize.

*   It is only if we begin with a conception of morality as a set of claims about how everyone has a reason to behave that we will not discover, at the end of our account, that the question of motivation has been left outside ethical theory—to be answered perhaps by a doubtful appeal to self-interest. The search for the foundations of morality ought to be part of a general theory of reasons for action. Whatever arguments are offered in this context to support a moral position would show that we have reasons to live in accordance with it. A theory which packs a strong motivational assumption into the conditions for using moral language, and then derives the content of morality from the logic of this language, has not provided a secure foundation for the morality it defends. The hard old questions have merely been excluded from the field of moral argument.

9. Prescriptivism, Constructivism, and Rights

David A. J. Richards

9.1 LARGELY under the inspiration of R. M. Hare, con- *
temporary moral philosophy insists on the profound unity of
metaethical and substantive moral inquiries. Our conception
of how to test and assess an abstract metaethical theory of
what ethical claims are and mean is, as Hare taught us it must
be, linked to the way in which the metaethical theory informs
critical understanding of substantive normative principles and
their applications both to easy and hard cases. Thus, Hare has
taught us to be sceptical of familiar forms of intuitionism (e.g.,
Moore, 1903; Ross, 1930; Ross, 1939; Prichard, 1949), not
only because of their questionable epistemic and ontological
commitments, but, more profoundly, because they rendered
mysteriously inexplicable how and why moral predicates
connect both to the world and to the moral psychology of the
persons who use them. We have justly come to expect more
from moral theory than we previously did, rediscovering the
ancient wisdom of moral philosophy as, at once, integrally
theory and practice. The measure of R. M. Hare's achievement is that he has made possible this rediscovery, and given
us one well-wrought exemplar of how to relive this ancient
wisdom which places moral philosophy at the core of humane
and civilizing learning.

The best way to pay tribute to Hare's achievement is, in my
judgement, critically to assess it from within the terms of
discourse he made possible: viz., does the view more
powerfully illuminate the linkages between its metaethical
and normative components than other perspectives? Hare's
most recent book is a naturally provocative stimulus to this
style of assessment for two good reasons.

First, Hare here elaborates his familiar metaethical position as one part of a two-stage or -level account of moral thinking. The first stage (combining the metaethics of universal prescriptivism and the normative ethics of utilitarianism) is the stage of the critical moral thinking of those with the time, inclination, and talent freshly to assess all moral issues in a systematically philosophical way. The second stage (ordinary, uncritical moral thought) is one in which people lack the luxury of philosophical reflection and must do their moral best to live a good life in accord with those lower-order practical maxims, norms, and rules which, when generally accepted and acted on, best realize what the critical morality of the previous stage would require.

Second, Hare deploys this two-stage theory of moral thinking in a quite clear-headed and argued defence of utilitarianism against a range of arguments which have led many good philosophers to suppose that utilitarianism fails to give appropriate weight to some of our central judgements of critical morality (for example, distributive constraints on utilitarian aggregation (Rawls, 1971; Hart, 1983:198), or the muscularity of arguments of rights as trumps over utilitarian arguments of policy (Dworkin, 1977)). Hare argues that the familiar arguments against utilitarianism erroneously confuse good arguments of the uncritical stage of ordinary moral thinking with good arguments of the critical stage. Properly understood, the soundest metaethical theory (universal pre-scriptivism) justifies preference–utilitarianism as the best substantive theory of critical morality. Critical morality, thus understood, itself justifies various rules, maxims, and norms of ordinary moral thinking (including distributive or rights-based constraints on utilitarian aggregation), and thus the appeal to such constraints confuses ordinary with critical moral thinking.

In support of this claim, Hare makes two points: first, familiar forms of these anti-utilitarian arguments appeal, for their plausibility, to unreal factual situations, precisely those with which ordinary moral thinking of the second stage has not to deal; and second, these anti-utilitarian arguments are themselves made in a style of intuitionist or, more broadly, intuitive moral argument which we have good reason now to distrust, as I earlier noted, in the absence of any systematic philosophical or explanatory account which connects these intuitions either to the world or to the moral psychology of persons. In *Moral Thinking*, the appeal to intuition is an expression of philosophical bad faith, a failure to take seriously both the theoretical and practical mission of moral philosophy as an essential tool of critical moral thinking. For Hare, such intuitive reasoning is an expression of theoretical failure, a kind of contemptible defence against probing more deeply into the metaethical foundation of ethical thought and the way it structures substantive moral principles. Utilitarianism is, on this view, the better critical morality because it is the fuller expression of this more profoundly elaborated kind of philosophical reason. In contrast, the intuitive reasoning of its critics appears philosophically shallow, superficial, undemanding, and, of course, question-begging.

Hare's challenge to the critics of utilitarianism can, I believe, be met and on terms not fairly regarded as improperly intuitionistic or intuitive. His metaethical theory of critical moral thinking does not, I believe, give the best, fairest, or most natural expression to his own internal ideals of critical thought or his general constructivist approach, and is not naturally associated with the substantive morality of utilitarianism in any of its forms. On the contrary, a metaethical perspective, more fully expressive of the internal ideals of critical moral thought, yields principles of substantive *critical* morality which precisely constrain the morally permissible scope of utilitarian aggregation in ways that critics of utilitarianism have justly urged. Accordingly, the claims of these critics do not draw their plausibility from a conflation of ordinary and critical moral discourse; these critics precisely identify anti-utilitarian constraints internal to critical morality itself. Hare's two arguments against these critics of utilitarianism are, on examination, unconvincing. *

9.2 In *Moral Thinking*, Hare sharpens his earlier views on the metaethical structure of moral language and thought to give clearer expression to the demands of critical moral thought, a development reflected in the treatment of the moral fanatic. The close examination of this development in Hare's views will, I believe, reveal the focal significance in critical morality of ideals of critical reason, ideals which Hare's current views do not naturally or fully elaborate.

In *Freedom and Reason* (157), when Hare had not fully distinguished critical and ordinary moral thinking, he at least lent credence to the idea that the formal requirements of his metaethical account (universal prescriptivism) would allow for the critical morality of the genocidal principles of a fanatic Nazi. Universal prescriptivism required that moral principles are those that a person would prescribe for everyone alike, including himself were he in the position of being disadvantaged by the prescription in question. If a fanatic Nazi entertained racist ideals calling for the genocide of mongrel races, a principle requiring such genocide would, on this view, be a moral principle if the fanatic would universalize such genocide even for himself (were he a member of that race). Such a degree of moral sincerity might be sufficiently uncommon to make the morality of the fanatic's principles a rather idle moral controversy, or so Hare then supposed. But many critics, including myself (Richards, 1971:83), argued that the critical morality of the Nazi's principles would not be established even by such sincerity, whether common or uncommon (the twisted idealism of Nazi ideology (see Arendt, 1973:305) inclined me to find such sincerity much less uncommon than Hare then supposed). Hare's criterion confused, on this view, a test for sincerity with the requirements of ethics (Warnock, 1967:37, 43; Richards, 1971:216; cf. Warnock, 1971*b*).

In *Moral Thinking*, Hare takes a stronger line against this moral possibility, one connected to a clearer conception that critical morality requires that the kinds of factual and other irrationalities central to the racist ideals of the Nazi not be given any weight by critical moral thought. The kind of racist ideologue, the morality of whose principles could be legitimated in *Freedom and Reason* (*FR* 157), could not be legitimated on this stronger conception of the demands of critical thought. These 'impure' fanatics, as Hare dubs them in *Moral Thinking* (*MT* 170), cannot satisfy the demands of critical moral thinking, for their views, however sincere, rest precisely on the failure to engage in the procedures essential to critical moral thought. These procedures include, Hare now argues, a kind of critical reasoning in examining the facts and desires essential to the agent's own preferences, and a willingness to change those preferences which cannot withstand the inquiries of critical reason (*MT* 180). Thus universal prescriptivism, as a formal test of critical morality, is now interpreted to reflect ideals of critical reason internal to such critical morality: a person, exercising such capacities of critical reason in forming a rational preference-structure, reasonably universalizes prescriptions applicable to the rational preference-structure of everyone alike, himself included. Accordingly, a critical morality of rational aims reasonably universalized gravitates, Hare argues, to a substantive utilitarian morality inconsistent   * with racist ideology.

But there is, I believe, an unexamined tension between these two developments in Hare's thought: first, his emphasis on the place of ideals of reason in critical morality; and second, his now whole-hearted defence of a substantive utilitarian morality. On the one hand, Hare now insists that the standpoint of critical morality must be interpreted to reflect and express the rational powers of persons who reasonably universalize the relevant principles. On the other hand, Hare argues that this strengthened metaethical theory requires the universalized prescriptions to have a certain content, namely, maximizing the satisfaction of preferences in the familiar utilitarian way.

The tension may be highlighted in the following way. A critical morality, expressing internal ideals of rationality and reasonableness, gives central normative weight, I believe, not to preferences as such, but to the distinctive place of a certain narrower range of goods essential to the exercise and expression of our rational powers as persons and the diverse ways persons, thus understood, realize their more ultimate aims expressive of such powers (Rawls, 1982:152). But, from this kind of implicitly Kantian perspective on metaethics,   * such internal ideals are naturally elaborated to universalize principles that would reasonably assure to persons that a lexically prior weight is accorded equal distribution of such goods, viz. the principles thus impose significant deontological constraints, grounded in securing such goods, on the ways in which utilitarian aggregation of preferences in general, or rational preferences in particular, may be pursued (cf. Scanlon, 1975; Rawls, 1982:159). The metaethical conception, naturally elaborated, is not only in tension with utilitarianism; it is, significantly, anti-utilitarian. How can Hare square his Kantian metaethics with his utilitarian normative ethics?

9.3 The kinds of objections to utilitarianism which Hare wishes to rebut are now familiarly explained in terms of a
* central blunder of utilitarian moral reasoning, namely, its failure to take seriously the separateness of persons (Hart, 1983:198). In our own personal lives, we often rationally endure substantial deprivations in one period of our lives (for example, educational training and discipline) in order to secure a more satisfying life in later periods; such trade-offs of current pain against future pleasure are often quite prudent. However, utilitarianism generalizes this intrapersonal form of rational prudence to encompass as well interpersonal impositions of substantial deprivation on some in order better to secure aggregate pleasure over all. But this, so it is argued, bespeaks the failure of utilitarianism to take seriously the separateness of persons: what is legitimate for one person within his own life is not the measure of ethically legitimate actions between or among persons.

This utilitarian failure is sometimes explained in terms of the characterististic association of utilitarianism, as a normative ethics, with the metaethical theory of the ideal observer (Richards, 1971:86–7). Ideal observer theories of ethics suppose that ethically right actions are those actions which would enjoy certain appropriately described kinds of approbation from a person who is omniscient, omnicompetent, perfectly sympathetic, etc. Since the ideal observer has perfect capacities of sympathetic identification, his approbations would, accordingly, reflect and be explained by the aggregate of pleasure over pain in the moral community at large with whose pleasures and pains he perfectly identifies. The
* approbations of the ideal observer would, in short, reflect the utilitarian principle in precisely the way that literally conflates the rationality of prudence with the reasonableness of ethics: the approbations of the ideal observer, expressive of the greatest pleasure over pain in himself, literally reflect (via sympathetic identification) the aggregate of pleasure over

pain in the moral community at large. Ethics, in short, is a kind of prudence in the generous soul of the ideal observer.

This kind of objection to utilitarianism is not intuitionist or intuitive in the way that Hare finds objectionable. It is an objection based on an alleged defect both in the structure and metaethics of utilitarian reasoning, viz. its failure to take seriously the ways in which ethical reasoning systematically differs from prudential reasoning, its connection to a meta-ethics which elides basic differences in ethics and prudence. *

Hare's theory is a useful test case for this kind of objection, for he, of course, not only does not defend any metaethics of the ideal observer, but is, rather, committed to a universal * prescriptivism which is, if anything, historically associated with the deontological moral philosophy of Kant (Kant, 1785). The interest of Hare's account is, precisely, this remarkable union of a Kantian metaethics with a utilitarian normative ethics, an attempt, like J. S. Mill's, to marry German profundity to British good sense (Mill, 1861:6, 65). If Hare can make his case for this way of justifying utilitarianism, he will have shown that utilitarianism follows from a moral perspective which does not confuse ethics and prudence and which insists, structurally, on the separateness of persons.

Hare construes the inference from universal prescriptivism to utilitarianism in a way, I believe, that fails to do justice to the fundamental fact of ethics, the separateness of persons. For Hare, as we have seen, ethics is what a critically rational person would reasonably prescribe as the universal principle applicable to himself and others in various contexts of choice and deliberation. From this perspective, Hare argues, every-one's rational preferences are of equal weight. Accordingly, such universal prescriptions would reflect the maximum aggregation of satisfaction of rational preferences, in short, the utilitarian principle. But the argument confuses the central ethical imperative, treating persons as equals, with the very * different idea that preferences or desires should be treated equally (cf. Richards, 1981:5). Only the former, not the latter, naturally, fully, and fairly gives expression to the way in which ethical principles impose constraints on our inter-personal life which we would fairly accept and prescribe as expressions of our common moral powers of rationality and reasonableness.

Kantian universalizability, of which Hare's universal prescriptivism is an elaboration, is a constructivist metaethics (Rawls, 1980): ethical principles do not track special properties in the world, but are the expression and acknowledgement of our common moral powers of rationality and reasonableness. The point is not, as Hare supposes, that ethical predicates cannot be given a cognitive or naturalistic account, or, as Mackie supposes (Mackie, 1977, ch. 1), that such predicates cannot objectively articulate values. A constructivist metaethics may be cognitivist, naturalistic, and objective (see e.g. Richards, 1971; Warnock, 1971*b*). Its constructivism is its characterization of ethics (cognitivist or non-cognitivist, naturalistic or non-naturalistic, objective or subjective) in terms of principles whose content depends, crucially, on what
* rational and reasonable persons would impose on themselves and all others (Kant, 1785), prescribe (*MT*), agree to (Rawls, 1971; Richards, 1971; Mackie, 1977), accept consistently (Gewirth, 1978), or not reject (Scanlon, 1982:103), as the universally applicable principles expressive of their common moral powers and the circumstances of interpersonal life. The fact of the matter in ethics, if there is a fact, is such a constructivist fact, not a non-natural property of the world or a chain of being or a natural hierarchy.

The distinctive power of this constructivist approach is the way in which it connects its metaethics to its normative ethics. In contrast to the ideal observer's conflation of all persons into the prudential calculations of one person, a constructivist metaethics requires that ethical principles are, crucially, those that all persons could impose on themselves, prescribe, agree to, etc. as the universally applicable expressions of their common moral powers of rationality and reasonableness in the circumstances of interpersonal life. As I earlier suggested, constructivist accounts, thus, familiarly give expression, weight, and place to ideals of the person internal to its metaethical approach, viz. the exercise of the moral powers of critical reason in the self-determination of a rational and reasonable life (Rawls, 1980). For example, such accounts give a central normative weight and place to the higher-order interest of persons, consisent with such ideals, in the formation, expression, and revision of the basic values of conscience which give shape and order to all the other pursuits in persons' lives, indeed make possible a personal point of view at all. Persons, understood on this model of constructivist metaethics, would only impose, prescribe, agree to, etc. political principles which would ensure that a good like conscience be guaranteed to all on terms of equal liberty lexically prior to arguments of utilitarian aggregation (Rawls, 1971:205; Richards, 1986). Otherwise, the very capacities for critical reason, which actuate the underlying metaethical conception, would too easily give way to values to which the conception gives no corresponding weight.

Hare's universal prescriptivism diverges from this natural elaboration of constructivist metaethics because of the way in which he chooses to cast the prescriptivist choice which we all must make, namely, each person rationally reflects on his own preferences, considers what his preferences would be were he the person affected by various actions, and universalistically prescribes a principle which gives equal weight to all preferences. But the formally constructivist premises are thus given a non-constructivist substantive interpretation, since the relevant preferences are those only of one person who, in principle, weights them like the generous prudence of the ideal observer. In a real sense, the argument does not take persons or personal point of view seriously, for the view gives weight to other persons not as persons but, externally and impersonally, as containers of preferences with which the prescriber projectively identifies. Preferences, not persons, are treated equally.

A constructivist theory may coherently impute to all rational and reasonable persons certain common goods, and even conduct its argument from the perspective of any one person and the demands he or she would make for that good (Rawls, 1971:139). But the construction of such common goods is itself dictated by the background ideals of the person capable of exercising the powers of rationality and reasonableness and must be of a kind that all such persons would impose, prescribe, agree to, etc.

Hare's appeal to the projective preferences of one universal

prescriber is not the constructivist search for those goods that all rational and reasonable persons would demand in an ethics whose legitimacy requires their free, reasonable, and public assent. It is, under the illusory guise of a neo-Kantian constructivism, a kind of ideal observer theory, construing ethics as a kind of imaginative identification of one generous soul with the projectively imagined preferences of others. The inference to utilitarianism is not, then, a genuinely construct-ivist inference. Indeed, from a constructivist perspective, many reasonable persons would decisively not accept, would
* indeed reject, a utilitarian principle which would put in peril guarantees of certain goods essential to personal integrity in order better to realize utilitarian aggregates.

Perhaps Hare's inference rests on a suppressed premiss rejecting constructivist ideals of the person in favour of a less unified conception of what a person is (cf. Parfit, 1984; but see *MT* 100). But controversies over personal identity are typically over how we would describe quite fantastically hypothetical cases of division, brain transplants, etc. Constructivist moral ideals, in contrast, attend to the world as it is and give expression to central concerns for rational and reasonable freedom of persons embedded in that world. Accordingly, these moral ideals have continuing appeal in the range of actual cases which arise irrespective of the range of cases over which philosophers of personal identity disagree. There would, of course, be some methodological irony in the fact, if it is a fact, that Hare's current utilitarianism does depend on these controversial arguments. For Hare, as we shall shortly see, is among the most methodologically demanding of contemporary moral philosophers in his insistence that moral philosophy must concentrate on actual not hypothetical cases.

9.4 The most arresting defensive move of *Moral Thinking* is Hare's use of the distinction between two levels of moral thought (critical and conventional) to defend utilitarianism as the best substantive critical morality. The now familiar objections to utilitarian ethics rest, Hare argues, on a confusion of these two levels: the objections rest on good conventional moral reasoning, but they are consistent with a utilitarian critical morality. If Hare were right on this point, it

might render idle the kinds of objections I have made to his *
universal prescriptivism. The strain between his metaethical
constructivism and his normative utilitarianism would surely
be much relieved if utilitarianism could give weight to and
even explain the leading objections to utilitarianism which
constructivist accounts have familiarly generated.

There are, however, two intractable difficulties with Hare's
use of the two levels to answer the critics of utilitarianism:
first, metaethical objections to the sharpness of such a line
between critical and conventional morality; and second, the
manipulation of facts to ensure the legitimacy of utilitarian
critical reasoning.

A constructivist metaethics, including Hare's, characterizes
ethical principles as, importantly, public, reasonable, and
egalitarian both in their substance and in their appeal (cf.
Baier, 1958). Accordingly, a sharp distinction between an
élitist critical morality and a populist conventional morality *
may, if carried too far, strain these metaethical requirements:
the élitist morality may be too non-public and inegalitarian to
be a critical morality; the conventional morality too unreasonable to carry any critical force whatsoever. Hare's
distinction between critical and conventional morality is
suspect for both such reasons.

Hare's defence of a utilitarian critical morality bears a
paradoxical relationship to his defence of a conventional
morality which calls for distributive and rights-based constraints on utilitarian aggregation. These features of conventional morality are, Hare argues, themselves justified on
utilitarian grounds on the ground that, given limited time and
temptations to abuse, the observance of these constraints
better aggregates utility over all. But if Hare is right and is
publicly seen to be right, these practices would surely erode:
persons will now understand that deontological constraints
are not issues of principle, but utilitarian strategies, and the *
scope and definition of the constraints must reasonably give
way to their redefinition by critical morality. The natural
utilitarian answer must be that such knowledge should not,
indeed cannot, be widely and publicly known, debated, and
understood (cf. Sidgwick, 1874:489). A critical moral theory,
which requires its own élitist constraints on publicity and

appeal, strains the very conception of a constructivist ethics of moral community.

The status of conventional morality, on Hare's conception, is no less anomalous. The self-understanding of conventional morality includes, Hare concedes, deontological constraints on utilitarian aggregation. Properly understood, belief in and action on these constraints are necessary, given limited time and temptations, to secure the aims of a critical utilitarian morality. But the demands of ordinary moral life are, more often than Hare supposes, consistent with considerable moral reflection, and critical morality surely requires that conventional morality, barbarously inhumane as it often is, must be searchingly tested by such critical moral reflection. Indeed, a constructivist moral conception calls, if anything, for moral principles that are perspicuously reasonable. But Hare's conception of a justifiable conventional morality is self-consciously not reasonable in this way and would be unstably connected to the only reasonable morality for Hare, namely, utilitarianism. Why should a conventional morality, so often or so probably unreasonable, have any critical force at all?

Hare presents two kinds of arguments against the familiar objections to utilitarian aggregation: first, such arguments rest on appeals to intuition without the systematic metaethical or normative argument on which Hare insists; and second, the familiar objections rest on hypothetical, not real, cases. We have addressed Hare's metaethical and normative arguments on their own terms earlier, and must now confront his leading attempt to reconcile utilitarianism with deontological judge-ments, namely, his contention that utilitarianism, properly understood, supports such judgements in all actual cases. The argument against utilitarianism appeals, in contrast, to purely hypothetical cases with which our actual morality has not to deal. Such arguments are, therefore, idle.

Hare makes a number of such reconciling claims in his attempt (*MT* ch. 9) to square his normative utilitarianism with such judgements as distributive constraints on utilitarian aggregation, and arguments of rights as trumps over policy arguments of utilitarian kinds. In each case, I believe, Hare appeals to factual assumptions which, if true, might explain how such deontological judgements might be strategies to maximize utility over all. Hare then rejects any objections to these arguments as resting on hypothetical, not real, cases. In contrast to the fantastically unreal reasoning of critics of utilitarianism, Hare stands, as it were, on the terra firma of facts as they are.

Hare's appeal for a more practical conception of moral philosophizing is, of course, estimable, but his appeal to facts, in defence of utilitarianism, is a bogus manipulation of the idea of real versus hypothetical cases to defend a questionable normative theory from some devastating and unanswerable objections. Hare's argument claims to defend our strong deontological judgements in certain cases by factual assumptions much more dubious than the normative judgements they allegedly support (cf. Richards, 1971:115). Indeed, plausible factual hypotheses can be made opposite to those offered by Hare which would render such normative judgements wrong on utilitarian grounds. We hold, critically, to these judgements, none the less.

I offer only one example from the range of those worthy of discussion. Hare takes note of the Kantian deontological argument (which H. L. A. Hart, of course, makes also in his classic contemporary discussion, 1968:1), namely, that familiar principles of just punishment require that only those persons be subject to punishment who have culpably committed the wrongful act so defined by a reasonably specific law, notwithstanding any argument of utilitarian aggregation to the contrary. But, Hare suggests, the place of such deontological constraints in our political morality is explained by the factual assumption: 'that a legal system in which judges have not been brought up to treat this principle as in practice unbreakable is likely to be a bad system for nearly everybody subject to it' (*MT* 163). But the factual assumption adduced is not merely dubious; it is almost certainly wrong. Hare simply repeats the 'spectacular *non sequitur*' (Hart, 1968:19) that Hart classically identified in Bentham's utilitarian rationale for these principles of punishment, namely, the confusion of specific deterrence of the putative criminal with general deterrent effects on non-criminals. It is quite plausible and probably true that an abandonment of the requirement of a culpable mind, in proof * of criminality, would make the administration of criminal justice much more certain and effective in ways that would secure higher levels of general deterrence which would amply compensate any disadvantage to a few people. None the less, the morality of criminal justice rejects such arguments not on utilitarian grounds, but on independent grounds of justice that utilitarianism cannot explain (see Hart, 1968:19–24).

Such suppositions of fact, contrary to Hare's, are, thus, not idle: they are tough-minded and fair assessments of fact, and the best critical thought about criminal justice takes such facts seriously and tries to explain why the complex structure of our values none the less requires that appropriate weight be given to independent distributive aims in criminal justice. Those deeply practical debates are not advanced by a normative perspective which oversimplifies the tensions between our critical moral values and tends to distort the interpretation of facts.

Above all, such dubious fact-mongering is not what we should expect from the aspirations for moral philosophy that Hare has insisted we should have, namely, systematically critical metaethical and normative argument rigorously attuned to the real practical issues of our moral life. Such ambitions, surely, should encompass a correspondingly rigorous and demanding attention to the rationality of the fact-finding on which an ethics of critical reason must rest, for * the distortion of our ethics by irresponsible inattention to fact is one among the more salient irrationalities of much conventional morality (see e.g. Richards, 1977:255; Richards, 1982: 94 ff., 168 ff.). Accordingly, a critical morality should assist us in understanding the complex connections between facts and values and the ways in which critical reasoning about facts and values may illuminate interconnecting distortions both of facts and of values. Certainly, the manipulation of controversial facts to reach the moral results we desire is all too human. It is not what Hare has taught us to demand from the critical thinking that moral philosophy makes possible.

If we resist the conclusions of a systematic moral philosophy sufficiently to tailor facts to avoid these conclusions, we should argue not over the facts, but over the kind of theory which requires such manipulations of fact to be acceptable. Our moral judgements are, perhaps, controlled by a deeper moral theory which guides the degree to which a decent person like Hare (or like J. S. Mill earlier) will and will not follow out the consistent implications of his normative utilitarianism.

These remarks are, perhaps, tendentiously intuitive in the way that Hare urges us, methodologically, to reject. I do not question his methodological rigour: I admire and respect it. But this consideration of counter-examples is embedded in a larger criticism of Hare's metaethics and normative utilitarianism which satisfies, I believe, the canons of philosophical argument which Hare requires of good argument in ethics. Neither his metaethics nor his normative utilitarianism is the best elaboration of the ideals internal to his constructivist orientation. Accordingly, the implausibility of Hare's discussion of counter-examples should reinforce the larger critical point: Hare cannot deal with these cases because the larger theory is internally flawed, perhaps at war with itself.

9.5 Good argument in ethics requires, as Hare has taught us, not isolated discussion of counter-examples, but detailed comparisons of divergent theoretical perspectives and their relative power to explain, organize thought, and advance discussion. Accordingly, I have discussed Hare's views in the context of a larger exploration of constructivist moral theories, of which Hare's theory is, for reasons earlier suggested, a rather paradoxical exemplar.

Hare's theory may well be wrong. But, if he is wrong, it is surely remarkable what minor differences in his assumptions at various points could have made his views less wrong, or even perhaps right. The profound influence and permanent importance of Hare's moral philosophy rest, I believe, on the general constructivist perspective he introduced into the best discourse on moral philosophy, and his methodological rigour in rediscovering the fertile union of metaethical and normative inquiries. The power of his contribution is seen in the way in which his work has transformed the subject of moral philosophy, and the remarkably creative stimulus his work has given to his often admiring critics in finding themselves and their views within the larger framework of constructivist discourse that Hare made possible. Those critics, like myself, who profited from Hare's generous criticisms of their views as students, know as well that the life of the man is one with the message of the work: integrity, rigour, clarity, and the broadest and most humane sympathies. His voice, as writer and teacher, has struck such deep resonances in so many of my generation because it has been, for us, the authentic contemporary voice, in its clarity and its critical demands, of the Socratic soul.

10. Levels of Moral Thinking

T. M. Scanlon

10.1 LIKE Professor Hare, I have found the idea of a two-level moral theory attractive, and some of the reasons which he has cited in favour of such a view have moved me as well. But the view which he arrives at contains elements which I would not accept. The aim of this paper is to explore the sources of this agreement and divergence.

    Several different lines of thought lead to the conclusion that there are different levels of moral thinking. For those who have adopted a moral theory like utilitarianism, with implications that are sharply at variance with ordinary moral thought, a 'two-level' theory can seem attractive as a way of explaining this divergence. The precepts of common-sense morality, while not strictly speaking correct according to the best moral theory, may be defended as principles which it is a good thing, from the point of view of this theory, for people to believe and act upon. Rule-utilitarianism has often been perceived in this way, as a means of reconciling utilitarian theory with ordinary moral thinking, whether or not this is what the proponents of that view actually had in mind.

    But one may also be led towards a two-level theory simply by a desire to do justice to the perceived complexity of ordinary moral argument. It is evident on reflection that no statable principle tells the whole story of the moral claim which it embodies. There is always more to be said about why the acts mentioned are wrong (or permissible or required), about which cases are to be recognized as exceptions, and so on. Thus the existence of a level of 'critical thinking' behind commonly accepted principles seems to be indicated by an examination of ordinary moral thought itself, considered in isolation from any moral theory, utilitarian or otherwise. Whether the critical thought employed or presupposed in ordinary moral thinking is utilitarian is of course a further question.

While these two lines of thought both lead to a distinction between levels of moral thinking, they support different views of the relation between these levels. The first is based on the presupposition that ordinary moral thought and 'critical thinking' will sometimes yield different answers about what one should do, and it is designed to explain this fact in a way that justifies our continued reliance on ordinary thinking even in cases in which the judgements it leads to are 'wrong'. The distinction between levels which this line of thought supports is thus quite sharp, and the relation between the two levels an instrumental one. The second line of thought, on the other hand, is compatible with the idea that the two levels of moral thinking are quite continuous with one another, 'critical thinking' being only the completion of less reflective moral thought, and that the two levels of thinking never yield conflicting practical judgements (or, rather, that when they do the judgement given by 'critical thinking' is always the unequivocally correct answer about what to do).

Both of these lines of thought are represented at various points in Professor Hare's work, though it is the latter which is predominant in *Moral Thinking*.[1] His view of the relation between critical and intuitive thinking, however, seems quite consistently to be the one supported by the first, more distinctively utilitarian rationale. One subject of critical thinking as Hare describes it is the question of what 'intuitive' principles it would be best for us to employ. But critical thought also, and primarily, yields conclusions about which acts are 'really' right. These conclusions are primary because it is with reference to them that the first sort of question (about the selection of intuitive principles) is to be answered. By determining what is right they define the goal of moral practice, and a set of intuitive principles is justified if trying to

[1] The idea that distinguishing levels of moral thought is a way of reconciling utilitarian theory with the normative content of common-sense morality is suggested in 'Ethical Theory and Utilitarianism' (H 1976a) and by a few remarks in *Moral Thinking*. See e.g. *MT* 43. But the overall strategy of that book, which argues for a distinct level of critical thinking as necessary to deal with cases of conflict and other challenges to common-sense principles, illustrates the second, and to my mind more convincing, rationale for distinguishing levels. See particularly sect. 2.5.

act by those principles would maximize our chances of performing acts which are right (*MT* 47). Conformity to intuitive principles, on the other hand, does not insure that an action is right—at most that it is 'morally rational'. None the less, morally good people will rely on such principles most of the time, not merely as 'rules of thumb' (i.e. convenient rough guides) but as principles which are taken seriously and cannot be violated without compunction (*MT* 2.2, 2.4).

This account of the distinction between the two levels of moral thinking strikes me as the least satisfactory element in Hare's two-level theory. He sometimes presents the distinction as one between the kinds of moral thinking appropriate to two different kinds of people: on the one hand, parents, and 'archangels': on the other, children, and 'proles'. Parents and archangels can engage in critical thinking because they have the opportunity to do so (their decisions need not be made in the heat of the moment) and because of their greater ability: greater knowledge of the relevant facts and greater powers of dispassionate judgement. Having the benefit of these advantages, they can attempt to discover the truth about what is right and, on this basis, choose intuitive principles which are to be 'implanted' into their charges, the children or proles. The latter, by contrast, should not attempt to discover the truth but should merely react, in accordance with these implanted principles, to the situations which confront them.

Without denying that there is such a thing as moral education and that parents do have to make decisions, employing what one hopes is their greater wisdom, about how to bring up their children, it must none the less be admitted that there is something quite unattractive about this picture (a criticism stressed by Bernard Williams, most recently in * 1985:106–10). Its most objectionable feature is the idea that attempting to discover the truth about what is right is something which is reserved for 'the wise', while most of us most of the time are supposed instead to react instinctively in accordance with implanted principles whose justification is purely instrumental. The terminology of 'archangels' and 'proles' does nothing to make this idea more appealing.

But this is just unfortunate terminology. What Hare is discussing is not really two separate groups of people but two points of view which the same person may adopt at different times. We are (almost all of us) sometimes 'parents' and sometimes 'children', sometimes 'archangels' and sometimes 'proles'. This makes the view more palatable, but does not remove the difficulty altogether. Certainly there is such a thing as moral self-education, and we do sometimes undertake, with varying success, to make ourselves more sensitive (or less susceptible) to certain considerations. Moreover, this process sometimes involves an element of approximation: we may, for example, undertake to make ourselves (or our children) hesitant to inflict pain on others because this is a good disposition to have on balance even though it may lead us (or them) to do the wrong thing in certain unusual circumstances. Finally, it cannot be denied that cases do arise in which there is no time for reflection and one must simply act on the basis of one's immediate reactions. But even conceding all this, it does not seem that the process of applying and acting on 'intuitive' moral principles is *in general* simply a matter of responding to such 'implanted' motivations. It does not seem to me, at least, that when I am applying common-sense moral principles I am doing something other than trying to discover what is 'really right'. Nor does it seem that when I employ these principles in an actual case I do so because if I were to try to think directly about morality I might well come up with the wrong answer. Thus, even when applied to a single person, Hare's distinction between the intuitive and critical standpoints involves a division of labour in moral thought which is at odds with at least part of our moral experience.

This leads me to look for an account of the relation between levels of moral thinking which adheres more consistently to the second of the two lines of thought mentioned above. Such an account should, first, allow for the possibility of 'critical thinking', that is to say for reflection which goes beyond intuitive principles and can deal with conflicts, questions of interpretation and justification, and so on. Second, it should allow for the fact that the justification of some principles involves what seems to be an instrumental element: in thinking about whether a course of action is wrong we must sometimes consider what things would be like if people generally believed that course of action to be permissible. But, third, it should not involve an implausible 'division of labour' in moral thinking. I believe that the main problem in developing such a view lies in giving a more satisfactory account of what is involved in accepting and applying 'intuitive principles'. I will approach this problem by considering an analogy with legal reasoning.

10.2 The Constitution of the United States contains in its * Bill of Rights a number of principles restricting the powers of government. Congress is forbidden to make laws abridging the freedom of speech, inhibiting the free exercise of religion, depriving citizens of life, liberty, or property without due process of law, and so on. Each of these rights is given a simple and general formulation: indeed, they are each stated in a few words. A great deal of 'critical thinking' is required to describe the justification of these principles and to work out what they require in 'hard cases', though there are of course some cases in which their meaning is quite clear. What is the relation between the kind of thinking involved in applying the Bill of Rights in cases of the latter kind—'easy cases'—and that called for when things get more difficult? One answer would be that in 'easy' cases the answer is obtained simply by noting that the law whose Constitutionality is at issue does or does not meet the description given in the Constitutional formula, e.g. that it does or does not restrict freedom of speech, while in 'hard cases' one must refer to something else (such as the intention of the framers, or the theory best explaining the Constitution and past decisions as a whole) which plays a role analogous to what Professor Hare calls 'critical thinking'.

I take it to be the consensus among legal scholars who * disagree about much else (in particular about what it is that is to play the role of critical thinking in Constitutional adjudication) that this suggestion is mistaken. Even in easy cases decisions are not reached by laying the law beside the Constitutional clause and seeing whether the one fits the description given by the other. This is clear from the example of freedom of speech; what is it for a law to abridge freedom of speech? In the most obvious and literal meaning of these words many clearly valid laws fit this description, since they decrease the freedom to speak. Once one moves beyond this obviously unsatisfactory interpretation, however, there is

nothing which could be called 'simply applying the words of
the Constitution'. The Constitutional formula is not, then, a
simple, general rule which, although it is only approximately
correct, can simply be followed in most cases, thereby
avoiding the need to engage in more sophisticated and
difficult 'critical thinking'. Rather, this formula refers to a
complex political idea about the limits of acceptable governmental authority: about the importance of expression, the
threats of it, and the role of law and government both as a
source of such threats and as a source of protection against
them. Exactly how this idea is to be understood is sometimes a
matter of controversy. There are many clear cases in which all
plausible theories give the same answer, and others in which
the content of the right referred to by the words of the
Constitution is less clear and more debatable. But the
important point for my present purposes is that whether we
are thinking about easy cases or hard ones the object of our
thought is the same—the same familiar but also complex and
elusive idea about the limits of governmental authority.

Even if these observations about Constitutional law are
correct, nothing directly follows about moral thinking. We
have at most a suggestive analogy. What it suggests is a way of
understanding the relation between relatively simple verbal
formulas and more complex 'critical thinking' which avoids
* the division of labour discussed above. The suggestion is that
such common-sense moral principles as 'it is wrong to kill' are
not simple self-contained rules but ways of referring to the
same moral ideas whose complexities are explored in 'critical
thinking'. Qualifications having to do with intent, justifications,
excuses, and so on, while not always explicit in any
formulation of the principle, are part of the idea referred to
(though their exact boundaries are never totally clear). If this
is correct, then taking these principles seriously will not
exclude critical thinking, and taking critical thinking to be the
way of discovering 'the moral truth' will not involve seeing
common-sense principles as unreflective tendencies to react
which we 'implant' in ourselves in order to minimize error.

There are, of course, important differences between legal
and moral thinking. No one would suggest that Constitutional
rights are stated in relatively simple, general terms because

judges must make decisions in haste and do not have time to consider fundamental issues. On the contrary, there are obvious practical reasons why constitutions require succinct, general formulations, and judicial decision-making is supposed *always* to be sufficiently deliberate and reflective to qualify as 'critical thinking'. Despite these differences, however, the model just described strikes me as a plausible account of the role of common-sense principles in moral thought. There is a need to instil in ourselves a tendency to act quickly and instinctively in certain cases, but this is not as central to the distinction between 'ordinary' and 'critical' moral thinking as Hare's account suggests.

10.3 While I do not accept Hare's account of common-sense moral principles, I agree that the justification of moral principles often depends both on the consequences that would ensue if people generally behaved in the ways these principles forbid and on the presumed likelihood that, in the absence of constraint, people would often behave in those ways. I need to explain, then, how this kind of argument differs from the instrumentalism and the element of mistrust which are central to Hare's account of 'intuitive' principles. Here again the analogy with legal rights is helpful.

The basis of the right to freedom of expression lies in the well-documented tendency of government officials, even when well-intentioned, to adopt policies which are unacceptably restrictive of individuals' opportunities to be informed and to make their own views known to others. In view of this tendency, reasonable citizens would refuse to grant governments authority to restrict expression whenever they believe it a good thing to do so: governments with this power are unreasonably risky. But the range of authority proscribed by this argument is not defined exactly. Wide agreement exists on some questions, such as that prior censorship of the political content of newspapers is unacceptable. In other cases there is considerable uncertainty, and different people (or different countries) may reasonably choose to accept different risks.

The conclusion of this argument is that certain kinds of * government action are wrong. Not just that it is a good thing for officials to believe that they are wrong, but that they really

are wrong. There will undoubtedly be some cases in which
restricting expression in ways that this right forbids would
have good consequences. But this does not make those actions
right or reduce the principle forbidding them to the status of a
useful fiction which, because of their tendencies to error, we
would like government officials to believe. It does not do this
because the question of right here is in the first instance a
question of what authority governments have. In setting these
limits—in deciding what authority it is reasonable to grant—
we take into consideration the things that we would like
governments to be able to do and the things that, given their
known propensities, we think it important to guard against
their doing. But when the argument for these limits is a good
one it is the limits themselves—not the goals which this
argument refers to—which mark the line between right and
wrong.

The analogous approach to the morality of individual
action takes the fundamental question of right to be: what
authority (and duty) to act is it reasonable for us to assign to
each other? In Hare's terms, what universal permissions and
injunctions do we have reason to accept? As in the case of
governmental authority, our answer to this question will take
into account such things as what we want to have happen,
what we feel it important to be protected against, our desires
for freedom of action, and our estimates of the consequences of
what we and others would be likely to choose to do in the
absence of restraint. On the view I am advocating, the
permissions and injunctions which it is reasonable to adopt
* determine what is right; they are not mere psychological
devices to move us as close as possible to some independently
determined standard of right conduct. These principles are
like what Hare calls intuitive principles in being chosen in the
light not only of our goals and desires but also our frailties, our
need to act without full information, and so on. My account
differs from Hare's, however, in that I do not take these
principles to be simple formulas which are applied literally. I
understand them instead, in the way described above, as
referring to more complex, incompletely articulated pieces of
argument about what authority to act it is reasonable to grant
(and to refuse to grant) one another.

I do not mean to suggest that there is a fixed set of moral ideas, which are the subject of intuitive moral principles and which it is the task of critical thinking merely to spell out and refine.[2] This is what critical thinking does in most cases, but it can also lead us to the conclusion that what we previously thought was an acceptable moral principle is in fact not acceptable (perhaps we only thought it was because we had neglected or underestimated what it involved for some people). The effect of reaching this conclusion is immediately to deprive the principle of its standing even at the intuitive level. It would therefore be misleading to think of such cases as instances of conflict between 'intuitive' and 'critical' thinking since they involve a simultaneous change in our opinions at both 'levels'.

I prefer this account to the one Hare offers because it seems to me to be more consistent with the way we normally think about moral questions. It allows for the possibility of 'critical thinking'—that is, of moral reflection and argument which goes beyond the invocation of simple principles. But it also allows us to take the moral beliefs embodied in common-sense moral principles seriously as beliefs about what really is right and wrong: we need not view the application of these principles in 'standard' cases as a blind reflex which we have been trained or trained ourselves to have. This view of the levels of moral thinking meets the requirements of the second line of thought described at the beginning of this paper. Whether it fulfils the first line of thought is less clear. Because it describes critical thinking as continuous with ordinary moral thought, it will provide a way of reconciling the latter with utilitarianism only if ordinary moral ideas are themselves already ideas about how happiness can be maximized. This has sometimes been claimed, though it seems to me doubtful.

10.4 The form of critical thinking which I see as continuous * with common-sense morality is not utilitarian—does not take maximum aggregate happiness as the standard for choosing moral principles. Rather, it takes the fundamental question to be whether a principle could reasonably be rejected (for application in our imperfect world) by parties who, in addition to their own personal aims, were moved by a desire

---

[2] I am grateful to Jonathan Wolff for pointing out the need to make this explicit.

to find principles that others similarly motivated could also accept (a view presented in Scanlon, 1982).

This view has considerable affinity with Professor Hare's metaethical theory since the question it takes to be fundamental is very much like the universal prescriptivist question, 'What universal imperatives do I accept for situations of this kind?' But it is in tension with two other theses which Hare has defended: the claim that rational application of the method of universal prescriptivism leads to utilitarianism and the claim that only utilitarian thinking can claim to be 'critical': any other form of moral argument will involve viciously circular appeals to intuition (*MT* 40). I will respond briefly to the first of these objections later.[3] Here I will address the charge of circularity, and illustrate the method I have in mind, by discussing several examples which Hare considers near the end of 'Ethical Theory and Utilitarianism' (H 1976*a*).

These examples are intended to illustrate how Hare's distinction between levels of moral thinking enables him to deal with some well-known cases which have been presented as problems for utilitarianism. These are 'the case of the man who is tempted, on utilitarian grounds, to use electricity during a power crisis, contrary to the government's instructions', 'the case of the voter who abstains in the belief that enough others will vote', 'the case of the person who only pretends to push the car' (letting others do the work and, presumably, saving him or herself for some endeavour producing more utility), and 'the case of the person who makes a lying promise to a dying person' (believing that utility will be maximized by reassuring the dying person that his wishes will be carried out and then not doing so).

Hare begins his discussion of these cases by observing that 'it would be impolitic to bring people up to behave like this if we were seeking level–1 principles with the highest acceptance-utility; if we did the result would be that nearly everyone would consume electricity under those conditions, and hardly anyone would vote' (H 1976*a*:129–30). He goes on, however, to offer a more ambitious reply, which he calls 'the chief answer to these cases'. This answer is given in two stages. First he

---

[3] In the concluding paragraphs of this article. Full treatment of the arguments in Chapters 5 and 6 of *Moral Thinking* would require a separate paper.

'goes back to the logical beginning' and asks whether he is 'prepared to prescribe, or even permit' that others should do these things when he considers them from the point of view of one of the people taken advantage of (those who are saving electricity, voting, pushing, or dying). His answer is an unhesitating, 'No'. Given, then, that the logical machinery of universal prescriptivism gives the 'right' answer in these cases, the second question is whether 'the utilitarianism based on it' gives the same answer. Hare's argument that it does concentrates on the fourth example (the death-bed promise), and turns on the observation that 'to frustrate a desire of mine is against my interest even if I do not know that it is being frustrated' (H 1976a:130). Thus the desires of the dying person concerning what happens after his or her death have to be taken into account in a utilitarian calculation. This solution is generalized to apply to the other cases mentioned by taking the desire in question to be a desire not to have other people cheating on one even when one does not know it. Hare concludes:

Whichever way we put it, whether in terms of what I am prepared to prescribe or permit universally (and therefore also for when I am the victim) or in terms of how to be fair as between the interests of all the affected parties, I conclude that the acts I have listed will come out wrong on the act-utilitarian calculation, because of the harms done to the interests of those who are cheated, or the non-fulfilment of prescriptions to which, we may assume, they attach high importance (H 1976a:131).

This reference to act-utilitarian calculation suggests that Hare's 'chief answer' involves the claim that the actions listed are wrong by the act- or specific rule-utilitarian standards employed at the critical level (not just that a principle forbidding them has highest acceptance utility). I agree that these actions are wrong, but I do not think that the argument just sketched yields this conclusion.

I agree with Professor Hare that an adequate moral theory must assign negative value to some actions which are contrary to a person's desires even when these actions have no effect on that person's conscious states. Acceptance of this point does not rescue an act-utilitarian analysis of the cases at hand,

however. It does not, for example, ensure that act-utilitarianism will give death-bed promises the force they have in 'common-sense morality', since the desire to have one's wishes carried out after one's death will count only as one element in the calculation, to be balanced against the (possibly numerous and varying) desires of others. Whatever force death-bed promises may have intuitively, it is not this weak and variable. Second, even if this calculation does happen to give 'the right answer', and even if we take the desire in question to be a desire that promises made to one on one's death bed not be false, nothing in the force that this desire has in an act-utilitarian calculation depends on the fact that a promise is involved or on the apparent acquiescence of the promisor. Such a calculation would have to yield the same answer in a case which involved, instead of a death-bed promise, a death-
* bed decree, backed by an intense desire that one's survivors live their lives in the way one had asked them to.

Similar problems arise in the other three cases. An act-utilitarian analysis taking into account the desire not to be taken advantage of might yield the right answer in the voting and electricity-shortage cases, where the number of 'victims' is large and the number of 'free riders' small. But it would have to give the same (hence 'wrong') answer in cases which were structurally similar but involved a desire on the part of the majority that everyone attend a brief ceremony honouring their leaders or that everyone abstain from using electricity (not because it was scarce but because the majority disapproved of its use).

The idea of a desire not to be *taken advantage* of suggests an element of resentment; but this moral attitude is appropriate
* only if the conclusion of the argument we are disussing is warranted, and a genuinely utilitarian analysis cannot turn on this special moral force. As the examples I have just given suggest, a successful argument needs to provide a way to distinguish this desire from other 'illegitimate' desires of equal intensity. The depth of the problem becomes apparent when we focus on the role which this desire is supposed to play in an act-utilitarian analysis of the cases at hand.

In some cases of these kinds a perfectly ordinary first-order interest is obviously infringed. This is so, for example, when someone makes a sacrifice for the sake of a common goal in the belief that similar action will be taken by others, but in fact the goal is not attained because others have not done their part. It is also true when, although the goal is produced, the person turns out without realizing it to have done much more than his or her share (and more than was ever intended) because others have held back. Here the agent has made a sacrifice for no gain, or a much larger sacrifice than was intended. But what if, as might happen in the voting and electricity-shortage cases, there are some 'free riders' but the goal is still produced with no increased cost to those who contribute? Who is harmed? An act-utilitarian analysis needs to find some loss to balance against the free riders' gain in such cases, and this is what the desire not to be taken advantage of is supposed to do. But just because it has this function of extending the concept of harm into cases where initially there seems to be none, such a desire has, in the absence of specific moral backing, a 'dog-in-the-manger' * quality.

I still agree, as I have said, with Hare's unhesitating conclusion that one would neither prescribe nor even permit that others behave towards us in the ways described in the four examples under discussion. But for the reasons just given I do not think that this conclusion can be reached (at least not 'unhesitatingly') by use of the method described in chapters 5 * and 6 of *Moral Thinking*, even bearing in mind the strong desire which people have not to be taken advantage of or 'played false'. Let me suggest an alternative, non-utilitarian analysis.

Hare's four examples all involve acting contrary to an expectation which others are relying on, but they differ in significant respects. In the voting, electricity, and car-pushing cases[4] there is a result which all want to bring about and which can be produced by common effort at a cost that each would be willing to bear. These facts are well known to the parties, and there is a general expectation that each will do his or her part to produce the desired result. In the car-pushing example this expectation is created and maintained by the intentional behaviour of the parties; in the voting and

[4] To what extent promising can be analysed in this way is a further question which I leave for another occasion.

electricity-shortage examples it results from an established institution or an official pronouncement.

Situations of this kind are common and subject to well-known instability. In most cases everyone's participation is not required: general compliance is sufficient to produce the desired result. Since everyone knows this, each is tempted to drop out, concealing this from the others and relying upon the assumption that they will do their part. The 'free rider' will then be free to enjoy extra leisure or devote his or her efforts to other worthwhile aims. This threat of instability calls for moral restraint: that is, makes it reasonable to refuse to 'prescribe or even permit' that people should act in the way * just described. This refusal is reasonable because (1) unrestrained behaviour of this kind would deprive one of the benefits of co-operative arrangements and leave those who do co-operate open to the double loss of fruitless contribution, and because (2) there are alternative principles which would, if generally adhered to, prevent these losses without imposing comparable special burdens on anyone.

These alternative principles, which it would not be reasonable to reject, can be stated in general terms, but it is difficult to spell them out in detail. The principle applicable to the car-pushing case is, roughly, that when you have intentionally and voluntarily led others to expect that you will do something, and you know that they are relying on this belief, you are not free to act otherwise without compelling reason. This last qualification is required in order to satisfy (2) above. What counts as a 'compelling reason' is clearly relative to the considerations at stake in the particular situation, and is not solely a matter of severity: forseeability when the expectation was created is also relevant, for example, since a principle is more burdensome if it requires one to accept losses which one could not have reasonably foreseen. These features are not *ad hoc* or perceived by some mysterious form of intuition. We recognize them when we reflect on the threat in question and the problem of devising a response that is not excessively burdensome.

The voting and electricity-shortage cases represent a slightly different problem. Clearly one could reasonably refuse to 'prescribe or even permit' people to act as they please in such cases. But it is more difficult to formulate the acceptable alternative principle, i.e. to say what 'such cases' are and what is required in them. Since the expectations in these cases are not created by voluntary action of all the parties involved, a principle requiring compliance with them may impose burdens that people have no reason to accept (as in Nozick's public-address system case, 1974:93–5). A defensible principle will therefore contain limiting conditions: that the benefit sought by co-operation is particularly important, that the scheme for securing it does not involve unnecessary interference with people's liberty, and so on.

10.5 I will not try to sketch such a principle here. My present purpose has been to describe a way of thinking about the cases Hare mentions that follows the pattern I presented above: a situation in which unrestricted discretion to act presents a threat, and a strategy for avoiding that threat at tolerable cost. This strategy is clear in central cases and admits of further elaboration, but there are other cases in which it gives less clear answers because there are competing strategies no one of which can claim to be uniquely acceptable.

It is the ability to satisfy condition (2) which differentiates a principle requiring fulfilment of death-bed promises from one requiring obedience to death-bed decrees and, in general, marks the moral difference between the desires which Hare has in mind and the other 'intrusive' or 'dictatorial' desires which I mentioned. The judgement that it is reasonable to refuse to accept a principle protecting the latter desires involves comparison and balancing of interests, but it is not a   * utilitarian judgement: what are compared and balanced are costs and benefits to individuals, not aggregate costs and benefits. Deciding in this way whether a principle can reasonably be rejected involves an ineliminable element of judgement, but this should not be seen as an objectionable   * appeal to intuition. To begin with, what is called for is not the apprehension of some special realm of moral truth, but a judgement in response to a well-defined problem, similar to a problem of strategy in which various factors must be balanced. Moreover, the scope left to judgement here is not obviously wider than that involved in utilitarian decision-making once the difficulties of weighing and aggregating different people's preferences and interests are taken into account.

I have yet to explain how I would deal with the 'dog-in-the-manger' problem, which was mentioned above as a difficulty for an analysis appealing to a desire not to be taken advantage of. A principle permitting anyone to exempt him or herself from co-operative arrangements is in a clear sense 'unfeasible': if acted on, it would deprive us all of the benefits of co-operation. This loss to each person gives them ground for rejecting the principle. But what of principles granting narrower exceptions, a principle exempting only me, for example, or only people born on 28 June 1940, from co-operative arrangements or from some particular class of such arrangements?[5] These principles would benefit me, or those
* sharing my birthday, seemingly at no cost to anyone else. To show that others have reason to reject such a principle I would, it seems, need to show that they would be made worse off by it. And how could I do this without appealing to something like 'the desire not to be taken advantage of', thereby leaving myself open to the objections I raised against Hare?

The crucial fact about these principles is that there are so many of them—a set for every person and every birthday, each of which would be favoured by some people and opposed by others for similar reasons in each case. These principles are in competition with one another since to adopt all of them would obviously be unfeasible. Each is opposed, therefore, by people who would prefer a competing principle favouring them, and their opposition is not of the 'dog-in-the-manger' variety.

Beyond this, however, it is important to distinguish between objections to the substance of a principle and objections to a means of selecting it as the one governing a given situation. Given the symmetry between the principles mentioned above, what selects any one or any group of them as the standard of right action in a given situation? In the

---

[5] Hare would of course rule out principles of the first kind on formal grounds. The present argument aims to show that, whether or not he is correct in this, such principles can also be rejected on the same grounds as principles of the second type.

cases we are most familiar with, some individual simply makes this selection unilaterally on self-interested or other grounds. In most cases, however, this kind of authority is something that others could reasonably object to quite apart from any objection to the principles chosen. Consider, for example, the family of 'mixed strategy' principles, which provide for sharing of the 'co-operative surplus' by having each person flip a series of coins, or roll dice, or employ some other chance procedure as a means of deciding whether to contribute to the common effort. Each of these principles is feasible, and each might, if established, be something to which no one could reasonably object. But this does not mean that no one could object to a person's choosing and acting on one of these principles unilaterally. To do so is simply to appropriate a portion of the 'surplus'. The same objection applies to unilateral selection of principles involving named individuals, birthdays, and so on.

This argument brings out an important difference between Hare's prescriptivist utilitarianism and the contractualist view I have described. In beginning with the question, what behaviour am I prepared to prescribe or permit, Hare's theory is closer to contractualism than to utilitarian theory of the traditional kind. But his account of moral judgement collapses the preferences of many individuals into those of one moral judge through a process of sympathetic identification, thus arriving at a utilitarian answer to the contractualist question. In the alternative I have proposed, on the other hand, the process of answering this question is seen as one of finding principles which could be agreed upon by individuals who, while they do not wholly identify with one another's preferences, are moved to seek agreement.

For a person so moved, considerations of symmetry have direct relevance. If I see that, corresponding to a principle which I would like to see adopted, there is an opposing principle which each other person would advance for exactly the same reason, and if I see that none of us would be willing to accept all of these principles and that no one of them is singled out by a reason which all of us, even if well-motivated, need accept, then, given the desire just mentioned, it would be unreasonable of me to assume the acceptability of the principle favouring me or to demand that others accept it. The same holds, *mutatis mutandis*, for everyone else in the situation. But this argument depends on the fact that in choosing principles we are seeking a basis for agreement between parties with divergent points of view. Considerations of this kind will play no role if one is to decide what to 'prescribe or permit' simply by feeling at one time the motivational force of all the preferences of the affected parties and then choosing in the way that the balance of these forces dictates.

Hare's view, as I understand it, is that this method is required if the decision is to be a rational one. But his arguments for this claim are mainly directed to showing (1) that the preferences of each affected person are among the facts relevant to a decision whether to accept a principle (*MT* 89–93), and (2) that knowing how a person feels in a given situation involves having a preference *now* as to what should be done if one were in that situation oneself. Even if these claims are accepted, however, there are still the further
* questions whether these are the *only* considerations on which a rational decision about which universal imperatives to accept can be based and whether a rational and impartial decision can be made only by combining them in the way described.

I believe that the answer to both of these questions is no. The alternative I have proposed counts the preferences of affected parties as relevant, though not the only relevant, information for a decision about which .principles could not reasonably be rejected. As the examples I have discussed indicate, this decision is not reached simply by summing up these preferences, but this does not prevent it from being both rational and impartial.

11. Reasoning towards Utilitarianism

Peter Singer

11.1 WHAT role can reason play in ethical decision-making? *
That has been the central question of ethics since Socrates
sought to refute the moral scepticism of the sophists. It is also
the connecting thread of R. M. Hare's work.

An exposition of Hare's position can be found elsewhere in
this volume, and so there is no need to provide one here. For
the discussion which follows, it is important only to note that
Hare's position emerged out of the non-cognitivist theories
defended by A. J. Ayer and C. L. Stevenson. A major
objection to these theories was that they could not allow
reason a role in determining basic moral positions. While
Hare shares with the non-cognitivists the view that moral
judgements do not state facts, he has always denied that this
view allows no place for reason in ultimate moral decisions. In
Freedom and Reason and *Moral Thinking* he has developed the
notion of universalizability to the point at which he feels able
to claim that it gives sufficient scope to reason to allow us to
reach, in principle, a determinate conclusion to any moral
deliberation. If universalizability really can do all that Hare
claims for it, his work must rank as the most important result
of recent ethics, perhaps even as the culmination of all
Western moral philosophy.

That so much should now be achieved, after so many
centuries of failure, may seem unlikely; but Hare's argument
is clearly set out and merits careful scrutiny. That is the aim of
the present essay.

11.2 Although J. L. Mackie wrote his *Ethics: Inventing Right* *
and Wrong before Hare had published the fully developed
statement of his position which appears in *Moral Thinking*,
Mackie's discussion of universalizability is still widely regarded
as pinpointing the key difficulties in Hare's position. Mackie

argued that there is not one single notion of universalizability, but three:

   i. The irrelevance of numerical differences
  ii. Putting oneself in the other person's place
 iii. Taking (equal) account of different tastes and rival ideals.

Probably only the first of these, and definitely no more than the first and second, Mackie claimed, can be said to be part of the meaning of moral terms, or logically implied by our moral concepts. Yet only the third notion of universalizability will suffice to bring us to the conclusion Hare seeks, that universalizability leads us to a form of utilitarianism. Moreover, Mackie, continues, even where a notion of universalizability is implicit in our moral concepts, there is a substantive decision involved in limiting one's actions to those one is prepared to prescribe universally. Nothing can logically compel us to make this decision (Mackie, 1977, ch. 4).

In *Moral Thinking* Hare denies that there are different stages of universalization; he says that there is, rather, a progression in the use made of a single property, namely the property of entailing identical judgements about all cases identical in their universal properties (*MT* 108). The difference is significant, for if there are three stages of universalizability as Mackie claims, those whom Hare calls 'fanatics' might claim that there is no reason to go beyond the first two stages. Such fanatics could still claim to hold a universalizable morality; they could, with Mackie's support, say that they accept the full notion of universalizability implied by our moral concepts; and yet they would, of course, escape the crucial third step of Hare's argument, the one which compels them to treat their ideals as if they counted for no more than any other ideal held with equal intensity. If, on the other hand, all three 'stages' are merely the progressive development of a single logical property, it would seem that anyone who accepts the first aspect of universalizability must also accept the second and third aspects of it. Then the fanatic would have to choose between rejecting universalizability altogether, and accepting all that Hare argues is implicit in the notion.

Clearly the most contentious step in this logical progression is the claim that rival ideals are to be given equal weight. This is the step which threatens all deontological systems of morality, for it seeks to compel deontologists to treat their cherished moral principles as just an odd set of desires. 'Let justice be done though the heavens fall' now becomes 'Let justice be done if justice will satisfy more preferences, including my preference for justice, than any alternative.' Carlyle once wrote, 'What have men to do with interests? There is a right way and a wrong way. That is all we need think about' (Carlyle, 1892). If Hare is right, Carlyle is utterly mistaken; it is interests, or preferences, which determine right and wrong.

How is this question to be resolved? Hare has consistently maintained that the basis of universalizability is to be found in the meanings of the moral words (*FR* 30; H 1976*a*, 114; *MT* 116). But if we ask ourselves whether ordinary people consider that a moral judgement must give equal weight to all ideals, irrespective of their content, the answer would surely go against Hare. To this extent, at least, Mackie is right. Very many ordinary people are not consequentialists: and even those who are, tend to regard deontological views as properly falling within the sphere of morality. How then can Hare argue that the moral words we ordinarily use require us to   *
disregard the content of the ideals we may hold? And even if somehow Hare could make out this claim, would the result not simply be to show, very clearly, that Mackie was right when he said that to decide to act in accordance with universalizable judgements is always a substantive decision which reason alone does not compel us to make?

I do not think that Hare can defend his position on ideals by appealing to our ordinary understanding of moral language. There is, however, another possibility. Ironically, Hare can make use of a point on which he and Mackie are in agreement: the fact that moral judgements do not state objective truths. In criticizing the idea that universalizability requires us to give equal weight to all moral ideals, Mackie wrote:

It is all too easy to believe that the objective validity of one's own ideals provides an overwhelmingly strong reason for taking no account at all of ideals that conflict with them, or of interests associated with the holding of such rival ideals (Mackie, 1977:96–7).

* Mackie is right. Hare's suggestion that all ideals should be treated equally, without regard to their content, is bound to be resisted by all those who claim that *their* ideals are objectively valid, while other people's ideals are false and mistaken. But of course Mackie himself is a moral sceptic; he does not believe that *any* ideals can be objectively valid. Once we grant such scepticism, what else can an ideal be except a certain type of desire? And why should we treat ideals differently from other desires when we universalize?

Hare also holds that there can be no objectively valid moral ideals. As we have already noted, Hare's position developed out of the non-cognitivism of Ayer and Stevenson. For Hare, moral judgements are prescriptions. Truth or falsity, in the sense in which it applies to descriptions, is not applicable to prescriptions. Because he rejects the idea that moral judgements are descriptive, Hare can reject the view that ideals are different from desires because they are true or false. Hare makes this point in his discussion of fanaticism in *Moral Thinking*. He has in mind a doctor who believes that he should prolong life at all costs, even in a situation in which the inevitable result is merely that the patient endures an additional month of suffering before dying. In showing how he can deal with such a fanatic, Hare writes:

First of all, our method is based on the falsity of descriptivism. If some form of descriptivism were true, the doctor might be able to say 'I just *know* that I ought not to let the patient die; what are his preferences against that?' But on the view here assumed to be correct, this is nothing more than an appeal to his own intuitions, which cannot be made without circularity, since they themselves are in dispute (*MT* 178–9).

Hare is here saying, in effect, that we cannot rely on universalizability alone to do all the work of dealing with the fanatic. It is prescriptivism which entails the falsity of descriptivism. The rejection of descriptivism has paved the way for dealing with fanatics, because it has undermined the chief prop to which they might have clung for support against Hare's insistence on the irrelevance of the content of their ideals.

Is there any other way in which this insistance might be

resisted? I read a paper containing some of the points just made to a seminar in Oxford in 1978; Mackie had seen the paper beforehand and prepared a response, which included the following:

Even if objectivism is rejected . . . third stage universalization doesn't go through. The point is that someone who shares my (or Hare's) view of the ontological status of values, as a second order view, can still endorse first order views which are close analogues of those held by an objectivist. He cannot speak . . . of true and false ideals, but he can still wholeheartedly endorse some ideals and reject others. He has no need to degrade an ideal which he endorses to the level of a mere preference, saying 'This matters only because I care   * for it'. What he says, in his first order judgment, is 'This matters' *tout court*, and since this claim does not involve even an implicit mention of himself, it is impervious to the kinds of universalization that exclude any differential attention to different persons and make the moral agent put himself thoroughly into each other person's place.[1]

It is no doubt true that someone can *say*, 'This matters, *tout court.*' But Mackie, of all people, should have been more critical of what people can say. His own defence of moral scepticism relies on the contention that when people make moral judgements they erroneously believe that they are saying something capable of being true or false. One of his arguments for regarding this belief as mistaken is that if there were objective truths which had some built-in action-guiding or prescriptive force, they would be very queer entities indeed. How, Mackie asks, can a truth about the universe constitute a reason for action, for all beings, whatever wants or desires they may have? How can 'to-be-doneness' and 'not-to-be-doneness' be properties of the world (Mackie, 1977:42)? This is Mackie's argument from queerness. In *Moral Thinking*, Hare suggests that Mackie is mistaken if he thinks the argument shows that belief in objective moral prescriptions is a *false* belief; what the argument shows, Hare says, is that it is an *incoherent* belief (*MT* 83–4). I am inclined to agree with Hare; but on either Mackie's or Hare's account, the argument can be turned on the person Mackie imagines as saying, 'This matters, *tout court.*' For what can such a statement mean? It obviously does not mean, 'This matters *to me.*' That would

[1] Mackie kindly provided me with a copy of his response.

concede that it was properly treated as a kind of preference. Nor would it help to say, 'This matters to every human being', or even, 'This matters to every sentient creature.' Then the remark would merely point to some larger group whose preferences need to be taken into the reckoning. But how can something *matter* if it does not matter *to anyone* , or to any group of beings? The answer, on either Mackie or Hare's view of the nature of morality, surely is that it cannot. The belief that something can matter, *tout court,* is just as incoherent as the belief that objective moral prescriptions can somehow be written into the fabric of the universe.

The upshot of this is that while some people may try to resist Hare's attempt to ignore the content of moral ideals by saying that *their* ideals *matter*, we should not heed such a claim. Either the ideals will matter because they affect the preferences of sentient creatures; or the claim is incoherent and the ideals cannot matter, beyond the effect that ignoring them will have on those who hold the ideal.

11.3 I have been arguing that as long as we reject the idea that there can be objectively true moral ideals, universaliz-ability does require that we put ourselves in the place of others and that this must then involve giving weight to their ideals in proportion to the strength with which they hold them. We should reject Mackie's claim that this 'third stage' of universalizability, as he calls it, can be resisted even without any appeal to the objective truth of one's moral ideals. I cannot see any other way in which one might resist the full application of universalizability. On the other hand, the very fact that universalizability can now be seen to have such far-reaching implications must make all the more attractive Mackie's fall-back strategy for resisting the idea that universal-izability can resolve ethical disagreement: the claim that to commit oneself to acting on universalizable judgements is a substantive decision which we are in no way compelled to make. We all know that we cannot get something from nothing. Rabbits do not come out of hats unless they were in the hats beforehand. If the notion of universalizability is strong enough to lead us straight to preference-utilitarianism, surely it must be the case that embracing universalizability already surreptitiously involves committing ourselves to preference-utilitarianism: and if this is correct, then all those who are not inclined to favour this particular normative theory will be able to reject universalizability without any qualms.   *

Hare recognizes that amoralism can be a consistent position. The amoralist either refuses to use any moral concepts at all, or uses moral concepts but refuses to make any prescriptions, saying only that something is morally indifferent. But Hare points out that there is a price to be paid for amoralism. He argues, in chapter 11 in *Moral Thinking*, that if we were charged with bringing up a child so as best to serve that child's interests, we would do poorly if we brought the child up as a calculating egoist. This is not the way to happiness; people do better, on the whole, if they possess a character which is firmly disposed to think of others and to follow one's moral judgement. Moreover if this is true in the case of bringing up a child it is also, Hare suggests, likely to apply to ourselves, in so far as we are able to modify our character and dispositions.

This argument is an empirical one, and Hare does not claim to have been able to establish it conclusively. I have elsewhere tried to defend a similar viewpoint, though with equally inconclusive results (Singer, 1979, ch. 10). I shall not repeat the arguments here, because most critics of Hare's argument from universalizability to utilitarianism will not wish to defend amoralism. They will, instead, seek to defend a position which allows us to say, on grounds other than those offered by preference-utilitarianism, that there are some things we ought to do, and others we ought not to do.

As a first move, such a critic might argue, 'Hare claims to base his position on an account of our moral concepts. But his account must be incorrect. For, according to Hare, our moral concepts require us to be preference-utilitarians. Yet most people are not preference-utilitarians. Hence I can continue to use the same moral concepts most people use.'

Hare's reply to this would presumably be that there is a good deal of confusion in the way we use moral terms, and this has made it difficult for people to see the implications of our ordinary moral concepts. Our imaginary critic might grant this, and then respond that if this is so, the clarity Hare has achieved has revealed the need for a radical reconstruction.

Once most people understand that our ordinary moral concepts lead to preference-utilitarianism, and understand what preference-utilitarianism is, they will be quite clear that they are more committed to preserving their rejection of preference-utilitarianism than to preserving the moral concepts they have been using. They will therefore adopt different moral concepts, adequate to expressing the diversity of normative views which people have expressed since ancient times, and not requiring that we be preference-utilitarians.

But is such a reconstruction of our moral concepts available? The rejection of descriptivism eliminates many possibilities. As long as this rejection stands, no reconstruction will allow us to support moral ideals by claiming that they are objectively true. On what basis, then, shall we assert our moral judgements? It seems that our moral judgements will still have to obtain their content from our own preferences, universalized. Nothing else can sneak in, because the only way in which it could sneak in would be by some claim that it is some kind of essential moral truth. In the absence of any coherent sense for such claims, they can only be treated as expressions of preferences.

This is, admittedly, a highly controversial claim, made much too briefly. It follows from the denial of the possibility of moral properties existing in the world independently of our preferences. The discussion of ideals in this paper has, I believe, brought out why such a denial implies that preferences can be the only basis for moral judgements. Some readers who resist the attempt to reduce the content of morality to preferences will base their denial on a belief in an objective moral reality of one form or another. To deal with their objections it would be necessary to present, once more, the case against such an objective moral reality; but this is something to which both Hare and Mackie have already given considerable attention. Other readers will hold that one can deny the existence of objective moral properties and still base moral judgements on something other than preferences. I am conscious that to forestall this possibility it would be necessary to say much more than I have said here. But I do not wish to say more, because it would be impossible to do the task properly in a brief essay. Instead, I shall raise a further question.

11.4 The restriction of the content of our moral judgements to preferences has taken us a giant stride towards the long-sought goal of demonstrating that reasoning can lead us to agreement in ethics; but unfortunately we are still not quite there. While we can reason our way to the conclusion that moral judgements must be based on some form of universalization of our preferences, there are still questions which can be raised about the nature of that universalization. The concepts Hare has analysed may not be the only possibilities. For instance, I can—all too easily—imagine people throwing up their hands in horror at the realization that these concepts require us to give the same weight to the preferences of non-human animals as we give to similar human preferences (*MT* 90–1). People might say, 'That isn't what we intended at all; we are only interested in a morality for humans. If you tell us that our concepts imply equal consideration for the preferences of animals, we shall simply adopt a new set of concepts, which implies universalizability up to, but not beyond, the boundary of our own species.'

Can this be done? If it can be done with the boundary of our species, why not with the boundary of our race, or even our nation? Might we not do better still by limiting our concern to members of our extended family? If we add the possibility of a boundary which marks not the end of all consideration, but a step down to a reduced amount of consideration, the variations become limitless. We might, for instance, have a set of concepts which discounts, by a factor of 50 per cent, the preferences of those who are not members of our family, and discounts the preferences of others by further percentages in proportion to the size of the group—tribe, nation, race, species, etc.—which include them.

If universalizability is simply a matter of the logic of the concepts we use, there can be no logical barrier against the creation of a new set of concepts which limits the scope for universalizability. Hare himself admits this possibility in the introductory pages of *Moral Thinking*:

I cannot forbid any philosopher, or anybody else, to start asking questions different from those which are expressed in terms of the moral words as we now use them. The new questions may be important and fruitful ones. But if it were being suggested that we should not just ask the new questions as well as the old ones, but give up asking the old ones, I should require to be satisfied, not merely that the new ones are important, but that the old ones are unimportant (*MT* 18–19).

The classification of some questions as 'important' and others as 'unimportant' bears out Mackie's point that a substantive decision is involved in choosing which set of concepts to accept. In the case of the kind of change we are discussing, it might not be too difficult to convince most members of a society—though presumably not Hare—that the questions asked by using the new, more restricted concepts were the important ones to ask, while the old ones really are unimportant. If members of a society simply do not care about the welfare of outsiders, whether of another nationality, race, or species, they will easily accept that some appropriately restricted set of concepts captures everything important about the questions asked by the set of concepts Hare has analysed, and leaves out only some unimportant matters with which they do not wish to be bothered. The same will be true if they care a little for some other group, and so adopt a set of concepts which includes an appropriate discount for the preferences of members of that group. (For simplicity of exposition I shall henceforth write as if the restricted concepts mark a total lack of consideration for those beyond the boundary; but the same points would apply to a boundary which marked a discounted consideration rather than the complete absence of consideration.)

Is there any way in which Hare could argue with a group of people who decided to adopt a new and more restricted set of concepts? Prudential arguments might work against the adoption of a narrowly constrained set of concepts, but for a
* dominant race, comfortably in control of a slave class of a different race, it would be much more difficult to make prudential arguments work. And how would one find prudential grounds for convincing a society to care about the preferences of non-human animals? One could, of course, condemn some forms of cruelty to animals, much as Kant did (1963:239–40), on the grounds that it might lead to cruelty to humans as well: but that is very different from allowing that the preferences of animals count for their own sakes. It seems

unlikely that there are prudential arguments for adopting concepts which extend universalizability this far.

So in the end, if we are to make a tight case for the adoption of a preference-utilitarian ethic, we will need more than the analysis of concepts and we will need more than prudential arguments. Is anything else available? Is it possible to argue, on other than prudential grounds, that concepts with narrow boundaries are unacceptable? The problem is that we cannot claim that they are *ethically* unacceptable, for then we would be arguing in a circle. Is there perhaps a case for saying that   *
they are *rationally* unacceptable? The problem is that the word 'rational' is notoriously tricky; it can all too easily be bent to include substantive moral commitments, or conversely a commitment to prudence. Suppose that we take Brandt's definition, of which Hare also makes use: 'I shall preempt the term "rational" to refer to actions, desires or moral systems which survive maximal criticism by facts and logic' (Brandt, 1979:10; cf. *MT* 214–15). Is there any way in which the adoption of some particular set of concepts can be shown not to survive maximal criticism by facts and logic?

This would, of course, be true of any set of concepts which was straightforwardly inconsistent; but to place a restriction on the scope of universalizability does not seem to involve an inconsistency in any strict logical sense. Can such restrictions perhaps be criticized for arbitrariness? This looks more promising. At whatever point universalizability stops, one can raise the question: 'Why stop there?' Why not also take into account the preferences of others, not of your family (tribe, nation, race, species, or whatever), who nevertheless have preferences similar in relevant respects to the preferences you do take into account? Only the boundary of sentience—the point beyond which there simply are no more preferences to be taken into account—seems to avoid this kind of arbitrariness. To stop short of this point can therefore be criticized as a refusal to take into account the relevant fact that other beings also have preferences which are similar to the preferences of those who fall within the scope of the restricted sense of universalizability.[2]

[2] I have discussed this notion of arbitrariness, and its connection with rationality, in Singer, 1981, chs. 4–5. In what follows I attempt to strengthen what I said there in the face of an objection which was put to me by Dick Sikora.

This is still not quite good enough. Those wishing to adopt the restricted sense may say: 'Our boundary is not arbitrary. It corresponds to the boundary of our concern. We just don't care about those who are not of our family (or tribe, nation, race, species, as the case may be). So for our purposes, the preferences of these others are *not* "relevantly similar" to the preferences of those for whom we do care. The fact that we care about someone is a highly relevant consideration. That is why we choose concepts which require us to take into account the group we do care about, and leave the rest out of consideration.'

This reply defeats the charge of arbitrariness. But it does so at considerable cost, for it concedes that the only basis for inclusion within the circle of the restricted concepts is that one is numbered amongst those for whom the group cares. There is no pretence here that the concepts employed should be acceptable to anyone, including those outside the circle. What we have is a form of group egoism, as broad or narrow as the group's concern may be. Accordingly those who defend a restricted notion of universalizability in this way are themselves defenceless against anyone who says: 'I don't care for all those who are within your sphere of concern. I care only for a smaller group. Hence I shall give no consideration to the preferences of those who fall outside my smaller sphere of concern.' It would be inconsistent to attempt to rebut such a move by insisting that the new, smaller boundary was arbitrary in a way that the larger, but still restricted boundary was not.

11.5 To take stock of the argument so far. If we use concepts with an unrestricted notion of universalizability, we have an argument against anyone who seeks to act on a more restricted notion. The argument is that the more restricted notion relies on an abitrary disregard of relevant similarities between those on both sides of the boundary line. The only defence to this argument is one which immediately opens the way to narrower and narrower notions, with no logical stopping place short of individual egoism.

We can now see that all of these new sets of concepts with restricted notions of universalizability are very different from the concepts Hare has analysed. They cannot be used to ask the same type of question. The restricted concepts can only be used to ask a form of the question, 'What will be best for me?' Depending on how restricted the notion is, the qualifying 'for me' may be broadened to include other groups for whom I care, but the nature of the question remains unchanged. The unrestricted concepts, on the other hand, can be used to ask a radically different question, in which my own interests and concerns do not figure at all.

If we recall Hare's words on the possibility of adopting new concepts in place of those he has analysed—'I should require to be satisfied, not merely that the new [questions] are important, but that the old ones are unimportant'—it is now easier to share Hare's view that the old questions are important. This may be, as Mackie would insist, a substantive decision; but the need we feel to defend our own concerns against those who do not share them is a powerful reason for deciding in this way. In seeking such a defence, we grasp at the only set of concepts which makes it possible to take a stand which is independent of our personal interests and concerns. This set of concepts must include an unrestricted notion of universalizability.

12. Hare on Intuitive Moral Thinking

J. O. Urmson

12.1 PROFESSOR Hare's *Moral Thinking* is an ambitious and exciting book, covering vast fields that this essay will for the most part leave untrodden, not because they are unworthy of exploration but because it has far less ambitious and exciting aims. In it I shall state what I understand to be Hare's account of the nature of what he calls the intuitive level of moral thinking, and then consider to what extent it gives an accurate and complete picture of such normal moral thinking as does not conform to the pattern of what he calls the critical level of moral thinking.

Hare (*MT* 25–6) distinguishes three levels of moral thinking. Of these the metaethical, which is non-substantial and philosophical, is of no concern to us now; more accurately, we shall be engaged in but not examining it. Substantial issues, he tells us, are deliberated on at either the critical or the intuitive level. At the critical level of moral thinking, 'no moral intuitions of substance can be appealed to. It proceeds in accordance with canons established by philosophical logic and thus based on linguistic intuitions only' (*MT* 40). These canons are 'the logical apparatus of universal prescriptivism' (*MT* 43). Since the only other form of moral thinking that Hare recognizes is what he calls the intuitive level, it presumably follows that when anyone is engaged in what would be generally regarded as moral thinking but recognizably fails to conform to the canons of the critical level, he must be engaged in intuitive moral thinking and Hare's account of intuitive thinking must be intended to cover all such deliberation—unless, of course, Hare is prepared to claim that thinking which does not perfectly conform to his account is not to be regarded as moral thinking at all.

So, I shall assume, the intuitive level of moral thinking is all moral thinking which does not conform, or attempt to conform, to the canons of the critical level. It is, Hare holds, a perfectly respectable form of moral thinking which he himself frequently adopts and which he thinks it desirable that others (except for archangels) should usually adopt. Our moral thinking will be flawed only if we operate exclusively at the intuitive level and never rise to the critical level.

What, then, is Hare's view of the nature of moral thinking at the intuitive level? So far as I can see, the picture is very
* simple, breathtakingly simple. We acquire, mainly by education, a number of 'relatively general principles'; these principles we usually follow unquestioningly so long as there is no conflict between them. If we have been well brought up this situation is satisfactory most of the time. But we are powerless to resolve conflicts between principles in a rational manner unless we resort to thinking at the critical level; otherwise we must resort to such irrational procedures as 'weighing' the principles. Further we cannot at the intuitive level rationally examine the principles that we at first uncritically accept, or rationally replace those found to be unacceptable.

There is no definite list, in Hare's opinion, of the relatively general principles which all men do, can, or should accept. What principles are desirably held is partly determined by the situation in which a person finds himself and the character he has; acts of supererogation are those performed by people who are able and willing to conform to principles to which we do not expect the generality of men to conform. But critical thinking will demonstrate that it is desirable for all ordinary mortals to have some set of relatively general principles and usually to obey them without question.

12.2 I have now outlined what I take to be Hare's account of the nature and role of moral thinking at the intuitive level. I hope that my outline involves no serious misrepresentation. Now, since my moral thinking (or what I take without doubt to be moral thinking) is rarely, if ever, conducted at Hare's critical level, I must surely ask how accurately Hare's account of the intuitive level, the only alternative, fits it. When I do so my doubts and difficulties soon arise.

Let us start where Hare does, with what he regards as one

insoluble problem for moral thinking, confined to his intuitive level, which he calls 'the conflict of duties' (*MT* 26) or 'the conflict of principles' (*MT* 32); so far as I can see these phrases refer, in Hare's view, to a single problem. Hare offers *
the following illustration:

I have promised to take my children for a picnic on the river at Oxford, and then a lifelong friend turns up from Australia and is in Oxford for the afternoon, and wants to be shown round the colleges with his wife (*MT* 26–7).

Hare calls this a dilemma and suggests that without his logical apparatus some heroic course of thinking, which will fail, has to be resorted to.

Faced with this situation I myself would not be heroic. I might ask my children to release me from my promise, or to put off the picnic until the next day; or I might presume on my friendship with Professor Hare to persuade him to allow me to offer him to the Australians as a greatly superior and charming guide, or . . . But in any case what principles 'of a *
relatively general kind' are supposed to be in conflict? Perhaps I have adopted, or accepted from my mentors, a principle 'Keep promises'; but what is the other principle? Not, presumably, 'Show Australian friends round Oxford', nor even 'Show people round places', though that is more suitably general. I certainly think that friends have some claim on one, and this is relevant here, but I certainly do not have a principle which requires me to do whatever my friends would like me to do. I can think of nothing relevant that the ordinary moral thinker would regard as one of his principles.

I might well decide, as Hare suggests, to take the Australian friends around, particularly if the children are unreasonably intransigent about allowing me to modify my promise. But, not being an official guide, I shall not regard myself as having a duty to do so. I may perhaps be under some obligation to them, perhaps because they have shown me round Sydney or Melbourne. If so, that is an extra reason for deciding to give them priority; but I might still decide to do this kindness to my friends even though I have no duty, no obligation, and no ready-made principle requiring me so to do. There may, indeed, be conflicts of principle, but this case does not

exemplify such a conflict and rather illustrates my contention
that morality is more complex than Hare allows.

12.3 At this stage Hare may well say that as *he* uses the
word 'principle' all moral conflicts are conflicts of principle.
They are certainly not all conflicts of members of a set of
ready-made maxims of relative generality and manageable
complexity; but no doubt as Hare often uses the word
'principle' he would be justified in this retort. But my main
criticism is that Hare includes, or appears to include, under
the term 'principle' a number of very different things.

I doubt whether there is a very rigid use of the word
'principle' in everyday life. But I think that many besides
myself tend to use it of some rules of conduct which we set for
ourselves or accept from others to be followed (ordinarily)
blindly. By following blindly I mean being unwilling to
consider arguments to the contrary. Principles need not be
moral. Thus I have a prudential principle which forbids me to
drink alcohol before 6 p.m. except when courtesy as a host or
guest requires it. This is for me a principle precisely because I
refuse to consider reasons for departure from it. I can always
think of dozens of what (at the time) appear to be good
reasons for starting earlier; if I could not I should have no
need of the principle. Of course, this principle, like most other
principles accepted by most people, might be violated in
readily conceivable circumstances; if atom bombs began to
fall on England at 5 p.m. I might decide to have a quick drink
before the end. Principles need to be just rigid enough to cope
with those problems they were designed to deal with, not to
turn one into an automaton. Some people have, or claim to
have, some completely rigid principles. Elizabeth Anscombe,
I understand, avoids boiling babies on account of such a
principle. A conflict between two such principles would
indeed present an inescapable dilemma. But what I am
calling a principle merely needs to be given unquestioning
obedience in the ordinary circumstances which it was
designed to deal with.

Keeping promises and truth-telling are two examples of
what many people regard as principles in my sense of the
term; but there are many relatively general moral adages
which I and many others accept, but certainly not as

principles. Consider, for example, the proposition that one should avoid causing inconvenience to other people, which most people, I imagine, would readily accept. But one often has to inconvenience some people to some extent, and that somebody would be inconvenienced by an action of mine is not a fact that would make me abstain from it without further consideration of the situation. That an action would inconvenience somebody is a reason, often one among many other considerations, that tells against its performance, a reason, but not a sufficient reason in all circumstances.

There are, indeed, conflicts of principle, such as Hare considers in his *Moral Thinking*. But very many situations of moral conflicts are not ones where two principles collide; more often there are many relevant considerations, none of them decisive, telling on both sides. All these considerations have to be taken into account, and the general welfare may be one, but only one, of them. Further there are many situations where the problem is not to decide which of two possible courses of action, already specified (children on the river or guided Australians), to adopt, but where the problem is what among a whole range of undefined possibilities will best satisfy a whole range of equally undefined circumstances. For many people questions like AID and surrogate motherhood can be settled by some ready-made principle, for example; but for others the problem is to try to marshal clearly all the morally relevant considerations and work out a policy. In Britain the Warnock Commission was presumably set up precisely * because of this perceived complexity. Only the dogmatic and the feeble-minded could fail to see that questions like racial discrimination, abortion, genetic engineering, divorce, warfare, are highly complex; in considering them morally it is certain that many considerations relevant in many different ways will be found, and it is very probable that we shall fail to notice all that are relevant. To try to deal philosophically with these situations in the light of a simple model of conflict between principles, already given and of relatively slight complexity, seems to me to be unwise in the extreme.

12.4 But even if Hare were to allow that there is often this kind of complexity in moral deliberation, we still have to meet his main objection to 'intuitive moral thinking' which is not

underpinned by 'critical moral thinking'. Hare speaks with
scorn of the attempt to deal with a conflict of duties by holding
that 'the conflict is to be settled by a judging or weighing
process to determine which ought, in the particular case, to be
conformed to. This is less a method than an evasion of the
problem; we are not told *how* to weigh or judge the rival
principles' (*MT* 34–5). He would, we may reasonably suppose,
consider that this objection applied with at least equal force in
the more complex cases to which we have been attending.

So far as I can see, there are no special objections to
weighing or judging in the moral sphere. Hare's objection is
merely a special case of the general objection to weighing and
judging without a decision procedure or other formulable
method, if there be such.

Presumably, then, we have here a 'scandal of moral
judgement' parallel to, for example, the 'scandal of induction'.
There are some, like Mill, who have attempted, with a total lack
of success, to give us canons of induction; others, like Keynes,
have produced such contrivances as principles of limited
independent variety to enable us to calculate new probabilities
from finite initial probabilities, with equal lack of success;
others, like Popper, have recognized these failures and have
claimed that induction is non-existent, or inevitably irrational.
But still scientists do base their hypotheses on evidence, using
their judgement, juries base their verdicts on evidence, that
they have weighed in the jury-room, and weathermen tell us
the evidence on which they base their forecasts. In all these
cases the evidence is liable to conflict or point in many
different directions, or is simply baffling, and it does seem that
some weighing or judging for which nobody can describe a
decision procedure does inevitably take place.

Just as evidence for fact has to be weighed, so has evidence
for value. In prudence we may have to decide whether a sum
of money should be spent on a new carpet, further insurance,
or new investments, and, if on investments, whether they
should aim at capital growth or income. Here again, in the
light of the complex facts and the complex needs of the family,
we have to weigh and judge. Nor, so far as I can see, can
Hare's 'critical moral thinking' avoid weighing and judging. If
we are to aim at maximum satisfaction of desires or needs, or

maximum welfare or maximum pleasure, do we not have to weigh the evidence? Does not one have to use one's judgement in trying to decide, by imaginatively putting ourselves in his place or any other method, what course of action would best satisfy the desires of an uneducated peasant in, say, New Guinea? Might one not have to use one's judgement, in a way not governed by any canons, to decide just how strongly or sincerely one's Australian friends wanted to trail round Oxford on a hot afternoon rather than to join the kids on the river?

It seems that the weighing of evidence and judgement are inevitable in all walks of life. So, though it would be desirable to have a better philosophical understanding of it, its presence in intuitive moral thinking does not seem to be a serious objection to the self-sufficiency of that type of thinking; or, if it does invalidate intuitive moral thinking, it invalidates also just about all our thinking outside pure mathematics.

Though it is not part of my main purpose, I here include a paragraph on Hare's attack on those who say that we may inevitably act wrongly or that an act may be both right and wrong; I cannot agree with him in his attack (*MT* 26–8), though I have no admiration for the philosophers whom he appears to have principally in mind. Let us consider the case where somebody has made incompatible promises to two different people, something which should not be done, may be done, and is sometimes done. As a consequence of this wrongdoing he must now, it seems, inevitably act wrongly and, if he fulfils one promise and breaks the other, he will simultaneously act rightly and wrongly. Plato pointed out that * a man may be simultaneously moving since he is nodding his head, and stationary, since he is sitting down, and one can be acting wrongly in breaking a promise to A and acting rightly in keeping a promise to B. There is no logical oddity in an act having contrary qualities in different respects. Perhaps, the world being the sort of place it is, we may find ourselves having to act wrongly through no fault of our own.

12.5 I now turn to the final point I wish to discuss, Hare's discussion of supererogatory acts (*MT* ch. 11). I deplore the introduction of this term, which has a clear use in theology where it belongs, into moral philosophy, and regret having, just once, used it in that way myself. For we now have, instead of the old over-simple trichotomy of acts into right, neutral, and wrong, a new over-simple tetrachotomy (I coin the word). Hare with his monolithic use of the term 'principle' does not even abandon the old trichotomy, nor can he with this simple apparatus. For him there is the man who has, at the intuitive level, a minimum set of principles and a man, with a more robust moral constitution or stronger moral digestion, who recognizes a larger set of principles which make greater demands on him. To act in accordance with these less common and more demanding principles is to perform supererogatory actions. So at the intuitive level all morally relevant action will either be obedience to a principle or disobedience.

But this is to ignore the vast array of actions, having moral significance, which frequently are performed by persons who are far from being moral saints or heroes but which are neither duties nor obligations, nor involve conformity to principle as I use that term. As well as acts of moral saintliness and heroism, this class includes many much humbler types of action within the reach of all of us. There are various types of action which we might call kind, considerate, chivalrous, charitable, neighbourly, sporting, decent, or acts of self-denial and self-abnegation; actions so described are in many circumstances neither duties nor obligations; to fail to do them would not be positively wrong (though, perhaps, un-neighbourly, unkind, etc.), nor are they dictated by what I call principle. Nor are these various terms synonymous with each other and with 'supererogatory'; there is, for example, nothing chivalrous about lending a bag of flour to a neighbour who has run out, and helping an old lady across the road would not naturally be called sporting. If we are to do justice to the rich complexity of moral life, part of which I have just briefly indicated, we need a much more rich and varied set of concepts than the small set to which Hare confines himself.

So I wish to dissociate myself both from those who speak as though there was a special variety of acts called supererogatory,
*   and from Hare's view that the only distinction to be made is between those people who accept fewer or more principles to guide their moral life. It seems to me that 'supererogatory' is

an unnecessary blanket-term used to cover a number of types of moral actions which are as worthy of distinction from each other as they all are from duties and obligations; and while one must naturally agree with Hare that there are people who make more exacting moral demands on themselves than others do, this distinction in no way corresponds to the kinds of distinction that I have been trying to indicate.

Let me end by summarizing my three contentions. First, in ordinary moral thinking we attempt to determine our duties and obligations with a more complex apparatus than Hare allows. Beyond simple moral principles there are all kinds of considerations of greater and lesser importance and with varying relevance which are ordinarily taken into account. Second, weighing and judgement are indispensable in all assessment of evidence, and relevant factors in matters of fact and questions of prudence as well as in morality. In all these areas it is very difficult to get philosophically clear on the nature of this weighing and judging, but this is no ground for denying either its existence or its indispensability. Thirdly, it seems to me that Hare simply fails to allow for whole ranges of * moral life which are not concerned with fulfilment of duty and obligation.

Professor Hare may, or may not, be right in claiming that morality must in the end be based on some such utilitarian thesis as he advocates: nothing in this paper attempts to prove him wrong. But surely the moral thinking that his critical thinking is designed to control and supplement is not the jejune unthinking affair that he describes.

13. Changing Places?

Zeno Vendler

13.1 THE ability to represent other minds, their experiences, feelings, preferences, and so forth, is a prerequisite of what Professor Hare calls critical thinking in the moral sphere. My remarks will be addressed to this topic, and are intended to prevent, or to remedy, some misunderstandings his account might occasion. *

I fully agree with him that such a representation cannot consist in merely knowing the physical conditions of another conscious being; what one has to know is, in Professor Nagel's phrase (Nagel, 1974), what it is like for them to be in that condition.[1] This knowledge, needless to say, will not be propositional: not something like knowing, in conceptual terms, that something is the case. Nevertheless, as it makes sense to say that, for instance, we know what pain feels like, or what coffee tastes like, so there is nothing wrong with the idea of knowing what it must be like, for a person or animal, to be in a certain state.

Can we ever know such a thing? Certainly not in the way we know their bodily conditions. For in this respect they are but part of the physical universe, causally linked to the observer and his senses in many ways. Along these paths information can be obtained in the usual manner. But there are no links connecting their subjective awareness ('what it is like to be . . .') with the observer over and above the ones that reveal the physical circumstances themselves. To put it simply: whereas one can find out, by simple observation or by scientific means, what an organism is like at a given time, as to its physical situation, behaviour, and even its neural state, one cannot discover, in the same manner, what it is like to be that organism at that point in time.

[1] 'But what is it that we have to know? The answer is "What it is like to be those people in that situation" ' (*MT* 91 f.).

Of course, it has to be that way: there cannot be an 'objective' (think of the etymology of the word) representation of a subjective state: it has no 'outside', it does not 'look', 'sound', or 'feel' like anything to another observer. A subject, as such, has to be represented subjectively: not as an 'it', but as an 'I'. In other words, one has to consider that being as another self. And the only way of doing that is to imagine being that individual.

But how do we know that we are right in our imaginings? 'Imagination is a very common source of error;' warns Professor Hare, 'it can just as well be of experiences and preferences which they do not have as of those which they have' (*MT* 95). There is a problem here, no doubt, and it is important to locate its source. It seems to arise from the impossibility of comparing the work of our fancy with the data of experience. If I imagine Joe's living-room, I can check next time I visit him whether I did it correctly or not. There is no similar matching of imagination and observation possible with respect to his mental state: if it were observable, it would not be a mental state.

Is, then, my imagination infallible in*this matter? Not at all, for I may fall short in ascertaining his physical circumstances, i.e. the comprehensive conditions into which I put myself. If I fail to notice your extreme myopia, or if I am unaware of the fact that your shoe pinches badly, my projection of what you experience will be defective. Not to speak of the 'traces of the past' preserved in your central nervous system, accounting for your memories, fears, inclinations, and the like, which certainly play a role in your current mental state. Obviously, these elements cannot be discovered by simple observation, but only surmised on the basis of words and behaviour.

13.2 'But what if I knew everything about a certain body— down to the last neuron in his brain; could I not still be wrong?' Hare's Archangel would be in this condition: he is supposed to know everything about all bodies and all minds (*MT* 44 ff.). But, I ask, would he know these two domains independently from one another, or would he merely project the experiences on the basis of his complete representation of the bodily conditions? The first option I do not understand: if the two representations are indeed unrelated, then what makes the Archangel sure that *these* experiences belong to *that* body? Concerning the other option, it leaves the problem where it was: would his projection be accurate? In other words: is there another, and more basic, way of being wrong in these matters, beyond the misrepresentations due to ignorance about physical conditions? Hare, probably, would say that the Archangel just knows both domains by a sort of fiat; the Archangel is just an idea.

Well, he had better be. Archangels, to begin with, are not supposed to have bodies. If so, then, presumably, they cannot have, and cannot imagine having, a toothache or a tickle. How, then, can such a creature represent, say, my experiences in the dentist's chair? Incidentally, this difficulty transcends angels and reaches the Creator; does God know what pain feels like, what coffee tastes like, or what I am experiencing   *
now? (And ignore the possibilities arising out of Incarnation by virtue of the *communicatio idiomatum*.) Professor Kripke suggests that God could have paired bodily conditions and experiences otherwise . . . (Kripke, 1980:153–4). But how did he know what are the things that he could assign, say, to C-fibre stimulation? He has assigned pain, for sure, but did he know what he was doing when he cannot *feel* pain?

But I am digressing. Let us return to the Archangel, this time nicely embodied. Still he is supposed to know everything about bodies and minds. The question returns: is that possible? I omit the difficulties concerning the exhaustive knowledge of physical states for an embodied individual. But what about subjective states? Since this Archangel has a body, it must be an organism of a definite kind. Accordingly, the experiences it can have in actuality, or entertain in fancy, will be restricted to the ones appropriate to that kind of organism. And the 'perfection' of this assumed body does not help. We are at a loss to imagine what it must be like to be a bat or a frog partly because our bodies are far more 'perfect', i.e. developed and sensitive, than theirs.

We have to conclude, then, that Hare's Archangel, embodied or not, embodies an incoherent idea: no perfect representation of another mind is possible. Short of being an organism at a given moment of its life, no one can fully know what it is like to be that organism at that time. Obviously, this restriction applies to one's own body beyond the confines of the present moment as well: one cannot perfectly recall, or fully anticipate, one's past and future experiences.

13.3 Yet we do project experiences, for ourselves and for others, beyond the intersection of the 'I' and the 'now'. Moreover, as I explain in *The Matter of Minds*, we have to do so if we are to be placed in the world at all (Vendler, 1984). My being this body, at this point in time, is a matter of fitting my current awareness into the pattern of experiences projectible for a certain body at a certain juncture of its life. I am Z. V., and not Hare or someone else, because the experiences I now have correspond to the ones I can project for Z. V., rather than for them, in my fancy. Without this move, my inner life would not be recognized as being 'hooked' to a body, and to this body rather than to those.

The vicissitudes one's body undergoes, moreover, provide the only means of expanding the resources of one's imagination for the task of projecting other minds; e.g. the only way of coming to know what weightlessness feels like is to experience such a state in one's own body.

We can be wrong, therefore, in representing the condition of another mind on three fairly distinct accounts. First, our representation of the body in question may be deficient, both as to its macrostate (think of the unnoticed myopia), and to its microstate (memory traces, etc.). Second, some of the external circumstances may be unknown (think of the pinching shoe). And third, lack of experience. Not even the most exhaustive scientific account of the drug-addict's condition (behavioural, neural, etc.) will reveal what his 'high' feels like, to the person who has never had that experience. This deficiency, of course, can be remedied (but don't try!). No similar improvement is possible, however, with respect to the awareness of creatures widely different from us: bats, fish, and the like. So we have to make do with what we have—like drawing the picture of a rose in black and white.

The important point is, however, that there is no 'fourth' way of being wrong, the radical way—i.e. that you all might be insensitive machines, or have experiences *toto caelo* different from my well-informed projections. For in that case I would have no assurance that I am this man rather than another, or that I have a body at all. I emerge as this man, at this time, as a result of the application of a rule projecting experiences for all suitable organisms. The validity of this rule, in other words, is a transcendental condition of all self-containing world representations. This is why I cannot be wrong in that fourth, radical, way.

This conclusion can be reached in another way too. As we mentioned above, to make sense of the idea of what a person (or animal) experiences at a given time, one has to ask the question: what would I feel if I were in the same situation myself? And we found that this 'situation' comprises two related ingredients: the structure of the organism on the one hand, and the external circumstances on the other. Admittedly, I can be wrong about either of these factors. But the mere fact that the being I thus represent is *another* organism cannot be an added source of error. There is no reason to think that the designation, *this* (mine) or *that* (yours) brings in a new element. Indexicality is not a source of qualitative differences anywhere. Therefore, if that body were in exactly the same qualitative state as this body, then that person would enjoy the same experiences as this person.   *

13.4 But what about the 'I', you ask. That creature is not just another body—it is another 'I' too. Thus, maybe, being in the same situation feels different to him! This objection captures a basic worry—and exhibits a fundamental mistake. It assumes that the other 'I' is a *thing* distinct from this 'I'. But how could that be? For the sake of argument, let us go along with that assumption: as our bodies are distinct, so are our 'I's': I have (am?) mine, and you have (are?) yours; let us play Descartes, in other words.

Unfortunately, this is bound to be a no-win game. Remember, the task to be accounted for is this: trying to imagine what it must be like, say, being you. Playing by the Cartesian rules, this enterprise must consist in one of two moves: either I must imagine this 'I' (me) being somehow 'attached to' or 'lodged in' your body instead of mine. But what on earth can this mean? Poor Descartes has suffered enough at the hands of his successors for proposing such housing arrangements; let us not prolong the agony. Then the other way: I may try to imagine that this 'I' (me) is the same thing as that 'I' (you). But if the two are distinct, they cannot be the same, and cannot be imagined to be the same. Try to imagine that Castro is Reagan, or that this dog is that dog. The patently impossible cannot be imagined.

Conclusion: there are bodies, and there are persons, but there are no 'I's'. If I imagine being you, I do not fancy 'transporting' something into your body, or 'mixing' two entities. What I do is assume, as far as it is in the power of my imagination, the coherent set of experiences corresponding to your present situation (your 'Humean self' as it were). But, as Hume pointed out, there is no specific experience of an 'I' in that totality. Nor is there one in mine. The 'I' as such has no content: it is the empty frame of consciousness indifferent to content. Consequently, by constructing in my fancy the image of what I would experience in your situation, I *ipso facto* represent your experiences. The result, as I repeatedly granted, may be inaccurate for a number of reasons—but the difference of 'I's' cannot be one of them.

13.5 There are passages in Professor Hare's book (some of them mentioning an article of mine (Vendler, 1977)), which suggest that he holds the same view about the 'I': e.g. ' "I" is tied to no "essence" ' (*MT* 121), 'actually the short answer to the problem about the meaning of statements about other people's states of mind is that terms like "I" and "you" have no descriptive content in the strict sense' (*MT* 123). I am going to show, however, that the way he understands these claims will not support the burden he puts on them, i.e. his interpretation will not account for the possibility of representing other minds. Indeed, there are certain remarks in his book which tend to undercut that possibility.

According to Hare 'I' lacks content because it is an 'indexical' term: 'when Jones and Smith both use the expression "I" to refer to themselves, they use it synonymously, though with different references' (*MT* 120–1). This is indeed true of 'I', and of other indexical terms: the meaning of, say, 'that' or 'here' is to be derived from their use, and is not affected
* by the references made. But, if I am right, our notion of the 'I' is by no means accounted for by the indexicality of the term 'I'.

What does it mean to say that the term 'I' is an indexical of
* self-reference? As Hare says, 'one could put on one's stove as a

warning "I am hot" and the "I" be readily understood as referring to the stove' (*MT* 120–1). To the same effect, one could have put on the stove 'This stove is hot.' In exactly the same way a speaker may voice his dissent by saying 'I don't agree' or 'This speaker does not agree.' It would not matter for the audience: the reference would go through.

The difference in these contexts between 'I' and 'this stove', or 'I' and 'this speaker', is the following: 'I' is purely indexical (although with an implication of personhood, cancelled in the stove case), but 'this stove' or 'this speaker' is not, because of the presence of a descriptive term, 'stove' or 'speaker'.

The question is this: how can the purity of the self-referential indexical, 'I', help me in my attempt to imagine * being another individual, or, what comes to the same thing, being in his exact situation? The problem we face here is due to a *de re* distinction between me and someone else. This person cannot be that person, and, accordingly, this person cannot be in that person's exact situation. And this distinction is by no means abolished or attentuated by the fact that we may, and ordinarily do, refer to ourselves by the same indexical term, namely 'I'.

Take another pure indexical: 'this'. I say, while pointing at two cats in succession, 'This is a cat, and this is a cat.' My doing so certainly leaves them distinct. Then try this: point at one cat nearby, then another cat at a distance, and say, 'This is a cat and that is a cat.' Now try to imagine that cat being this cat. It won't go in the *de re* sense. But in this case, owing to a difference between the meanings of these indexicals, one might try to imagine that cat being closer, i.e. falling within the scope of 'this'. So in this queer sense one can imagine 'that cat' being 'this cat'.

This gives us an idea: 'you' (and 'he') and 'I' are indexicals in the way 'that' and 'this' are. Thus, perhaps, imagining being you involves something like 'moving' you into the 'I' position. Only whereas it is clear what 'move' is involved in fancying that cat being in the 'this' position, it is not yet clear how to bring another person within the scope of the 'I'.

Hare says 'It is not . . . legitimate to argue that, since "I" in Jones' mouth and "Jones" in anybody's mouth refer to the same person, and since "Jones might be in Smith's precise

situation" is self-contradictory (as we have conceded), therefore "I might be in Smith's precise situation", said by Jones, is
self-contradictory' (*MT* 120). I agree with Hare's conclusion;
I wish to point out, however, that it does not follow from the
mere fact that the term 'I' is a pure indexical. Somethig else
* has to be said: it has to be explained what it is for an
individual to be in the 'I'-position, i.e. what is the relation I in
fact have to Z. Vendler, or in fancy to that other person, by
virtue of which I can call them 'I'.

13.6 Before taking on that problem, however, I shall
review some of Hare's remarks which definitely point in the
wrong direction by allowing something like distinct Cartesian
'I's to sneak into the picture.

I begin with his example of the bicycle-owner versus the
car-driver (*MT* 109 ff.). I, the driver, want to move the bicycle
to be able to park my car. Am I allowed to do so? In order to
arrive at a verdict by critical thinking, I have to represent the
bicycle-owner's mind, at least as far as the relevant preferences
go, by imagining being in his place. Thus there *seem* to be two
different situations envisioned: one in which I am the driver,
and the other in which I am the bicycle-owner. Hare says this,
'Note that, although the situations are different, they differ
* only in what *individuals* occupy the two roles; their *universal*
properties are all the same' (*MT* 111). 'No', I say, it is the same
situation, with the same individuals; the only difference is
which of them is I: in imagining being he, I imagine the same
situation from a different perspective. And that constitutes
fancying being he. Because, I ask, what are those 'individuals'
which occupy the two roles in such a way that they can
'switch'? They seem to be distinct 'things', *à la* Descartes,
otherwise they could not switch roles; the very word 'occupy'
evokes the notorious 'is lodged in' . . .

This is by no means a unique text, or an *obiter dictum*.
Consider these lines:

Given two cases differing solely in that in one of them individuals *A*
and *B* occupy certain roles, and in the other the roles are reversed,
any universal principle must yield the same prescriptions about
them both. In order to yield different prescriptions about the two
cases, the principle would have to contain the names of the
individuals, and would therefore not be universal (*MT* 114).

Once more, 'individuals' play 'roles', moreover they can be, and are ('*A*' and '*B*'), named. Yet, Hare claims, the two cases are not different in any of their 'universal properties' (*MT* 114). So, it seems, *A* and *B* are distinct *solo numero*: either they are bare particulars, or share all their properties. But, in Leibniz's name, how is that possible?   *

It seems that Hare holds the bare particular view: 'terms like "I" and "you" have no *descriptive* content in the strict sense; that is to say, if you and I just changed places, the world would be no different in its universal properties' * (*MT* 123). I already objected to the 'that is to say' in this passage: from the fact that the referring device has no descriptive content it does not follow that the thing referred to has no properties. I only give this text to show that Hare seems to regard the 'individuals', you and me, *A* and *B*, as bare particulars.

He implies, finally, that the switching of these particulars would constitute different possible worlds.[2] Thus if, say, you * and I were to change places, we would be in a different world, albeit not in a qualitatively different one: there would be no difference in 'universal properties'.

I wonder, by the way, whether he would say the same thing about switching dates rather than subjects. He is aware of the analogy between the 'I' and the 'now' and implies that fancying being someone else is similar to imagining being at another point in time (which we often do, of course) (*MT* 101, 127). 'There is thus no possibility of discounting the future, because we have to imagine it as present', says Hare correctly (*MT* 101). Now I ask: does such an exercise envision another possible world? My answer is that it does not, as the switching of subjects does not. The perspectives on the world are different in either case, not the world. To put it differently: another moment of time is brought into the 'now' position by * the efforts of the imagination. But, the question returns, how do we do this?

13.7 It is time, then, to face the main issue and give an

---

[2] '. . . the hypothetical case in which he occupied the position of his victim . . . The question which arises, therefore, is whether moral principles . . . have to apply to all cases both actual and hypothetical, or only to actual cases. To use the fashionable terminology, do we have to be able to apply our moral principles to all logically possible worlds, or only to the actual world?' (*MT* 113).

account of the 'I' and the 'now' beyond the mere indexicality of
the words 'I' and 'now'.

Let us consider, first, the pure indexical word 'now'. In
normal use it refers to a definite moment in time, the time of
the utterance, which can be otherwise specified as, say, XXX
(imagine here a date, hour, minute, etc.). In other words, our
utterance of 'now' may be co-referential with a token of 'XXX';
'Now it is XXX' may be a true statement of identity. Of course,
there are other ways of referring to that moment: e.g. by
saying 'this moment'.

Now think of the other indexical, 'I'. This is normally used
to refer to the utterer, e.g. to Z. V. Thus again, an utterance of
'I' may be co-referential with a token of 'Z. V.'; so 'I am
Z. V.' may express a true statement of identity. Finally, to
complete the analogy, 'this speaker' may have the same
import as 'I'.

But then think of the enterprise of returning to the past, or
anticipating the future, in imagination: e.g. reliving my first
day in school, or savouring in advance my forthcoming
vacation in Puerto Vallarta. Hare is right: 'we have to imagine
it as present.' In other words, one has to represent those
events as occurring now. Let us say, my first entrance to
school occurred at the time YYY. Therefore, in that flight of
fancy, now is YYY. What does this mean? It surely does not
mean that I imagine XXX (the time of my imaginary
excursion into the past) to be YYY, or that I somehow move
XXX to the place of YYY. What it does mean is that I imagine
having the same relation, the same kind of access, to the world
at YYY which I actually have to the world at XXX. Mainly,
that it is open to my senses: I 'see' the schoolroom, I 'hear' the
bell, I 'feel' shy, etc. Needless to say, such an exercise may
reach beyond one's lifespan altogether; as in the TV show *You
Are There*, one can imagine Caesar being stabbed by Brutus. In
other words, any moment of the past or the future can be
brought into the 'now'-position by the effort of fantasy. And
now we understand what this amounts to.

My point is that imagining being someone else involves a
similar move. Say I imagine being Fidel Castro, i.e. in that
flight of fancy I am Castro. Again, this does not mean that
what I imagine is that Vendler is Castro, or that *he* is in

Castro's exact situation. That is absurd and cannot be imagined. What can be is having the same relation, the same access, to Castro's experiences and Castro's mind that I actually have to mine, i.e. Vendler's. In some detail: I imagine feeling the pinch of his army boots, seeing what he is looking at, enjoying the cigar in his mouth, entertaining his (presumed) memories, preferences, etc. as mine. Thus I bring him into the 'I'-position as it were.   *

As I suggested above, I am able to do these things not because the word 'I' is a bare self-referential indexical, but because the 'I' is an empty frame of awareness, indifferent to * content beyond the mere formal requirements of a unified consciousness.

The word 'I' refers to Z. V. in my speech acts, as 'this speaker' might, but it cannot refer to that contentless 'I', simply because it is not an object in the field of experience, but a mere subject to which no reference can be made. The word 'I' is indeed a (nearly) pure indexical, and 'I' is a pure subject, but these two claims are by no means identical, and the second cannot be derived from the first, as Hare seems to * think.

When I say 'I am Z. V.', I could say 'This speaker is Z. V.', or even 'This thing here is Z. V.' In all these cases I say something about a thing in the world to which I refer in various ways. But when I think: I am Z. V., or I am this thing, the thought of the 'I' cannot be replaced by any name or description. For if I try, say, by the thought of Vendler, or this speaker, the realization that I am Vendler, or this speaker, is still left out. The awareness that I am this thing consists in the following: when this body is pinched I feel pain, when these eyes are illuminated I see light . . . and when I want to reach out these hands move. Thus I, as subject, have a 'special relation' to this individual (Z. V.) in the world. This person is, in fact, in the 'I'-position. But, as we just saw, I can put Castro, or anybody, there in fantasy, by imagining having the same relation to his body, and his mind, as the one which I actually have to mine.

Accordingly, I can imagine being you, but not *me* being you, or *you* being *me*. For these 'you's' and 'me's' denote distinct individuals, which cannot be mixed or exchanged. Thus you and I cannot 'change places' without disturbing the 'universal properties' of the world. Of course, we can change places in the trivial sense of the phrase ('swap' seats, jobs, wives, etc.), but not without altering the world. But, as I just explained, in fancying being you or Castro, I do not touch the world: I merely switch perspectives on it.

This is the reason, by the way, for my maintaining throughout this paper that imagining being in exactly the same qualitative conditions as another person is the same thing as imagining being that person. As far as I can see Hare shies away from viewing them as the same. And indeed, given the bare particular view, my assuming your role in imagination would not amount to fancying being you.

If you ask, finally, as you are bound to ask, what is this 'I' which is supposed to have a 'relation' to your mind and body, my answer is that I cannot say, because it is not a 'what' or a 'such', about which something can be said non-metaphorically. For all the things one can describe, or to which one can refer, have to appear to this 'I', and 'it' cannot appear to itself. This is the reason why I mention 'it' in scare quotes: 'I'; I am talking metaphorically.

13.8 How do my revisions affect Hare's account of critical moral thinking? If anything, they make it easier.

If I understand him correctly, the application of such thinking to a moral conflict proceeds as follows. First, represent the inner state of the participants with their preferences and aversions concerning possible actions to be taken by some of them. Second, sum up the preferences and aversions with respect to each outcome, and choose the one for which the former outweigh the latter by the widest margin.

In all this I agree with Hare, and he agrees with me that the representation of the minds of the participants consists in putting myself in their exact circumstances. We also agree that the fact that I happen to be one of the participants of the scene should not make any difference.

But then, where do we disagree? He says, commenting on the solution of the car versus bicycle case: 'We see here in miniature how the requirement to universalize our prescriptions generates utilitarianism' (*MT* 111). What does he mean by universalizing here? I have already quoted Hare's previous remark concerning the same case: 'although the situations are different, they differ only in what *individuals* occupy the two roles; their *universal* properties are all the same' (*MT* 111). Thus for him, as I see it, universalization consists in an abstraction from the identity of the individuals involved, namely, that in the first situation I am the car-man and you the cycle-man, and in the second I am the cycle-man and you are the car-man. Now this is the move I do not understand and cannot follow. To me, as I explained above, there is only one situation with two persons involved, with their individuality unchanged and intact. What changes in the course of the critical thinking is my perspective on the situation: I view it first from the point of view of the one man, then from that of the other. And, if I am in fact one of them, this makes no difference for the moral choice. Thus I do not 'abstract', but simply omit a designation as irrelevant. Indeed, decisions can be made, by the same procedure, for situations in which I do not figure at all.

Being a participant, of course, will make an epistemological difference: if I am actually the car-man I 'know' his mind, but only project that of the cycle-man. But this has no moral significance.

So there is no need for 'trading places'. For one thing, whereas I know how to imagine being in your exact situation (we do such things all the time) I have no idea how to imagine *you* being in my exact situation. Who is this 'you' who would be shorn of all its attributes and yet remain the same individual? To put it pompously, I allowed for a transcendental 'I', but I refuse the same courtesy to a transcendental 'you' (or 'he' for that matter).

As I said above, critical thinking can proceed whether or not I am a participant in the examined situation. But if I am, I am bound by the verdict. This is, in part, what it means to be a participant. I am this man, since *I* see what these eyes look at, *I* feel what this body undergoes, and these arms move when *I* want to reach out. In exactly the same way, *I* am obliged to do what moral reflection enjoins this man to do in a situation in which he is involved.

14. The Structure of Hare's Theory

Bernard Williams

14.1 I hope that Dick Hare is disposed to accept seriously *
intended criticism as an expression of interest and respect,
since I have expressed in this form my interest in and respect
for his work at what he may reasonably regard as excessive
length. Trying in a recent book (Williams, 1985) to describe
moral philosophy and some significant modern contributions
to it, I found it appropriate to criticize his views at various
points of the argument. Here I shall try to examine the
structure of his theory as I understand it, and in the course of
this I shall make some of these criticisms again, but in a
different form, responding to what I take to be the overall
shape of his theory. The design of this book gives him the
opportunity to reply, and this is the best reason for my
repeating some of my points.

14.2 I take Hare's theory[1] to have a structure that
(allowing for some compressed formulations) can be set out in
the following way.

(*a*) Moral language has certain necessary features.

(*b*) It is necessarily (i) prescriptive and (ii) universal; and (iii)
these features are enough to determine the nature of moral
thinking at a basic level.

Because of (*b*i) and (*b*ii),

(*c*) moral thinking involves identification with everyone's
preferences[2];

© Bernard Williams 1988

[1] I shall discuss the theory presented in *MT*. I shall not be concerned except in 14.7
with the development of Hare's views.

[2] Hare makes simplifying assumptions about the class of preferences to be
considered: see *MT*, ch. 5. This is an important matter, raising questions about the
motivation of utilitarian theories in general (cf. Williams, 1985:86–9; Sen and
Williams, 1982, Introduction), but I shall not pursue it here.

and because of (biii), this is all there is to basic moral thinking. Hence,

(d) basic moral thinking is equivalent to a quasi-first-personal deliberation, governed by decision-theoretical criteria, over all preferences.

Basic moral thinking, that is to say, is properly represented
* by what I have called *the World Agent model* (Williams, 1985:83 f.). But,

(e) within the World Agent model, items of different levels can be evaluated: particular actions, type-actions, policies, principles, dispositions, etc. In particular, its criteria can be applied to the activity of this basic moral thinking itself.

When they are so applied, the result is that

(f) everyday moral thinking should not all take the form of basic ('critical') moral thought; some of it should involve an 'intuitive' expression of dispositions.

The result is a two-level theory.

14.3 I have presented (f) as a consequence of the rest of the theory: immediately, of (e) together with some supposed empirical facts. I think that this is correct in terms of the theory's logical structure, but it does not adequately reveal the importance of the part played by the two-level view in recommending the earlier parts of the theory. (c) and (d) are not obviously true. Moreover, even if some conception such as that of an *impartial consideration* of all preferences followed from moral language or, independently of that, was thought to constitute basic moral thinking, it might still be thought that (d), and (c) when taken in a corresponding sense, involved an implausibly strong interpretation of that conception. In face of such objections, the two-level view helps to make (c) and (d)
* acceptable, by saving the appearances that seemingly tell against them. Various features of moral experience that suggest a different view are conceded their place at the 'intuitive' level, while (c) and (d) hold true at the basic or 'critical' level.

This is the same strategy as Sidgwick adopted, to try to show that utilitarianism, properly understood, did not have the unpalatable consequences that it seemed to have when advocated as a simple one-level theory. However, the doubts about (c) and (d) have wider effects. The fact that (c) and (d) are not accepted by many careful thinkers makes it not merely unobvious but implausible that they follow from the nature of moral language:[3] it casts doubt, that is to say, on the role of (b). If the two-level strategy helps to defend (c) and (d), does it thereby defend the role of (b)? Here there is an interesting contrast between Hare's position and Sidgwick's. Sidgwick believed that (c) and (d), or something of the same sort, followed from a purely rational intuition to the effect that there could be no antecedent reason to prefer some one part of attainable good over any other part, and he thought that one came to see this truth by concentrating one's mind on it. His theory was intended to produce an acceptable balance between very general principles on the one hand and, on the other, spontaneous moral reactions to familiar types of situation. In particular, it was meant to help the theorist in justifying, and in that sense understanding, those reactions in terms of the general principles; it was also to help in defending the principles against the apparently contrary force of the reactions. While the epistemology of intuitions remains incurably obscure, Sidgwick could put this process into some relation to one's grasp of the basic principles as he conceived of it, by saying that the two-level theory, in giving a place to experiences that seemed to tell against the basic principles, helped to concentrate one's mind on those principles.

Hare's use of the two-level theory to make (c) and (d) more acceptable is much like Sidgwick's. But Hare's use of it has nothing to do with the way in which he derives (c) and (d) in the first place. The two-level theory does nothing to make more plausible the claim *that they follow from the nature of moral language*—that is to say, to justify the role of (b). Suppose that it is true that if one thinks hard about (c) and (d), with the help of the two-level theory, one will become convinced of them: that is not enough. It is enough for Sidgwick, but it is not enough for Hare, if he is to justify the role of (b). What needs to be true is that by thinking harder *about moral language*

---

[3] For this objection, see Mackie, 1977:97; Nagel, 1982. On Hare's very demanding *
conception of impartial concern for others' preferences, see Williams, 1985:89–92.

one will become convinced of them, and the two-level theory offers no help in that.

Besides asking whether considerations about language will yield this result rather than some other, we can ask why something called 'moral language' should be expected to reveal anything, or anything reliable, about these matters at all. Language consists in human practices; human beings (as the theory itself insists) have suffered and do suffer from many illusions about the relations of value to the world and so forth; if language can embody or imply any propositions at all about
* such things, why should it not embody illusions?

Merely as a moral theory, it might seem that Hare's system could do as well without involving (*a*) and (*b*). It could proceed by seeking what Rawls calls 'reflective equilibrium', by balancing the general theoretical material against features of moral experience, with the help of the two-level theory. In fact, Hare has strongly resisted this method, for reasons that I shall come back to in 14.7.

14.4 The two-level theory has its own difficulties. In what way are 'critical' and 'intuitive' thinking supposed to be embodied? In Sidgwick's version of indirect utilitarianism, the two styles of thought correspond to a social distinction between two classes of people, the utilitarian élite and the rest.
* In that version—'Government House utilitarianism', as it may be called—there are clear distinctions between the thoughts of the two classes of people. For one thing, the purely logical or semantic distinction between first-order and second-order thought is mirrored in the fact that the élite thinks about the practices of the others, but the others do not reflect on the special thoughts of the élite—in particular (as Sidgwick makes clear) because they do not know about them. Moreover, the élite are special not merely in the sense that they have second-order thoughts; they also think in a different way about particular practical issues, since more of their thoughts about those issues express direct utilitarianism, and fewer express common-sense principles.

This is not how Hare represents the distinction between the two levels of thought. Elsewhere (Williams, 1985:106–10) I have said that he regards the distinction rather as one between two times, that of practical activity as contrasted with the cool hour of reflection. However, this is not quite right. His distinction is indeed intended as a psychological rather than a social one: it picks out two styles of thought, both of which can be represented in the mind of one person. But it does not merely pick out two times of thought corresponding to those styles, since Hare supposes that a person can think in both styles at one time. Morever, he believes that there are in this respect various kinds of people, who approximate in different degrees to one or the other of two archetypes, revealingly called the 'archangel' and the 'prole'. The first of these characters uses only critical thinking—which means, his powers are such that he needs no other. The second uses only intuitive thinking, because he is incapable of critical thinking (*MT* ch. 3, especially 3.1 to 3.3). Thus there are some people— more like the archangel, and more like Sidgwick's élite—who can think at the critical level more of the time; and this is seen as a valuable capacity, while thinking at the intuitive level is seen rather as a necessity and an imperfection. How much of the time it is advisable to think in one of these styles or in the other is a question that Hare seems to think depends on empirical factors and is of no philosophical interest.   *

I do not believe that this account is coherent, or that the styles of thought Hare seeks to describe could provide what his theory requires. It is important to make clear what the objection is. It is not an objection (how could it be?) to all styles of reflective or second-order thought, nor to the mere idea that such thoughts might be interwoven with other thoughts in the course of practice. Hare is of course right to say that a general in action can jump between tactical and strategic levels of thought (*MT* 52). But strategic and tactical thoughts, unless the general is in a muddle, do not conflict, nor is there any conflict between the activities of thinking in the one style or the other. Nor do reflections of moral philosophy necessarily have to conflict with first-order practical thoughts: those of contractualism, for instance, characteristically do not. The objection is specifically to Hare's kind of theory, which represents the intuitive responses as deeply entrenched, surrounded by strong moral emotions, sufficiently robust to see the agent through situations in which sophisticated reflection might lead him astray, and so on; and yet at the same time explains those responses as a device to secure utilitarian outcomes. The theory ignores the fact that the responses are not merely a black-box mechanism to generate what is probably the best outcome under confusing conditions. Rather, they constitute a way of seeing the situation; and you cannot combine seeing the situation in that way, *from* the point of view of those dispositions, with seeing it in the archangel's way, in which all that is important is maximum preference satisfaction, and the dispositions themselves are merely a means towards that.

In saying that you 'cannot combine' these two things, I do not mean that as a matter of psychological fact it is impossibly difficult. People indeed have thoughts that they describe in these terms—Hare himself has said that he does. The point is that the thoughts are not stable under reflection; in particular, you cannot think in these terms if at the same time you apply to the process the kind of thorough reflection that this theory itself advocates. That is not a merely psychological claim. It is a philosophical claim, about what is involved in effective and adequate reflection on these particular states of mind.

It might be said that the difficulty arises only because the depth and strength of the 'intuitive' dispositions have been exaggerated. If the intuitive responses are seen only as presumptive rules of thumb, then the difficulty disappears, or at least is less severe.[4] That is right, but the position it provides is not Hare's. Moreover, it would not allow Hare to make all the use he does make of the two-level theory. Like Sidgwick, as I said earlier, he uses the theory to save the appearances, explaining people's ordinary reactions in relation to the basic utilitarian principles. But the more the theory represents the intuitive reactions as merely superficial, provisional, and instrumental, the fewer appearances it saves: it does not explain what people do feel and think, but suggests something else in the same area that they might usefully feel and think.

14.5 It is important that the two-level theory in its present form is not a unique solution, given the rest of the material, to

---

[4] If a utilitarian theory is not to raise the difficulty at all, it should not go much beyond the 'gas bill model' discussed in Williams, 1972.

the problem of what everyday moral thought should be. Its logical status, I suggested earlier, is that it is supported by the basic position together with some empirical material, and if there are difficulties with it, then some other solution may turn out to be better supported. If basic moral thought is defined in archangelic terms, then *some* stand-in for it is needed in everyday practice, since full archangelic thought requires an indefinite amount of knowledge and deliberative power (it is all the more exacting because Hare interprets so ambitiously the idea of being impartially concerned with everyone's preferences). Yet Hare himself cannot see critical, non-intuitive, thought exclusively in archangelic terms, since   *
he thinks that it is something that most of us can conduct some of the time, and when it is seen in that light, it indeed becomes an empirical question, as he claims, to what extent a stand-in is needed. But then it must also be an empirical question what the stand-in should be.

It is obvious (as indeed it is from the history of utilitarianism) that there are many candidates for the stand-in, many styles of everyday moral thought that might in practice produce the best results. Deep dispositions, which Hare favours and which produce their own special problems, are only one. There are rules of thumb, direct utilitarianism applied to a limited constituency of beneficiaries, and others. Proceeding downwards from the account of basic moral thought, and taking the appropriate empirical facts into consideration about the effects in practice of different kinds of moral practice, one might arrive at any of these solutions. The fact that Hare arrives at this particular stand-in rather than some other may not simply be the product of empirical belief. It may be that he is drawn to this solution because it is at least prima facie better than others at saving the appearances of moral experience. But further argument is needed to show that the position one gets to by proceeding downwards from the top of the system, and the position that best saves the appearances of   *
moral experience, are likely to be one and the same. If the method of reflective equilibrium is adopted, then of course there is a rationale for saving the appearances—that is part of the idea. But if the method is that of travelling down from moral language to basic principles, and from them, in the light

of empirical facts, to the most desirable forms of everyday moral thought, there is simply no guarantee that the appearances deserve to be saved.

14.6 I raised (in 14.4) a difficulty with the two-level theory in its present form, in which it favours deep dispositions. The difficulty is, in summary, that one could not think at the 'intuitive' or everyday level in the way that the theory requires while one was fully conscious of what one was doing: in particular, while one fully understood in terms of the theory itself what one was doing. This is, if real, a difficulty; but why exactly does it constitute an objection to Hare's theory? It might be seen as not yielding an objection, but merely as showing something about the theory, that it cannot work if people, in full reflection and all the time, believe it. Such properties of ethical theories, in particular of utilitarian theories, have been studied by Parfit (Parfit, 1984, Part I), who argues that they do not necessarily mean that such theories should be rejected. But this still leaves problems of who is to accept such theories, and in what spirit; and if it is not possible that any, or many, people should accept them, what the status of the theory then is, and the purpose of the theorist in announcing it.

In the case of Government House utilitarianism, the answer to these questions is straightforward. The theory is addressed to the élite, and there is no problem about the élite's fully believing it, all of the time. The hard problem is a political one, of how to run a modern society that is controlled by such an élite—in particular, running it decently, in accordance with values that the élite might (otherwise) be expected to endorse. Hare's theory, however, is addressed to people who are expected themselves to have dispositions which they cannot both exercise in the way that the theory requires and at the same time understand in the terms that the theory provides. If they are being asked to attend to this theory, they are also being asked, in some significant degree, to forget it. There could be a theory that asked to be treated in that way, but it is obvious that Hare's does not. On the contrary, his is meant to appeal to and to sustain a spirit of critical reflection and self-enquiry, and Hare makes it clear that he intends his philosophy to contribute to moral improvement through self-criticism. It is because the theory has these aspirations that the difficulty is also an objection.

14.7 Hare in his earliest theory separated his description of moral language from any determination of the content of moral principles. He was also disposed to see that separation as an application of the fact–value distinction—indeed, more than that, as a prime expression of it. Philosophy itself had to be on the 'fact' side of the distinction: both because that accorded with a general picture of philosophy as linguistic analysis, and, in particular, because philosophy's announcement of the fact–value distinction would lack the critical force it was supposed to possess if it were itself an expression of value.

In the later theory which I am considering, the description of moral language, together with empirical information, is thought to determine the content of moral principles; and the degree to which the description of moral language determines the nature of moral thinking, even without empirical information, certainly serves already to eliminate substantive alternatives. (Hare says that what is determined at this level is the *form* of (basic) moral thought: but then many substantive questions about it must be questions about its form.) Because Hare associated his earlier formulations so closely with the expression of the fact–value distinction, these developments have led some critics to say that Hare has changed his mind about that distinction. However that may be—I think in fact that Hare can answer this claim—the relevant points here are that he has not changed his mind about what philosophy is, and that he has a stronger view now than earlier about its powers.

Hare has always wanted, and earnestly wanted, moral philosophy to have a practical effect, to make a difference. He does not think it an obstacle to this that on his view moral philosophy is, roughly, a branch of philosophical logic. On the contrary: moral philosophy can make a difference only because it has authority, and it can have authority only because of its neutral status as a logical or linguistic subject. He has always held this in some form, but his present theory gives a very special explanation of what this authority is. The crucial belief now is that this neutral subject can yield foundations.   *

It is this belief that explains his scorn for those who use the method of seeking reflective equilibrium and start their moral philosophy from people's 'moral intuitions'. Hare does not primarily object to this, as some utilitarians do, because these intuitions are too conservative; the 'intuitive' principles that he puts back at the end of his enquiry tend, in some areas, to be more conservative than those that would have been elicited in the first place. Similarly, the objection cannot simply be that their method is not critical or radical enough, if this is taken in some general sense: in a general sense, some of these philosophers are notably critical or radical. His objection is that, whether conservative or radical in the outcome, the intuitions and the theories elicited from them by these philosophers are mere prejudices: which means, they lack any foundation. This provides one sense in which he does think that these enquiries are not sufficiently critical or radical—the Cartesian sense, that they have not gone back to foundations.

* Hare's present view of moral philosophy and its relation to practice has, then, several strands, with different histories. He now believes:

  (i)   moral philosophy is (roughly) a logical or linguistic subject;
  (ii) it provides foundations;
  (iii) it helps us to reflect clearly on our moral thoughts, and in particular—because of (i)—to think about what we mean;
  (iv) when we do so, we discover (ii).

Hare has always believed (i). He has not always believed, as he now believes, (ii) and (iv). However, he now believes that in some part the authority of moral philosophy derives from (ii); as we have just seen, his rejection of other methods rests on this.

I earlier discussed the difficulty about the two-level theory and I suggested, in 14.6, that the reason why that difficulty was an objection to Hare lay in the view that he took of philosophy. In terms of the present schema, it is an objection in virtue of (iii). Hare has always accepted (iii); indeed, before he came to believe (ii), it had to do all the work of explaining why philosophy, as a neutral study of language, had authority and relevance to practical life. (iii) in itself presents no difficulty, at least of this kind. Others may be less inclined than Hare is to stress its purely linguistic aspect, but everyone can recognize it as a worthy declaration of the Socratic impulse, an expression of the values of social and personal transparency. When Hare moved to believing (ii) and (iv), however, it became possible for (iii) to be in conflict with the conclusions of (i). It was bound to be an open question whether the foundations that (i) now yielded were such that the practice recommended by (iii) could be thoroughly carried out. Hare has always assumed that (iii) was an obvious statement of the aims of philosophy, and also that the results of philosophy, as the objective subject described in (i), could be consistently, and no doubt usefully, known by anyone. He now has no assurance that these two things, the external view of what morality is, and the internal representation of it in moral practice, will necessarily fit together.

Some other objections I have mentioned turn on rejecting the idea that a linguistic enquiry will yield foundations. I shall not discuss here the question whether morality should be expected to have foundations, nor the paradox that Hare (and he is not alone in this) should move to a foundationalist view of morality while philosophy has been moving to taking a less foundationalist view of everything else. The present point is only about method. I have already mentioned Hare's basic reason for thinking that philosophy should not proceed by reflection (in the first place, at least) on our moral 'intuitions', opinions, or experiences. His reason is that they are merely *ours*: as an objection, it rests on his belief in foundations. His particular insistence on a linguistic enquiry, as opposed to such reflections, rests in some part of the general point (i); but the special form taken by his linguistic enquiry reveals that it is itself conditioned by the search for foundations, and by the desire to get away from what is merely 'ours'.[5]

To those who do not agree with Hare that a linguistic method can yield foundations, he does not provide any purely methodological reason why they should not start from 'intuitions'—a reason, that is to say, independent of the

[5] The point is explicit at *MT* 17 f. For the very special character of the linguistic enquiry, cf. Williams, 1985, ch. 7.

substantial point on which he and they disagree. They may themselves believe in foundations, but think that the way to find them is by starting from our moral opinions. Or they may not believe in foundations at all, and merely be concerned with the implications, presuppositions, and incoherences of those opinions. In relation to either of these groups, Hare is in a situation familiar in philosophy (it was Descartes's own situation), that his objection to their method rests only on what he believes to be the actual results of his own.

Just because Hare's conclusions govern his method, and his conclusions are so foundationalist, he does clearly answer in his own terms a question that other philosohers often merely ignore. Why should the critical reflection to which moral philosophy is committed be expected to issue in an ethical theory? Hare has a conception of moral philosophy and its aims that naturally issues in such a theory. Those who reject that conception, but still seek a theory to systematize our moral opinions, owe both him and the rest of us an account of why they expect our best understanding of our ethical life to take such a form.

Part III

Hare

15. Comments
R. M. Hare

1. Introduction

C. D. BROAD, in a letter to me about my contribution to his
similar but grander volume, referred to it as 'the me-volume in
Schilpp's Library of Moribund Philosophers'. The appearance
of such a volume carries with it a premonition of impending
senility; but at least it is not a *Festschrift* (which nobody ought
to be awarded until he has retired from active service). Since I
am now more active than I have ever been, I have looked
forward with relish to the congenial activity of replying to
such a distinguished set of critics, who have been kind enough
to do me the honour of contributing their discussions of my
ideas. I have been relieved to find that for the most part the
stale old criticisms of utilitarianism and prescriptivism are
absent from this volume, except in so far as the contributors
(Professor Hudson in particular) have mentioned them only
in order to answer them summarily themselves, thus saving
me the tedious task of answering them yet again. I am grateful
to him and to others for defending me on some points as well
as criticizing me. This does not indicate that the editors in
their selection of people to invite were looking for yes-men.
They were looking for critics who would take the subject
further than I had been able to, and they have found them.
Often criticisms and answers to them are the best way of
doing this, and I shall try to play my part.

Inevitably I am able to agree more with some of the
contributors than with others; and since expressions of
agreement take up less space than answers to objections, this
has been one reason for a somewhat unequal allocation of
space between the critics in my reply. Another is that some
critics have made more points that need comment than others.

But quantity does not always correlate with importance, and I have learnt a lot from all my critics.

I shall start with an introductory section discussing some general points, mainly about the development of my views, which need to be understood if I am not to be misinterpreted. Then I shall devote sections to each of the contributions. We have had some discussions among the editors, the other contributors, the publishers, and myself about the style of these. I have followed the majority view, which is the same as my own. Some of the contributors regret that I have not adopted the conventional style in such volumes, and written continuous essays in answer to each of the critics, but have commented in note form. I must therefore explain my reasons for this choice of style.

The first is that I am concerned above all for the serious student of these issues, who will wish to have my replies to particular points that the critics have made, and to be able to locate them easily. In a continuous essay he could not do so without a protracted search. The second is that continuous essays would inevitably have to be much longer to contain the same substance. Instead of numerical references to the critics' texts, I should have had to rehearse in summary the arguments of theirs to which I was replying; and the same holds for references to arguments in my own earlier writings. From volumes of this sort to which I have contributed, my impression is that this need either to cite particular arguments of the critics or to ignore them, coupled with the constraints of space, has made some of the 'replies to critics' in them rather cursory.

Some people have suggested that I might write a restatement of my position in the light of criticisms. If by this they meant that I was to *alter* my position radically, I am unable to oblige, because it remains substantially the same. Where the critics have shaken me, I have acknowledged this; but to restate my position as a whole would have been a pointless repetition of what I have written and published already. It will be more useful to clarify particular points and answer, or accept, particular criticisms; and for this the commentary style is most appropriate.

I recognize that it also has disadvantages. The less studious reader will undeniably find it a bore to have to refer from the text to my notes and back, and may even miss out my notes altogether. But I do not much mind if readers who do not want to follow the arguments save themselves the trouble. There are in most of the replies longer continuous passages to which they might give what attention they can spare. Lastly, in case anybody thinks that I have been discourteous to my critics in writing notes instead of essays, I must point out that this is what we commonly do to Plato and Aristotle (as in the Clarendon series of commentaries), taking their arguments one by one and treating them briskly but seriously.

It may be helpful if I start on an autobiographical note. It is often suggested (e.g. by Professors Nagel (*102/7*), Richards (*116/−13*) and Williams (*194/18*)) that in later books of mine I have changed my views substantially from those expressed in earlier ones. It would be no discredit to me if I had, because many famous philosophers such as Kant and Plato have done the same. But it might lead to misinterpretation if it were assumed that I have changed my position when I have not; and in fact I have done so perhaps less than has been thought. After in my youth discarding completely an entire book I had written, as containing mostly rubbish, and the second half of my T. H. Green Prize dissertation as not much better, I was lucky enough, when I started writing *The Language of Morals*, to hit right at the beginning on a line of enquiry which I have subsequently seen no reason to abandon. Though my ideas have developed and expanded, and I have found new ways of defending them, I have not had actually to reject very much that I wrote earlier. Where I have done so in any important way, I have tried to give indications of this. If those who think I have changed my views would look for chapter and verse in earlier writings where there is an inconsistency with later, and tell me about them, they would do me a service. But actually references are seldom given.

I will give just three instances of this kind of claim. In a notorious passage in *The Language of Morals*, I said that we have to decide for ourselves what principles to live by (*LM* 68 f.). This has been seized upon by many critics (though not in this volume) as an advocacy of irrationalism, and it would follow that in my later books, which are highly rationalistic, I have changed my view, and abandoned this irrationalism. But I never said that one has to decide *irrationally* what principles to live by; and in fact the end of this passage (like *LM* 15 f. and 45) implies the opposite:

> He has to decide whether to accept that way of life or not; if he accepts it, then we can proceed to justify the decisions that are based upon it; if he does not accept it, then let him accept some other, and try to live by it. The sting is in the last clause. To describe such ultimate decisions as arbitrary, because *ex hypothesi* everything which could be used to justify them has already been included in the decision, would be like saying that a complete description of the universe was utterly unfounded, because no further fact could be called upon in corroboration of it . . . Far from being arbitrary, such a decision would be the most well-founded of decisions, because it would be based upon a consideration of everything upon which it could possibly be founded.

I still think this, and in fact the whole of my subsequent work has been devoted to eliciting the rationalism that is implicit in this passage. The 'sting' is the feature of moral judgements which I call prescriptivity; and the fact that what we are deciding on are principles brings with it universalizability. The latter thesis is explicitly advocated in *LM* 131 ff. and 157, though not under that name, and with 'general' wrongly used to mean the same as 'universal' (the error is later acknowledged in *MT* 41 and refs.). On these two features my developed account of moral reasoning was later based, and there are hints of it not only here but in other places in that early book.

I may add that the thought that I was an irrationalist when I wrote *LM* is due mainly to the confusion of supposing that the only way to be a rationalist is to be a descriptivist. No progress can be made in moral philosophy by those who are the victims of this confusion, which I have throughout my career been trying to dispel. See e.g. H 1976*b* and *MT* 206 ff., and on Singer *151/12*.

Another claim that is commonly made is that between *Freedom and Reason* and *Moral Thinking* I changed my views on the nature of fanaticism. What actually happened was that I developed a new weapon against the fanatic, but one entirely consistent with what I said in the earlier book. There (*FR*

171 f.) I isolated the 'pure' fanatic (as I called him in *MT* 170), and said (out of caution) that such fanatics 'are extremely rare'. I later (e.g. *FR* 184) admitted that they would always be with us. That was because I had not at that time thought of the move made in *MT* 181. This consists in facing the 'pure' fanatic with a dilemma. Either his fanatical ideals or desires are strong enough to outweigh all the desires of all the other people affected by his actions, or they are not. If they are not, then (for reasons quite consistent with *FR*) he will lose the argument. If they are, then his claim can be supported on utilitarian grounds, so that his existence would be no objection to my theory. The new development here (not a change of view) is that the contingent improbability of finding a fanatic with such strong desires has been shown to be so high that for practical purposes he has vanished from the scene. He is still, as in *FR*, theoretically irrefutable, but, for the theoretical reason given, no objection to the theory, and in practice possible to ignore, as was already claimed in *FR* 185. The change is not in the characterization of the fanatic, but in the introduction of a new move against him, which shows that he cannot be *even* as much instantiated as was (for caution's sake) admitted in *FR*.

A third mistake about the development of my ideas has been so widespread that I must mention it in this introduction, although I have also noted it in my comment on Nagel *102/8*, and when writing about Mackie in my comment on Singer *147/−5*. It is commonly thought that I have changed my understanding of the thesis of universalizability. This is not so. As H 1984*b* makes clear, the thesis is the same now as it was in my earliest (unpublished) paper on the subject, and has been maintained consistently ever since. There is a change from H 1955*a* (noted in *FR* 35) on the question of whether the doctrine applies to all evaluative words or only to moral uses; but that does not affect the point I am presently making.

It is thought that I now want the thesis to do more than before, and am therefore interpreting it in a more powerful way, to require impartiality in some substantial sense when making moral judgements. This would be a change from *FR* 30 ff., in that it would make the thesis into a substantial moral principle, and not just a logical requirement. I have always set my face against doing that, because the principle would then require a moral intuition for its support, whereas the logical thesis relies for support on our linguistic intuitions alone (see *MT* 10 ff.).

It must be stressed therefore that the new move made in *MT*, chs. 5 and 6, does not depend on a changed interpretation of universalizability. It depends on the addition of a new thesis altogether (what is called in Gibbard *58/3* ff. the Conditional Reflection Principle). This is explained and justified in *MT*, ch. 5, and the justification does not rely on universalizability (see *MT* 108). It is then used, in *MT*, ch. 6, in combination with the *old* thesis of universalizability, to provide a strong foundation for moral arguments and for substantial impartiality. Both theses are logical, but they are different, independent theses.

The last piece of autobiography I shall inflict on the reader is this. It has become common in recent articles on philosophy by journalists, and indeed in the writings of some professional philosophers, to proclaim the advent of a new era in which philosophers actually turn their attention to issues of practical relevance, whereas in recent years, it is implied, they concerned themselves only with verbal disputes. Sometimes they are contrasted in this respect, to their discredit, with the famous philosophers of the past. On this, see H 1986*b*. Since some of this mud might stick, and be intended to stick, to me, it may be as well to set out the true facts as I see them.

From about the turn of this century there have been two main classes of philosophers, whom I will call the romantics and the analyticals. The former (who include most Marxists) have written quite a lot about practical issues, but have done almost nothing to illuminate them. What they have done is to satisfy the cravings of those who desire not illumination but excitement; and on the whole they have, by making the issues even more confused than they would in any case have been, done more harm than good. This is because they have not tried, and have not even desired, to express themselves in such a way that one can understand clearly what they are saying and determine whether it is right or not. The policy I follow, when confronted with a piece of writing by such people, is to read enough to determine whether the author wants his views to be understood and rationally addressed by his readers; and if, as is usually the case, the evidence shows that he does not, to stop reading.

The analyticals by contrast have sought to make themselves clear and to expose themselves to scrutiny. Wittgenstein was perhaps an exception; but he was in any case half a romantic. Some of his followers have managed to elicit some important insights from his devious and obscure writings; others have aped the worst features of his style. It has to be attributed partly to his influence that philosophy, even in analytical circles, is not now usually written with the clarity which used to be demanded.

It is true of most analytical philosophers, including myself, that they concerned themselves very much with the meanings of words and with logical rigour. This was in reaction from the excesses of the romantics of an earlier generation, and was almost wholly beneficial. It is also true that in this search after clarity and rigour some of them (like Professor Ayer) looked askance at kinds of language, such as moral discourse, which did not seem to them to carry a clear meaning on their face; so they restricted their logical enquiries, as Aristotle (*De Int.* 17a2) had, to statements of fact expressed in indicative or declarative sentences, and admitting of truth or falsity in some readily explicable sense. There thus arose a school of moral philosophers, the emotivists, who denied that there could be rational moral argument.

In conscious reaction to this tendency, I and a few other analyticals sought to show that an account could be given of the meaning of moral statements which, though not assimilating them to the kind of descriptive statements that logicians had been treating as privileged, nevertheless made it possible for them, and arguments containing them, to be assessed rigorously. I believe that we have succeeded in this. But what I must above all make clear is my motive for wanting to do it.

I entered moral philosophy, and indeed philosophy itself, because I was confronted (as I still am) with serious moral questions, and wanted to answer them in a rational manner. But it was absolutely clear that there was no hope of doing this without first finding a way through the logical difficulties raised by the emotivists. I therefore devoted most of my work

in the early stages to these conceptual and linguistic problems.
But I did not stop being troubled by practical moral issues. I
thought and wrote about them from the beginning, and
actually published my first essays in this genre three years
after *LM* (H 1955*b*). These were lectures given earlier in
Germany and then on the BBC Third Programme, on such
problems as the duties of citizens whose governments act
immorally. However, I did not trust myself at that early time
to publish much on practical issues, because I was not so
confident then as I am now that I had a theory of moral
reasoning that would withstand scrutiny. Without such a
theory, whatever one writes on practical issues is bound to be
insecure.

As soon as I became more confident in my understanding of
moral reasoning, I wrote more on practical issues; the last
chapter of *FR* (1963) is about racism, and was a revision of a
paper on that subject that I read to a seminar I put on with
Professor Kirkwood on the subject. This was not the first nor
the last of the many that I have held (often with experts in
other disciplines) on practical moral questions. I currently
devote about half of my philosophical work to such questions,
and my bibliography shows the results.

Because I have always had a desire to help, as a
philosopher, with practical problems, the development in my
writing that I have described must not be confused with a
somewhat more recent shift in attitude among analytical
philosophers generally, which has caught the attention of
journalists. It is certainly true that a great many of them have
now started to write about practical issues. But for the most
part (there are exceptions) that is not due to any increased
confidence in their understanding of ethical theory. Indeed,
many *have* no theory, and do not seem to feel the need of one.
For want of it, much of what they write on practical issues is
unhelpful, because, lacking any grasp of how one should
reason morally, they have constant recourse to their own
moral intuitions; and in controversial matters (abortion for
example) intuitions are conflicting, and no appeal to them will
carry weight with those who do not share them (see H 1975*b*
ad init.).

Therefore, although no doubt some of those who have

written about practical issues have done so from the same motives as myself, in others one must look for different explanations. One could be a mere change in fashion—an urge to do something different. Another could be the desire to avoid the attacks made on analytical philosophers by radicals. These had drawn a supposed contrast between the verbal trivialities of the analytical school and the 'relevant' writings of the romantics. As I have said already, the romantics had in fact not written much that was helpful, because they, like their radical admirers, were after excitement not illumination; and the analyticals had at least done important work on the foundations of argument, including moral argument. But one can understand how an analytical philosopher might be stung by these reproaches into writing *something* about practical issues, however handicapped by his lack of any way of telling good arguments from bad.

Though I am pleased that philosophers now write more about such issues, I do not think they will do so successfully unless they have the desire that philosophers ought to have to give their views rational support. But my main point is that my interest in these questions is not new. I have throughout my career been thinking about them; I do so now with more confidence; and I leave it to others to judge, from my writings in this field, whether I know how to argue about them. If there is a bandwaggon, I was on it long ago. But I should prefer to be judged by my success in illuminating the issues, rather than in following any fashion.

The only other general remark I wish to make besides these autobiographical ones is this. I must draw attention to a distinction made on *MT* 178 between two kinds of question. The first is whether some thesis of mine is correct. The second is whether, if correct, it will achieve the results that I claim for it. It is obviously begging the question if a critic, when seeking to show that it does not achieve these results, uses arguments which assume the falsity of the theory.

For example Professor Nagel (*108/7*) seems to be advancing the following argument. Many people acknowledge agent-relative obligations (e.g. to give priority to their own children). Therefore my theory which (at the critical level) does not admit such obligations, must be wrong. He suggests (correctly) that I would answer this objection by claiming that such obligations are only to be acknowledged at the intuitive level and do not affect the critical level, my views on which Nagel is here attacking.

The question then becomes: *if* my two-level theory is correct, can it answer the objection? My claim that it can is not refuted by saying, as Nagel does: 'If someone . . . claims that there are special obligations and permissions far in excess of what utilitarianism would allow, he can't be refuted by an appeal to the logic of the moral concepts that they both share; because Hare's crucial logical claim, that to prescribe universally is to express a universal desire of a particular kind, embodies the central moral view which is in dispute.' For, first of all, this logical claim embodies no moral views, and certainly not this one, and Nagel has not shown that it does. And secondly, it is clear that *if* my two-level theory were correct it *could* answer this objection by assigning such special obligations to the intuitive level. In order to prevent this answer being made, Nagel has to *assume* that the two-level theory is not correct, which is a *petitio principii*.

Nagel might object that it is I who am guilty of such a *petitio*, because I am assuming that my two-level theory does square with the facts of moral language and moral experience. But this is to misunderstand the argument. My theory of moral reasoning is founded, not on any appeal to, or attempt to square it with, what people generally think about moral questions. It is founded on an examination of the meanings they attach to words, which are revealed most securely, not by what they think right or wrong, but by what they think self-contradictory or what they think logically entails what. So, though the theory can draw some support from the substantial moral opinions that we find people having (see on Williams *191/—6* and refs.), it does not need this support. All it needs is to be able to explain how, given that that is what they mean by the words, and that those are the logical properties that they attribute to them, and given the other facts of their situation, they can have come to those opinions. The explanation may even involve attributing to them ignorance, muddle, and worse; and it does not have to (though it is nice if it can) leave their opinions unscathed.

So it is not open to anyone to argue that, because people hold opinions different from what the theory would support, the theory must be wrong. And, as I said, the argument we are considering is about what the theory will establish, *if* correct, and not about whether it *is* correct. If it is correct, it does really have certain consequences, and can really explain the phenomena of our moral life. But its correctness is *established*, most securely, by an appeal, not to these phenomena, but to the logic of the moral concepts, which we learn by asking what, according to the way people use words, is consistent with what.

Similar moves are commonly made in connection with the very question discussed on the page (*MT* 178) on which I made the distinction that I have been labouring; the question of whether I can deal with the fanatic. My theory of moral reasoning itself is constructed with the aid of logical considerations alone. The question then arises: can the theory deal with the problem of the fanatic, *if* it is correct? If it is correct, the consequences are as I stated above, and it is not open to any objections based on the logical possibility of fanaticism, because it gives a clear account of such a phenomenon. It is no argument against me to claim that this would not be so if it were *not* correct. Its correctness is not what is at issue a that point, but whether *if* correct it would deal with fanaticism.

This enables me to counter a related move, as I do in the preceding passage on *MT* 178. The fanatic might claim that he has a moral conviction that he should pursue his fanatical ideal at whatever cost in suffering. This, he might claim, enables him to resist the argument put forward by me, that he cannot universalize the prescription to cause such suffering in such a case. But it is part of the theory that at the critical level (which is what we are here talking about) no considerations can rationally be appealed to except those of logic and the facts. Moral intuitions, however firmly held, are ruled out as arguments unless they can be rationally supported, which he has not done. *If* this element in the theory is correct, we *can* so deal with the fanatic. If it is incorrect, and moral convictions unsupported by reason are admissible as arguments, then of course the fanatic will win; but what is at issue here is not whether the theory is correct (that is argued elsewhere) but whether it can, *if* correct, answer this objection.

I must end this introduction by expressing my thanks and admiration for the way in which the editors have got this volume together, and steered it through the inevitable difficulties and delays. The initiative was theirs, but I took it up with alacrity, and they have assembled a set of critics of just the sort that it is a pleasure to reply to. The volume was originally to have been called *Hare and Hounds* (defined by Webster (1919) as 'a sport in which . . . the hares . . . scattering bits of paper . . . are chased by others, the hounds, who must, to win, catch them before they return to the starting place'). The title was abandoned as suggesting too much hostility and aggression on the part of the critics; they have indeed been extremely nice to me, and I must apologize to some of them for biting them in a rather unharelike manner. But I hope I have succeeded in returning to the starting place, or even perhaps to one a little further on.

2. Comments on Hudson

9/−6 I cannot thank Professor Hudson enough for the excellent job he has done with his 'restricted space'. My space is restricted too, so I must content myself with a few detailed amplifications and explanations. Hudson's and my references may guide the reader to the fuller accounts given in my writings.

10/−15 I did, and do, follow the emotivists in their rejection of descriptivism. But I was never an emotivist, though I have often been called one. Indeed, I started my career as a moral philosopher by trying to refute the emotivists, whose irrationalism I could not accept. But unlike most of their opponents I saw that it was the irrationalism, not the non-descriptivism, that was mistaken. So my main task was to find a rationalist kind of non-descriptivism, and this led me to establish that imperatives, the simplest kind of prescriptions, could be subject to logical restraints although not descriptive. For more about the relation between descriptive and prescriptive (or evaluative) meanings see H 1986*c*.

11/−19 See also my reply to Warnock in H 1979*d*.

11/−14 I return to the subject of universalizability and the related property of supervenience in H 1984*b*.

12/1 'Indisputable' here has to mean 'logically or conceptually indisputable'. It is not enough that we would all agree in the substantial moral opinion (if that were what it were) that we ought not to discriminate morally between like cases. See *FR* 30 to which Hudson refers.

12/−14 For the distinction between 'universal' and 'general' see also H 1972*a* and *MT* 41. These terms are often confused (I was guilty myself in *LM*). Intuitive principles have, in order to fulfil their role, to be fairly general; but critical principles can be as specific as is needed. One of the sources of the confusion of these critics is a failure to distinguish between the critical and intuitive levels of moral thinking, and a consequent attribution to universalists like me of the absurd view that even at the highest critical level we have to employ the rather general principles that are appropriate in intuitive thinking. In critical thinking one can apply a highly specific but still universal principle even to the most unusual cases, although they may be too unlike ordinary cases to fall under the general principles that we apply to these.

Generality is necessary for intuitive principles, first because if they were not to some degree general we could not learn them; but secondly because, since moral problems resemble one another only in their general features and not absolutely exactly, a highly specific principle would apply to only one, or at most a very few, situations, and so could not serve as the kind of general guide we need. But in critical thinking we can focus on the specific details of a particular problem and find the right answer in that case. In order to do so we may imagine hypothetical cases, absolutely identical in their universal properties, but with the roles reversed, and look for a universal principle covering such cases that we can accept. The fact that there cannot be identical actual cases is no bar to this.

13/1 'To act in accordance with it' and, of course, to have it acted on by others.

13/14 When writing *MT* I divided these ingredients somewhat differently. I had come to see that the inclinations or preferences of all the parties were one kind of relevant matters of fact (*MT* 90 f.) This is important methodologically, because it adds to the tally of ingredients that can be factually ascertained. It is true that both the agent and others can *change* their preferences or inclinations; but that they at any one time have or would have them can be taken as a datum. This does not diminish the freedom and the responsibility of the moral thinker to change his preferences if the moral thinking leads him to.

13/−9 See on Griffin *83/−12* and on Nagel *104/−15*. Charles Taylor (1982) spends a whole paper elaborating this confusion. For a good account, see Griffin 1982. The point is that although we can value many different things, we can at least usually say which we value more than which; and this 'preference-ordering' is all that the utilitarian needs.

14/20 It is important to understand that *moral* preferences and the prescriptions which express them can enter our moral thinking at two different points. (1) They appear first in the crude data about people's preferences from which the thinking has to start. We may find, for example, that someone has a strong moral conviction that wives ought to obey their husbands in all things. He will undoubtedly suffer sorrow and pain if his wife does not do so, because he will think she is doing wrong. This sorrow and pain counts in the reasoning that the moral thinker has to do; but it counts only in the same way as the sorrow and pain that the wife would have to endure if she did obey. (2) When the moral thinker has 'gone the rounds of the affected parties' and represented to himself all these sufferings, he will then have to make a reasoned moral judgement on whether the wife ought to obey or not. The mistake of these critics is to think that (1) is a significant moral consideration in the same way as (2) is. (1) is of course significant; it is part of the data for moral reasoning; but it is not significant *qua* moral conviction (the wife's non-moral preferences count just as much, strength for strength). (2), on the other hand, is significant in a stronger way; since the moral judgement is the conclusion of rational moral thinking, it cannot be abandoned without impugning the reasoning and having to do it all over again. That is why we have to pay much more (indeed a different sort of) regard to the moral deliverances of our own and others' critical thinking than to our and their intuitions. The latter may indeed serve as a useful and humanly speaking indispensable heuristic guide; but the former, if the thinking has been rightly done, give a definitive answer.

15/23 This account of my reply needs some amplification; see *MT* 218–26 to which Hudson refers. My method of reasoning is not a *derivation* or *deduction* of moral conclusions from premises about people's preferences. The judgement it leads to is, rather, what all those who think rationally and are in possession of the facts will say, i.e. the moral prescription that they will accept. They will accept it, not because it is the logical consequence of those facts, but because, assuming that they are not amoralists and therefore are going to make *some* moral judgement about the situation, the full representation to themselves of the preferences of all those affected, and the prescriptions that they thus come to for what should be done to themselves were they in those people's positions, turn out to be logically inconsistent with any other judgement than the one that they then make. This is not a derivation of the moral judgement from facts, first of all because an amoralist could dissent from it (*MT* 219), and secondly because what the imaginative representation of others' positions leads us to are prescriptions, not facts about prescriptions, and these two things are logically distinct. I am not deriving the first from the second; I am saying that one who is making a moral judgement about a situation will, if he is rational, and is informed about the situation, make *that* moral judgement. This implies no equivalence in meaning, or even one-way derivability, between prescriptive and descriptive expressions. My position is thus rationalistic but not descriptivist. But for a full account I must refer the reader to *MT* 218–28.

16/7 It would be a travesty to say that I have omitted reference to human wants (i.e. desires). The whole point of prescriptivism is that it makes moral judgements equivalent to a certain kind of prescriptions, and prescriptions are the expressions of preferences or desires in a broad sense. There must therefore be an intimate relation between (1) moral prescriptions and (2) other prescriptions and preferences of the agent and (via universalizability) of other people. See H 1972*b*: 92 ff.

16/16 Another and complementary reply is that moral reasons are not the same as prudential reasons. The latter have, perhaps, to be traced back exclusively to desires or preferences, present or future, of the agent. But the former have also to take into account the preferences of others affected. Could anybody who understood what morality is deny this? There are prudential reasons for thinking morally (see *MT* ch. 11); but prudential and moral thinking are distinct.

16/−11 It could be wished that moral philosophers would give up needs as a basis for their theories. They will not bear any weight. The word 'need' is etymologically connected in many languages with words for 'necessity' (e.g. the German '*Not*' and '*notwendig*'). If I need something, it is a necessary condition for the realization of some end. To say that somebody needs something is always to say something incomplete, unless we specify what he needs it for, or what it is a necessary condition for. Very often this does not have to be specified because it is so obvious, and that is what has misled these philosophers. But for completeness it has to be specified. This is apparent in the form of the objection here considered. We need food for survival, and survival for 'human flourishing'. We do not need 'human flourishing' (whatever that is) for anything, and therefore it is improper (as anybody who knows the language and can decipher that expression will recognize) to say that we *need* it. We desire it. It is our end or purpose, not a means to an end. To call it a need would imply that it was instrumental to something else. What *constitutes* 'human flourishing' is another question—a question of value which cannot be settled by appealing to needs.

18/12 My answer to both these objections could be summed up by quoting Aristotle against the self-styled 'Aristotelians'. He defines *telos* as *prākton agathon* (good to be achieved by action; *EN* 1141b12, cited in *LM* 99). Therefore settling on an end, like deciding what 'human flourishing' is, is answering an evaluative question. We cannot therefore without circularity answer all evaluative questions by appealing to a *telos* as given. The *telos* of actions is what we desire (*boulometha*) for its own sake (*EN* 1094a18); so there are no ends without desires.

18/−11 For a fuller answer to this criticism, see H 1986*c*. The criticism should attract only those who want to tie themselves hand and foot to the morality of the society, church, or coterie in which they happen to find themselves. It is, as I say there, a primrose path to relativism.

19/−8 My own answer to this criticism is, like Searle's paper reprinted as Hudson (1969). Its main point is that we could not have the institution of promising, nor the word 'promise' in its current sense, unless we accepted the constitutive rule of the institution, namely the substantial moral principle that one ought to keep promises. This is therefore a suppressed premiss in Searle's argument. It is a mistake to think that, because we could not have a word in our language without accepting some substantial principle, the principle itself holds analytically.

21/14 It is not quite accurate to equate my distinction between intuitive and critical moral thinking with that between the acceptance of received opinion and its revision. Even after we have criticized and perhaps revised our intuitive principles, we should still go on using them in our day-to-day intuitive thinking. But Hudson is right in seeing critical thinking as a liberation from the *necessity* of following received opinion.

22/15 For my view on the relation between critical and intuitive moral thinking, see especially on Frankena *51/−13*. For more about the fanatic, see on Gibbard *64/−8* ff.

3. Comments on Brandt

33/19 Up to this point Brandt has given a fair and helpful summary of *MT*. The criticism which follows turns on the question of what has to be my state of mind before I can be said fully to have represented to myself the state of mind, including the preferences, of another person. This is crucial to my own argument, which depends on the premiss that I have *not* fully represented it unless I have formed a preference that, were I in his position with his preferences, those preferences should be satisfied. The premiss is further discussed between Gibbard (*60/−18* ff.) and myself (on Gibbard *64/−8*, the source of the 'big funeral' example of *35/4* below). I wish to stress that I only have to have formed *a* preference. As I explain in H 1984*f*, this preference has to compete with other preferences that I may still have. In *36/15* below Brandt seems to misunderstand this, attributing to me a view that gives a veto to the preference of any single person affected by a proposed action. But since many people are likely to be affected, including the agent himself, all their interests have to be sympathetically considered; none exercises a veto.

Brandt's main objection here is that it must be an empirical and not a conceptual claim that I shall form this 'conditional preference', as Gibbard calls it, if I fully represent to myself the state of mind of the other person (as is necessary for full information about the proposed action, a condition of informed moral judgement). But this is not so. I am treating it as a logically necessary condition for full representation (see *MT* 99). Brandt's example of the thirsty man in *34/16* shows that it is hard (as indeed it often is) fully to represent to oneself one's own future deprivation-states and preferences. The same applies *a fortiori* to one's own hypothetical deprivation-states, were one in the situation of another person with his preferences. It does not show that, if I did fully represent one of these to myself, I might still fail to have the same desire now for then as I should have then for then. For example, if I am told I am going to be whipped, or should be whipped if I were in the other's position, but do not want not then to be whipped as much as I shall or should then want to be whipped, I am just not fully representing the experience to myself. This is a conceptual and not an empirical claim; it is indeed 'a priori psychology'. No doubt causal (e.g. physiological) factors favour or impede full representation; but the connection between full representation and having the desire is conceptual.

This is because the experience that is being represented is a desire. If we try to represent to ourselves what it is like to have a certain desire, we have not succeeded unless there is something in our *present* experience to correspond to what we are trying to represent; and this has to be a desire too. We can utter the words 'I shall be desiring not to be being whipped';

but we shall not really be *thinking what it would be like* unless there is a desire of equal intensity in our present experience, namely the desire not to be being whipped if we are in that situation. The difficulty of fully representing to ourselves absent states of experience (our own or other people's) is one of the main obstacles to good moral thinking—that is obvious. Any theory which makes moral thinking easier than it is in this respect must be wrong; see on Nagel *101/1*. The remedy, for humans, lies in sharpening our sensitivity, and above all in cultivating considerate habits of thought for use at the intuitive level.

33/23 Brandt's point in parentheses, that my argument to act-utilitarianism requires that we have to form a conditional preference corresponding to the *ideal*, not the *actual* preference of the other person, cannot be dealt with fully in the space available. Briefly, the answer is that act-utilitarianism seeks to maximize utility over time for the persons affected. If, therefore a person's present actual preference, if realized, would lead to the frustration of a greater future preference, it is not prudent or ideal. I therefore excluded it by my 'requirement of prudence' (*MT* 105). This 'simplifying assumption', as I called it, could be dispensed with if, instead of universalizing over persons, we universalized over temporal phases of persons. This longer route was taken in an earlier draft of *MT*, but I avoided it in the final version because of its complications. It is clear that if we put ourselves imaginatively, not only in the other person's present position, but in all his future positions, we shall (as he would if prudent) give weight to his preferences at various times in proportion to their strengths, and that thus his actual present preference will be outweighed in our thinking by his future stronger preferences. Thus it will be *as if* we had formed a conditional preference corresponding to his ideal, not his actual, preference. See also on Harsanyi *96/−18*.

On irrational preferences of others, to which Brandt recurs on *36/−5*, my position therefore remains the same as in *MT* 105 f. Brandt has himself given a good account of these (1979, ch. 8), from which I did not think I was dissenting. In *MT* I specifically mentioned Brandt's 'cognitive psychotherapy' as a means of discarding all but prudent preferences. Brandt and I both think that the preferences which have to be considered are those which survive this 'cognitive psychotherapy'. These may include some bizarre ones, but these are not irrational by Brandt's definition, provided that they 'would not extinguish after cognitive psychotherapy' (1979:113), so he cannot be thinking of them here. In my view it is morally right to give equal weight to such bizarre preferences, because, however bizarre, they are important to the people who have them. They may of course be outweighed in our moral thinking by other competing preferences with whose satisfaction they might compete; but this is allowed for in my theory. See *MT* 104 ff.

33/−4 In another parenthesis here Brandt suggests that the *identity* of the other person might make a difference to whether I would form conditional preferences corresponding to his, for the case in which I would be in a position just like his in its universal properties. But how could it? For I am to imagine *myself* in exactly *his* position, with all its universal properties. If I do not form, now, a conditional preference that were I in that position the preferences which a person in that position has should be fulfilled, I am not thinking of the person whom I am imagining being in that position as *myself*. See *MT* 96–8. I cannot see why Brandt thinks that his daughter/chairman example tells against this. Moral thinking requires us, in order to be fully informed, to put ourselves imaginatively in the places of those affected by our actions, and I can do this with sufficient vividness in the case of my daughter and even my chairman in these circumstances. It also requires us (because of universalizability) to ignore their *individual* identities, while taking account of their universal properties (which Brandt rather unhappily calls 'abstract' properties, *27/−1*). If this is done, how is this case different from those discussed by me? The 'vast complications' arise only if individual identity is treated as a universal property, and so has to be reckoned with in moral thinking; but this it cannot be.

36/18 Hypothetical self-interest for the case where one is in someone else's shoes is not selfish; so Kant cannot be accused of egoism.

36/—17 I agree that my theory is equivalent to *a certain form of* Ideal Observer Theory. See *MT* 44 and refs.

36/—2 For a prescriptivist like me there is no further problem of showing why anyone should be interested in whether one ought or ought not. Holding as I do that 'ought' in its relevant uses is prescriptive, and that (*pace* Nagel *104/4*) prescriptions if sincere are expressions of preferences, I think it impossible that one should not prefer universally what one sincerely prescribes universally, i.e. thinks that (in the relevant sense) one ought. The relevant sense is that in which we are asking 'Ought I?' when we are taking the question seriously. If we want to ask different questions, we can, but the serious 'ought'-question remains to plague us (see *MT* 18 f.).

38/3 The fact that diminishing marginal utility makes the strengths of the preferences of different parties for a given outcome different poses no difficulty for my theory. We have to take into account the preferences which each party has, given *his* situation, as affected by this factor. The problem of how to determine how much they are affected is part of the general problem of interpersonal comparison; see below on Griffin, and *MT* 121 ff.

38/18 Of course the fact that there are three persons involved, not two, alters the situation; but this is no objection to my view, which allows alterations in the situation to be taken into account in moral thinking, to the extent that they affect the preferences of the parties.

38/—9 I do not make, but explicitly reject, the suggestion that we have to think of the agent as occupying many positions simultaneously (see Brandt's quotation from *MT*, below).

39/13 See on Vendler *173/15*. Objectors on logical grounds to putting oneself imaginatively in the shoes of more than one person should read the whole of Blake's poem cited in *MT* 99, and notice what Blake thinks God can do. I have admitted that a divine or at least archangelic mind is required for perfect moral thinking (which is why humans need the intuitive level). But even humans can sometimes form a sufficiently good idea of what it is like to be each of several other people in a given situation; they can then think what it

would be like for them themselves to be in those persons'
shoes, and form their preferences accordingly. To balance
these preferences against one another seems then to create no
insuperable problem. This process of thought is what is
dramatized in C. I. Lewis's construction. I also mention the
alternative proposal (*MT* 129) that they might think of
themselves as having equal chances of being in each of the
situations. Brandt does not refer to this proposal, which is due
to Harsanyi (ref. on *MT* 128). Neither proposal gives us
exactly what is required in order to understand the situation
of the perfect moral thinker. The Lewis proposal has the
disadvantage that the *order* in which we were to occupy the
different lives might make a difference. For this reason I said
that we were to think of ourselves as occupying them in
random order. This alteration, by introducing equiprobability,
makes this scenario very like the other. They are both only
devices for getting us to think as Blake says God thinks:

> He doth give His joy to all;
> He becomes an infant small;
> He becomes a man of woe;
> He doth feel the sorrow too.

Blake evidently sees no difficulty in God summing up and
balancing all these feelings.

39/−8 It makes a difference that my theory operates not with
the notion of 'happiness/well-being' but with that of (global)
preference-satisfaction (see Griffin, 1982, 1986). Here again
the link between preferences and prescriptions is important
(*36/−2* above). We can prescribe other things than happiness
for ourselves, but can we sincerely prescribe other things than
what we (all in all) prefer? Is not our all-in-all prescription, if
sincere, the expression of our all-in-all preference?

40/6 The suggestion that somebody's moral thinking might
give weight to some ideals (e.g. equality) which were
independent of what anybody preferred is dealt with in *MT*
(esp. 176 ff.) under the heading of 'fanaticism'. So far as ideals
are the reflection of preferences, they get weight in moral
thinking, on my view, in proportion to the strengths of the
preferences and the numbers of those who have them. The
issue therefore is whether someone can rationally give an ideal

any more weight than this. See on Singer *157/9*. My argument
is that he cannot do this *rationally*, because giving this weight
involves the introduction into the argument of premisses
supplied by moral intuitions for which reasons cannot be
given. See *MT* 40. It can be admitted that if equality increases
preference-satisfactions, there will be a good argument in
critical thinking for adopting intuitive principles which
promote it. And the archangel will encourage us to cleave to
these intuitions in all ordinary situations. But if somebody
says 'I am just never going to admit into my critical thinking
any derogation of the pursuit of the ideal of equality', and
gives no reason why equality should have this priority, he is
thinking irrationally. That is what the person in Brandt's
example seems to be doing.

40/−11 The reasoning will 'come out where the act-utilitarian
would' if preferences count in it according to their strengths
(as they rationally must, because no reason can be given for
any other weighting). I here invoke something analogous to
the 'Principle of Insufficient Reason'. If some super-fanatic
has *such* a strong preference for equality that it outweighs all
the preferences of all those who will suffer from its pursuit in
this case, then a utilitarian will allow him to have his way
(*MT* 181). For example, if in the car/cycle example the cyclist,
when he thinks of the affluent motorist not having to walk to
the store, is so shocked and appalled that his suffering
outweighs that of the motorist if he walks, it is rational to say
that the cycle ought to be left where it is. That is what the case
has to be like before we can rationally say that the motorist
ought to be made to walk; but this is in accordance with
utilitarianism. If we go beyond this, and allow the cyclist
without argument to bump up the weight to be given to his ideal
above what critical thinking can justify, we are being
irrational. This is the *rationale* behind the opinion (which
Brandt and I share) that 'equality should be brought about
only to the extent that maximizing long-run benefit requires'
(*41/−19*). But for the problem posed by the fanatic see further
on Gibbard *64/−8* ff., where I discuss an alternative solution
before returning to that favoured in *MT*. The question at issue
there is whether preferences which are not for one's own
actual or hypothetical *experiences* are subject to the 'Conditional

Reflection Principle' and therefore enter into our moral thinking. Clearly the egalitarian cyclist's preference for equality is of this 'external' kind, and what we say about it will depend on our answer to that question.

41/—4 See on *33/23* above.

4. Comments on Frankena

43/13 Frankena, in this initial account of my views, uses a method which one might call 'exposition by misinterpretation'. This, though legitimate and sometimes even helpful, may mislead the reader unless accompanied by a warning. He starts here with an explanation of my two-level theory which is so oversimplified as to amount to a travesty. He then (*45/17*) introduces the necessary complications and qualifications. Most of them he initially extracts from my writings; but where he thinks these unclear, he asks for further elucidations, which I shall try to provide. I fear that an incautious reader, in spite of the later disavowals, might think that Frankena is attributing to me the crude views with which he starts. But I do *not* think that intuitive principles should always be 'acquired somehow but not by the use of any kind of critical thinking or reflection' (*44/1*; cf. *MT* 47 ff. and *passim*); I do *not* think that intuitive principles can be treated as overriding (*44/17*; cf. *MT* 60); and I do *not* think that 'theoretically at least, MT can take either form and so need not have a two-level structure' (*44/19*)—at any rate, not if 'can' means 'can with any hope of suiting our human condition'. This initial account is of a theory which holds, unlike mine, that the two 'kinds' of MT (as Frankena calls them) could for humans exist in isolation from each other.

48/19 What Frankena calls 'thesis A' is also oversimplified. I have indeed in *MT* 46 subscribed to the thesis as an account of 'right' in one of its senses. But it is also possible that we sometimes *within* intuitive thinking call acts right if they are in accordance with our intuitive prima-facie principles and wrong if they are not. See on Scanlon *129/6*. 'Prima facie right' would be a good term for this use, which might commend itself to an intuitionist like Ross. As I have said many times, the account which intuitionists give of intuitive moral thinking is not in itself wrong but rather incomplete; its fault is to imply that this is the only level of moral thinking that we need. When intuitions are in conflict or called in question, we need a way of deciding what is right that is independent of intuitions. Critical thinking supplies this.

49/11 ff. On rules of thumb see *MT* 38. The expression, as Williams (*190/–12*) realizes, should not be used in speaking of my theory. Frankena himself cites my reason for distinguishing between rules of thumb and my 'prima-facie principles': that the breach of rules of thumb does not excite compunction, because they are not 'associated . . . with very firm and deep dispositions and feelings'.

He also says that, for all that, the two might have logically and epistemically the same status. But I do not think that Frankena has given a correct account of the logical and epistemic status even of rules of thumb. The right way to choose a rule of thumb for when to plant parsnips is, as he says, 'on the basis of previous experience'; but this experience should not consist of trying out different rules of thumb and rejecting those that give bad results. Experimental horti-culturalists do not start with rules of thumb at all; they carry out tests of various planting times, ascertain the quite complicated rules by following which one gets the most profitable crop (depending on the fluctuations of the weather, market prices, etc.), and only then work out a simpler rule, easier to remember and follow, which will yield an approximation to this optimum.

Sometimes the right procedure for choosing rules of thumb is not empirical at all. In gunnery the 'rule of ranging' which bids us 'bracket' rather than 'creep' ought not to be based merely inductively on the bad results of past creepings and the good results of past bracketings, but rather on the geometrical truth that if we have bracketed the target (i.e. landed one round short of it and one beyond it) we have added to our knowledge: we know that the target lies between those two ranges; whereas, however many rounds creeping up short of the target we fire, the target may be thousands of yards further off for all we know. Hence the rule to start with two rounds 400 yards apart and then, if they bracket the target, one half-way between, and so on.

So Frankena's suggestion (1) is wrong, not merely because my prima-facie principles have different emotional accompaniments from rules of thumb, but also because he has not correctly specified the right way to come by rules of thumb *or* prima-facie principles. Of both, what I say in the passage he cites *(51/−11)* is correct, but, as I say, the explanation follows later, and the italicized words do not bear the interpretation he gives them. So his suggestion (1) is to be rejected.

50/7 Suggestion (2) appears to differ from (1) mainly in that the cases considered are not actual and previous but hypothetical or foreseen. Both kinds of case can test a principle; but in my view the principles we should have are not those that survive such tests in single cases, as a Popperian method would require; rather, we look at the global effects of cultivating or adopting a principle (see below). In *FR* 87 ff. I was not speaking about how to select prima-facie principles by critical thinking, but rather about how to test *critical* principles by seeing whether we could accept their logical consequences.

50/−8 Suggestion (3) is nearer the mark. But though I have learnt a lot from Brandt, I cannot find in my text, even in the passage which Frankena cites, any justification for this complete assimilation of my views to Brandt's. As I explain in *MT* 43 and refs., and on Harsanyi *92/20*, my view combines the valid features of rule- and act- utilitarianism; and one of these is brought out in this passage. But though Brandt's method may not involve the use of CMT which Frankena calls CMT1, my own procedure, explained in the next note, does make use of it.

51/−13 In order to evaluate Frankena's suggestions (4) and (5), it will be clearer to start by explaining what my actual recommended procedure for selecting prima-facie principles is like. We may then be able to see whether his ranging shots have bracketed the target. I must admit that in *MT* I was more concerned with establishing that there has to be a two-level structure of the kind I sketched, and that the highest level (Frankena's CMT1) was of a utilitarian sort and justified by the logic of the moral concepts, than in explaining in detail how we should use it in order to select prima-facie principles for use at the intuitive level. To that extent my account was unclear. I am grateful to Frankena for making me clarify further the relation between the levels of thinking, although I think that it is only by some rather perverse interpretations that he produces an appearance of inconsistency between the hints that I gave of what the relation should be.

Let us start by supposing that the procedure of selecting prima-facie principles is being used by a perfect, archangelic thinker, but that the principles, once selected, are to be used by a human thinker. The archangel will be able to do CMT1 perfectly. He will also know all the circumstances in which his pupil will have to use the prima-facie principles selected, and what will be the consequences of all the actions he performs as a result of adopting them. These consequences will include the consequences of the series of acts involved in the cultivation of the dispositions to obey these principles. And he will have the same information about the comparable acts of cultivating and observing the principles by other members of his pupil's society. He will know the likelihood of all these people actually observing on different occasions the principles they are trying to cultivate. And he will know the probability of these different kinds of occasion occurring in the lives of the different members of the society.

So far I have only scratched the surface of what the archangel has to know in order to make a good job of selecting prima-facie principles. But I have done enough already to show why I did not think it possible in a short book to go into the matter in detail, and also why human beings, unlike archangels, cannot do this kind of thinking very well (though they can do it after a fashion, and after many generations do succeed in getting for themselves a serviceable set of principles, albeit capable of improvement).

Armed with information of this sort the archangel, who, it must be remembered, is an act-utilitarian, will opt for the set of principles for a society, and modified sets of such principles for each individual within the society, such that the cultivation of the disposition to observe them will lead to the maximal satisfaction of the preferences of those affected. This satisfaction

will be made greater or less by the following factors at least.
(1) The immediate costs and benefits of the acts which
constitute the cultivation-process (e.g. the rigours of self-
discipline, the sufferings of the young while being brought up
not to be nasty to their little sisters, etc.). (2) The extent to
which, when they have made a shot at cultivating these
dispositions, the members of the society will actually succeed
in acting accordingly. (3) The costs of securing, or trying to
secure, future compliance when they have not succeeded.
(4) The extent of the benefits (i.e. preference-satisfactions)
that accrue from such compliance as takes place, and also the
extent of the costs. (5) The probabilities of all these
consequences occurring. (6) The 'expectation effects' in
Harsanyi's sense (*91/15*).

Obviously I have only made a beginning; but the archangel
will need to know at least all this. How will he then select the
principles for the education of his pupils? Remember that he is
an act-utilitarian. He will therefore concern himself with the
consequences for good or ill, taken together, of all the *acts*
which constitute this whole education-process, and all the *acts*
to which the education leads. I think that this is what a wise
human educator does when deciding how to educate his
children; but of course the archangel can do it incomparably
better.

I should have made my view on all this clearer if, instead of
taking over the expression 'acceptance-utility', which I now
see to be ambiguous, I had used the more cumbrous
expression 'utility of cultivating and (perhaps only incompletely) following'. The utility in question (expressed in
terms of preference-satisfactions) is that of the whole series of
acts comprising the cultivation and following (probably
incomplete) of the dispositions. It is thus apparent that
Frankena's suggestions so far are all for one reason or another
defective.

Even this brief summary does something to justify my claim
that I am both an act- and a rule-utilitarian. For the
dispositions I have been speaking of are close to what are
called in the literature 'rules'; and the utility of having them
enables me to answer (as in *MT* 130 ff.) those tedious critics
who go on claiming that an act-utilitarian like me will have,

on unusual occasions, to commend or condone acts contrary
to these good dispositions (e.g. truthfulness). But I am still an
act-utilitarian, because what we are, essentially, selecting are
acts of cultivating and following the various dispositions. In
judging these acts (which has to be done globally in the light
of the consequences of the whole nexus of acts) we are to use
critical thinking (Frankena's CMT1). There are not two
kinds, but only two uses of critical thinking (he himself says
'using' in *53/—3*). The thought-process I have just sketched
consists in amassing a lot of information and then judging acts
morally in the light of their probable consequences.

It might be claimed that the archangel will not need to
concern himself with probabilities, because he knows with
certainty what would happen. This is not, however, a real
difficulty. For an omniscient being probability collapses into
frequency. The archangel will know the frequency with which
certain types of circumstances will arise, and the frequency
with which certain kinds of acts will have certain kinds of
consequences. In explaining to his pupil the reasons for the
choice of the various principles selected, he will naturally
translate these frequencies into probabilities; he will say
things like 'If you form the habit of telling lies, you will
probably do more harm than good'; but he will know the
frequencies of harmful and beneficial lie-telling on which this
calculation of probability is based. Only in this way does my
account bring in frequencies.

51/—6 I might equally have said 'if one is an act-utilitarian'.
The above account, while benefiting from the rule-utilitarian
insights of Brandt and Harsanyi, is perfectly consistent with
act-utilitarianism. And the words that Frankena omits from
the quotation that follows ('say in effect the same thing') are
crucial to an understanding of my Kantian utilitarian
position. My method is not rule-utilitarian in quite Brandt's
sense; but it is, in the sense that it justifies the cultivation and
following of dispositions (rules) by the utility of these (series
of) acts of cultivation and following, and bids us *at the intuitive
level* do our moral thinking (decide what we ought to do) in
conformity to these rules. It thus secures the advantages
claimed for rule-utilitarianism.

52/19 'More often' implies a 'frequency'-theory. Frankena does not cite passages from *MT* in which I imply this; but if there are any, they were slips. It is the global consequences of cultivating and (as fully as humans are likely to) following the dispositions that have to be judged by critical thinking when the archangel is selecting the dispositions, and not the mere frequency with which they will lead to acts occurring which are such as critical thinking would approve. One reason is that a single really bad act (say a brutal murder) would obviously outweigh a great number of peccadilloes, as Frankena sees (below). Another is that the series of acts has to be judged globally; on this, see Griffin 1986. The quotations at the end of this paragraph do not justify the ascription to me of a 'frequency'-theory; 'the greatest possible conformity to what an archangel would pronounce' is not secured by committing one murder and so avoiding a score of peccadilloes; but this *would* maximize the frequency of (single) conforming actions.

53/6 'The *net* cost vs. benefit of the *series* of acts' is right. But the subsequent working out of this idea by Frankena would tie me to something that I do not wish to be tied to: the view that the global utility of a series of acts is the same as the sum of the utilities of the single acts in the series. Griffin (l.c.) is good on this.

53/−11 Though I try hard to keep the theses advanced in my *books* consistent, and to flag places in which a change of view is expressed, I have felt at liberty to try out tentative theses in my published papers, to be perhaps modified when they are incorporated into books. However, I do not on this point see any inconsistency between what I say in H 1979*b* and *MT*.

53/−2 Acts of cultivating dispositions are, as already explained, one kind of acts, and are judged like the others by critical thinking in its global assessment. Almost all acts are to some degree self-educative (see Aristotle, *Nicomachean Ethics*, 1103a34). The distinction made in H 1979*b* was not intended to imply otherwise. Some acts are *especially* self-educative (for example, acts involved in learning to suffer fools gladly). But the assessment of these by critical thinking is no different in principle from that of those which are so to a lesser degree. The distinction is therefore somewhat overworked in

Frankena's (6a). We should, on this suggestion, end up applying CMT1 to pretty well all our acts to some degree, so that (6a) and (6b) would not be so different. For example if we found ourselves *not* suffering a fool gladly, we should pull ourselves up *both* because it led to less than optimal consequences on that occasion, *and* because we were getting into bad habits. For this and other reasons Frankena's (6b) is preferable to his (6a), and indeed gets quite close to the position which I actually prefer.

54/−10 The difficulty here is the same as that of using CMT for any purpose—a difficulty which I have always acknowledged. That is why, in discussing here how CMT should proceed, I have supposed that it is being used by an archangel. As I said earlier, humans can do it after a fashion, and (for want of archangels to advise them) have sometimes to try to, when they are in the right circumstances and frame of mind. And over the generations we have achieved something like it. We should not be misled, by the fact that what this has resulted in are some pretty firm moral convictions, into thinking that we need not do any critical thinking ever again. Our forebears were, perhaps, quite wise, but not infinitely so.

56/−1 I must say in conclusion that both Frankena's contribution and my own commentary on it bring back happy memories of conversations I had with him during a wonderful week I spent at Ann Arbor in November 1984 discussing my ideas with him, Brandt, Gibbard and others. I am immensely grateful to them all for helping me to clarify my thought; but I cannot at this stage say with confidence how many of the clarifications are due to them and how many to myself.

5. Comments on Gibbard

59/4 'A conditional preference is a preference I actually have for a hypothetical circumstance. It may not be a preference I *would* have if I were in that circumstance.' Here Gibbard, unlike many writers, gets this important point right. See *MT* 95.

59/−2 I have always, I think, taken universality, as used in my arguments from universalizability, in the sense of Gibbard's *strong universality.* His *weak universality* seems to me an implausible thesis, and is not enough to support my arguments. In what follows I shall therefore argue on the basis of strong universality, i.e. his *stringent reading.*

60/−6 When I wrote *MT* I was conscious of leaving 'unfinished business' (*MT* 104 f.). I had a strong inclination to apply the Conditional Reflection Principle to all preferences, but, because of difficulties connected with Prof. Dworkin's 'external preferences' (1977:234), decided not to make such a comprehensive claim. Gibbard not only interprets my intention correctly, but suggests what may be a way out of the difficulty (see below).

62/17 Here too Gibbard, unlike many writers, gets me right. See *MT* 99.

64/−8 I greatly admire the elegant formality with which Gibbard has addressed a problem that has long troubled me—in effect that of the fanatic, coupled with another problem which is in some respects analogous, that of external preferences. For the analogy between the two problems, see *MT* 104–6. Gibbard's constant K represents a combination of what in my more informal discussion of the fanatic (*FR*, ch. 9, *MT*, ch. 10) I called 'fanatical ideals', with what I called, following Dworkin, 'external preferences' (*MT* 104). K is the balance of the preferences we may have after what Gibbard calls 'basic preferences' and what he calls 'sympathetic preferences' have been accounted for. 'Basic preferences' are preferences that are self-pertinent and rationally required (Gibbard gives as an example the preference not forthwith to suffer—*63/9*); sympathetic preferences are those we acquire, owing to the operation of the Conditional Reflection Principle, as a result of our representation to ourselves of the basic preferences of others.

Gibbard contemplates the possibility of two kinds of preference which are neither basic nor sympathetic. One of these consists of preferences which are self-pertinent but not rationally required, like Cheops's preference for a big funeral (*61/11, 70/12*). This is, also, a preference for something other than an experience of the preferrer. Gibbard thinks it possible that I, or someone else other than Cheops, might fully represent to myself the situation of Cheops with this preference, but nevertheless not myself acquire a preference that, were I in the situation of Cheops with Cheops's preferences, I should have a big funeral.

This would imply a restriction on the Conditional Reflection Principle, as stated on *MT* 99 and cited by Gibbard (*60/−17*). I did not in *MT* want to place any restriction on this principle, although I did provisionally exclude from consideration preferences that are incompatible with the 'requirement of prudence'. This demands an overriding preference for the maximal satisfaction of our now-for-now and then-for-then preferences. It would have the effect of ruling out from consideration Cheops's preference for a big funeral, which is a now-for-then preference. I decided similarly to exclude provisionally all external preferences (*MT* 104–6).

The other, overlapping, kind of preference which could be included in *K* is the preference of the fanatic that things should universally happen, independently of how they affect his or anybody else's experiences. I say 'overlapping', because, like ordinary moral preferences, it is universalized, and therefore entails some external preferences for what should happen to other people. Contrast the desires mentioned on Harsanyi *97/2* (first para.).

Such a fanatical preference will not be a basic preference as defined; nor will it be a sympathetic preference, since these are all the result of representing to ourselves others' basic preferences. As Gibbard says (*67/−4*), if I could show that *K* was null (i.e. that there were no preferences except basic and sympathetic ones) I should have proved an important part of my utilitarian thesis. The possibility that *K* might not be null was the reason why in *FR* I thought that the fanatic was a problem for me, and why in *MT* I swept the problem of external preferences and autofanatical now-for-then preferences temporarily under the carpet. I said on *MT* 106 that this was unlikely to make a practical difference to our moral thinking; but I postponed the task of showing this.

As a result of Gibbard's discussion I am inclined to choose between two alternatives. The first is to continue to insist on the 'requirement of prudence' of *MT* 105, and exclude all other now-for-then preferences from consideration except that which it imposes, namely 'a dominant or overriding preference now that the satisfaction of our now-for-now and then-for-then preferences should be maximized'; and also bar from consideration all external preferences. Gibbard has provided me with a very good way of doing this, if I chose to take it. This would be to say that these excluded preferences, since they do not obey the Conditional Reflection Principle, simply cannot enter into moral thinking of the sort that I am giving an account of. In this kind of thinking, Cheops's preference for a big funeral will cut no ice. And the same will be true of the fanatic's preference, for example, that homosexuals be put in prison whether this enters into his experience or not. On homosexuals see on Harsanyi *96/—18*.

This short way with now-for-then and external preferences seems attractive. We could just disregard in our moral thinking preferences like Cheops's. There would be a minor disadvantage, in that I should no longer have available what I used to think a convenient answer to the 'death-bed promise' objection to utilitarianism. I shall return to this and other similar objections in discussing Scanlon *138/15*. The objection points to the counter-intuitiveness of the position, to which utilitarians are thought to be committed, that death-bed promises can be disregarded if that marginally increases utility. The answer is that if utility is interpreted as preference-satisfaction, the strong preference which the dead man had that the promise should be honoured will count in our moral thinking, and so make it come out with a more intuitively acceptable answer. In universal-prescriptivist terms, I shall not readily prescribe that people should break promises to me even after I am dead, so I shall not readily prescribe universally that this should be done. This answer would cease to be available if preferences, and thus prescriptions, for events after one's death were ruled out of court.

But it may be that the utilitarian does not need this answer; he can rely on the general answer to charges of counter-intuitiveness provided in *MT*, ch. 8, which seems to apply to this case. We have an intuition that important promises should be kept, and it is good that we have it; therefore we are outraged that a promise should be broken when the promisee attached great importance to it. The cultivation of a disposition to disregard death-bed promises would do more harm than good. It is clear how the argument would proceed. So perhaps I ought to forget about the 'convenient answer' and avail myself of Gibbard's short way of getting out of difficulties with external and now-for-then preferences.

However, this will not do for the fanatic. We cannot rule his preferences out of court so easily. This is because, as Gibbard sees, they are strongly universal, albeit, in his expression, idiosyncratic (*72/13*, cf. *FR* 162). If somebody has such a great preference that homosexuals be put in prison, that he is prepared to prescribe that he himself be put in prison if he were a homosexual, even if he fully represents to himself the sufferings of the homosexual in prison, we cannot argue with him. Admittedly, he cannot argue with us either, if we are not bound to form preferences similar to this for the case where we are in his position. This will be so if the Conditional Reflection Principle is qualified in the way just suggested to exclude from its operation external preferences (of which this fanatical preference is one).

Dissatisfaction with this impasse inclines me to do without the 'short way' just described and instead go on taking the line followed in *MT* 176–82. This consists in treating the fanatic's idiosyncratic universal preference in just the same way as all the other preferences which enter into our moral thinking. Either it is great enough, even given the strong universality requirement and the Conditional Reflection Principle and full representation of the preferences of others, to outweigh all the others' preferences, or it is not. If it is not, he loses the argument. If it is, then the existence of this super-fanatic (unrealizable in practice) is no counter-example to utilitarianism or to my theory, because in his extraordinary unrealizable case both would prescribe that he should have his way.

In other words, I have the alternatives of either taking the 'short way' of saying that external preferences do not count in moral thinking (in which case we are left, *vis-à-vis* the fanatic, in the theoretically weak but practically tolerable position of *FR*); or else saying that external preferences do count, in which case I shall have to find a longer way of avoiding the counter-intuitiveness of allowing them to count. When I wrote

MT I thought that such a longer way might be found, and it still may be. So on the whole I prefer to wait for this way, and deal with the fanatic as in *MT*.

69/−3 I agree that on the assumption that rational preferences are all either basic or sympathetic, my utilitarian conclusion follows. But I am not clear whether this is an empirical assumption. It contains the word 'rational'. A preference is rational, as defined by Gibbard (*61/−10*), so long as the person whose preference it is would retain it if he were ideally knowledgeable. But what counts as being 'ideally knowledgeable'? Suppose that someone claims to realize fully everything involved (*69/−2*). Are we sure that his claim can be true if he does not form a corresponding preference for his own similar hypothetical case? For example, suppose that I realize fully what it is like to be Cheops wanting a big funeral. Is it entirely an empirical question whether I shall have the same preference as Cheops for the case where I am Cheops? Perhaps if I *fully* represent to myself my own hypothetical state, were I in Cheops's state of preference, and am really thinking of the person in it as *myself*, I shall form a like conditional preference. If I do not, perhaps it will be said that I have not entirely fulfilled these conditions—that I have not become ideally knowledgeable or rational (*70/11*). See on Brandt *33/19*, para. 2, though that is a rather different case.

So the argument to the conclusion in *72/−1*, that if different archangels have different personal ideals then not all archangels will agree, depends on the assumption—the empirical nature of which I have just been questioning—being both empirical and false.

72/−1 Archangels with idiosyncratic universal preferences are fanatics (no offence meant!). I have discussed above alternative ways in which I might deal with them.

6. Comments on Griffin

74/−15 ff. The 'primary goods' approach and the 'objective list' approach are closely related and likely to share the same faults. How close an 'informed desire' approach is to an 'objective list' approach will depend on what is on the list.

The fault of some objective lists is that no method has been given for constructing them. They may just have been picked out of an intuitive bag, which contains no *information* at all. If, on the other hand, the list were constructed on the basis of an appeal to informed desire, then the approaches would be close. But, as we shall see, it is important to be clear on the question, *about what* desire has to be informed. Has it to be informed just about the descriptive properties of the object of desire? Or has it to be informed about their *desirability*? If the former, then different people's desires might be fully informed, and yet they still might not desire the same things. So on that alternative no 'objective list' could be constructed. See below on *82/6* for how to overcome this obstacle to agreement. If the latter, then we shall need a prior list of what things are desirable, in order that the information with which the desire is equipped can be certified as correct. But in that case, in order to construct an 'objective list' of goods, we should have already to have an 'objective list' of desirables.

76/18 This is a very clear statement of the problem that faces me. My solution to it relies, first of all, on a *tu quoque* addressed to anybody who sees no difficulty in *intra*personal comparisons of preference-strengths, but cavils at *inter*personal ones. Most of us take it as obvious, unless we are radical sceptics about the reliability of memory, that we *can* make *intra*personal comparisons between the strengths of our own preferences at different times. But, since even our very basic preferences many change, it cannot be that this requires us to assess the strengths on the basis of our preferences *at the time of making the comparison* (see the example of my reflection in retrospect on my Italian holiday in *MT* 124 f.). That is, it must be possible to do this without appealing to our current preferences.

But, I argue, the interpersonal case is analogous. Given the same sort of true imaginative representation of others' experience as our memory gives us of our own, we ought to be able to compare them likewise. But if we assume, as Griffin allows me to, a solution to the 'other minds' problem, we can in principle have such a true imaginative representation. I leave undiscussed the question of what the solution is, and of *how* we are to achieve this true representation; I think that this is a problem which nearly all philosophers have to face (*MT* 118 f.). But, given a solution to it, we have a basis for interpersonal comparisons just like that which memory gives us for intrapersonal ones.

This does not, so far, go all the way to solving the interpersonal comparison problem, because, as Griffin sees, we still have to be able to compare the preferences that we imagine ourselves having in respect of their strengths. But, as Griffin also sees, we have by this manœuvre at least divided up the problem. So, if we can assume the solution of one part of it, what remains may be more tractable.

77/−15 Here Griffin innocently makes a move which will get him into great trouble later on. He assumes that all preferences have to be *on the basis of* something. In a sense this is true, because we have to know between what we are forming a preference. But this requires only a *descriptive* basis; we have to know what the experiences between which we are forming a preference are, were, or would be like. We do not have to have a basis for our preference in the sense of a temporally or even a logically antecedent preference-set. When presented with a choice between two entirely new and unfamiliar experiences that I have just had, I can say which of them I prefer. What I say will express the preference I have formed; but in order to form it I did not have to have it already; nor does the preference somehow act as a logical basis for itself, or justify itself. I do not form the new preference on the basis of a preference; I just form it. See *MT* 125 and H 1979c.

Because he makes this false move, Griffin is led to think that, lacking any other basis for my preference, I have to appeal to 'the framework of a set of values that apply to everyone'—i.e. to an 'objective list'. But I can prefer one thing to another without having a basis of *this* kind; so the problem for which he adopts the dubious solution does not arise.

Putting this point together with the one I made on *74/−15 ff.* above, we can say that he slips, from the true thesis that in order to form an informed preference we have truly to represent to ourselves the descriptive properties of the experiences between which the choice lies, to the false thesis that we cannot form it unless we have a true list of values, i.e. of what is *preferable*. This confuses knowing what the experiences would be with knowing how desirable they would be or which would be preferable, and thus confuses forming a preference informed by the former piece of knowledge with forming it on the basis of the latter (supposed) piece.

At this point it is important to notice that the nature of the problem is not quite what Griffin supposes. His solution (telling how much *a particular person* prefers something by appeal to our knowledge of how much *people* prefer it) cannot be a solution to *this* problem. For what we are trying to decide is what *this person* prefers or values, and that is (in one sense of that confusing word) a subjective question. Griffin seems to be looking for an objective answer to it; but we do not need that, though we do need a *factual* answer to it (which would be objective in another sense of the word in which even subjective facts are objective). An 'objective list' of values would be of no help here, unless we assume what is clearly false, that *anyone* is bound to prefer what *most people* prefer.

The question of objective vs. subjective values is thus hardly relevant to Griffin's problem, and I shall therefore go into it, not here, but when commenting on Singer's discussion of Mackie's views (Singer *151/12*).

78/6 ff. What is needed for forming a preference is not a 'point of view'; we form the point of view *in* forming the preference. What is needed, rather, if the preference is to be informed, is true knowledge of what we are preferring to what. This is provided on my assumptions.

78/−9 We have not merely to 'give shape to our inchoate and unenlightened desires'. This would imply that they already existed to be given shape to, which is not always the case. Sometimes we have to, and can, form new desires. On *88/−16* Griffin says something different and more correct: 'In first forming a preference between the options, I give expression to a value. I do not consult a value that is already built into me in the form of a utility function of one sort or another; on the contrary, I create and give shape to part of my utility function', i.e. to a value in the 'subjective' sense (see on Singer *151/12*).

78/−2 See on *77/−15* above. So far from its being the case that 'without [the values] I would have no preferences', it is rather the case that without the preferences I would not have the values.

79/−13 'How do I get these two strong desires on to one scale?' See *MT* 128 f.

80/16 See on *77/−15* above. It is not requisite for informed preference-ordering that we have a scale of preferability or desirability to 'appeal' to; so, *a fortiori*, we do not need a 'ground for interpersonal comparisons' consisting in 'the things that are desirable for persons generally'. What have 'persons generally' to do with it?

81/7 There is no space to discuss in detail Griffin's treatment of the 'Socrates/fool' example. It still seems to me that either I or Socrates himself can, by forming true representations of the lives of Socrates and the fool, form also a preference, unbiased by antecedent preferences of our own, between the two lives, on the hypothetical assumption that we were going to live them.

82/6 I cannot be sure in what sense these are not personal preferences. Griffin's use of the expression here is clearly different from Dworkin's (1977:234). They are at any rate preferences of the person who has them, but between hypothetical situations, in the light of his 'perception of the nature of the two lives'. They are formed 'from scratch . . . from an understanding of the objects before us'. With this I agree; but (see on *74/−15* ff. above) 'understanding' means understanding of their nature, not of their objective or generally accepted value; and though the judger judges from his own particular point of view, the exclusion of appeal to his own antecedent preferences or values means that any judge who truly represented to ,himself the situations-cum-preferences would form the same order of preference. This order of preference is thus objective in the sense that all rational informed judges, judging from a universal point of view which excludes their own other preferences, will share it.

In short, 'objectivity' (by which I mean here merely uniqueness and agreement by competent judges) is to be achieved, not, as Griffin thinks, by *bringing in* the preferences of people in general, but by *keeping out* both these and the other preferences of the judger, and making him attend merely to the preferences of the people whose preferences he is comparing. All competent judges will agree, because we have, while giving to all of them all the relevant information about what they are comparing, withheld from them the only thing that could make them differ, namely their own other preferences.

82/13 The judger's personal preferences are irrelevant, in so far as they consist of the 'other preferences' I have just excluded. But in so far as they consist of the preferences for hypothetical states of himself which he forms when he fully represents to himself the situations he is comparing, they are the only things relevant to an 'objective' interpersonal comparison of preferences (though other preferences might be relevant to a *moral judgement*, e.g. the preferences of other affected parties including himself: see H 1976*a*:120). They are still preferences *of his*, and are relevant because he has to do the judging.

83/15 For the 'ancient question' ('Are things valuable because desired, or desired because valuable?') see on Singer *151/12*. I agree with Griffin that the right answer is, 'Neither'.

83/−12 People do indeed value irreducibly different things, and therefore there is no single overarching value; see on Nagel *104/−15* and Hudson *13/−1*.

84/7 As I said on *77/−15 s.f.* above, we are concerned here with a question of what values or desires a particular person has in the 'subjective' sense (see on Singer *151/12*). So Griffin's pursuit here of 'objectivity', even in the mild form of intersubjectivity, is hardly to the point. But I agree that the distinction between 'objective' and 'subjective' marks no important difference here.

84/19 The answer to the question 'How do we determine whether one person's preference is stronger than another's?' may involve two stages of inquiry, which have to be distinguished. The first consists in obtaining a true picture of the other's state. It is at this stage that we may usefully appeal to information 'based on causal knowledge of human nature' of what preferences *people generally* have. For example, if people generally do not like eating mud, we may fairly confidently predict that a particular person will not like it. I think that

Griffin may have made the mistake of confusing this predictive stage, at which we can legitimately appeal to the fact that certain values are generally accepted, with the next, comparative, stage, at which, having satisfied ourselves that we have a true picture of his state, we then ask how his preferences compare in strength with those of another person of whose state we have also acquired, by similar means, a true picture. At this later stage, since we are asking about *these people's* preferences, and not about those of *people generally*, the latter have ceased to be relevant. The two stages are distinguished in *MT* 124 ff., but, because they are interwoven in the discussion, it is perhaps unclear. The predictive stage has already been taken to be superable with the hoped-for solution of the other-minds problem. *MT* 124–6 deals with the comparative problem. The predictive problem is taken up again briefly on *MT* 127, and the rest of the chapter is about the comparative problem. I must apologize for not making this clearer.

85/1 'Any' seems an exaggeration. If Griffin is going to argue in this way, he will end up with a list of 'primary goods' which contains only items which all people agree on, and will thus find important individual differences in desires slipping between his fingers, while he is attending to the 'profile of general prudential values'.

85/−13 How small is this corner? Even if it is small, it is crucially important for theory. I do not want to have my individual preferences steamrollered by any 'general profile of human desires', useful as the latter may be to anyone who is trying to *predict* what my individual preferences may be.

86/17 Griffin has my permission to try to *predict* whether I will like oysters by appeal to the general profile; but I do not want him to tell me that I do not like them when I do, or withhold them from me because people generally do not like them. I know whether I like oysters without appeal to 'the whole scheme of human desires', although appeal to this might help Griffin (a little) when he is trying to guess whether I *will* like oysters.

87/1 Griffin has not succeeded in overcoming this defect in the objective list theory. For unless we can ascertain the desires of individuals without reference to the list, or to the general profile, we can never construct the list or profile in the first place, since it has to be based inductively on particular instances.

87/−4 For myself, when I am (prudentially) planning my own future, I ask what *I* shall like, not what *people* like, although the latter might help me predict the former.

88/−2 The solutions are indeed different, and I prefer mine; but Griffin has certainly shed a great deal of light on the problem.

7. Comments on Harsanyi

89/16 I put forward the 'archangel' as a device for studying critical thinking, and not for studying 'moral decision-making by humans in the face of real-life risk and uncertainty', which, on my view, should normally be done at the intuitive level. I am therefore not open to this objection.

90/16 I argued in *MT* 5 ff., 80 against Brandt's dismissal of everyday moral language as a source for the logic of moral reasoning. It provides a stronger basis than he thinks. Moral words in ordinary language, like all words including logical words, have a variety of uses. But this has not prevented logicians from constructing logical systems on the basis of central uses of 'and', 'not' and 'all', and it should not deter moral philosophers from constructing theories of moral reasoning on the basis of central uses of 'ought'. In both cases, the logic and the reasoning will be recognized as an account of our thinking only if the central uses appealed to are indeed those we use when asking questions that we do ask. As an example of the founding of logic on our understanding of words, suppose that I ask 'Have all our guests left?' I know that the answer 'Yes' will be wrong if one of the guests has not left, because I understand the logic of the words 'all', 'not', etc. What I am claiming is that the same kind of thing can be true of words like 'ought'.

90/−14 ff. Some of the questions which follow are answered in my writings on the basis of the same linguistic or logical intuitions (i.e. of the same understanding of the terms or concepts) as were used in constructing my theory of moral reasoning. These are capable, I think, of yielding answers to them all, though I would not yet claim to have found definitive ones. The answer to the question about unborn babies is adumbrated in H 1975*b*, and it receives, I hope, a clearer answer, based on logical considerations, in forthcoming papers of mine (H 1988*a*, 1988*c*). An answer to that about uninformed preferences is suggested in *MT* 102 f.; see also H 1976*a*:119. Antisocial preferences are discussed in *MT* 140 ff. and below. A discussion of rule- and act-utilitarianism follows immediately. All these answers are generated by the theory, which is itself generated by the logic.

90/−4 Harsanyi is, with Brandt, a pioneer in modern times of rule-utilitarianism. I am proud to follow them in advocating such a theory, but in a version which, unlike theirs, is compatible with a kind of act-utilitarianism at the critical level. See H 1972*a*:13, *MT* 43. I agree almost entirely with Harsanyi's sections 7.2 and 7.3, which contain an explanation of the distinction between act- and rule-utilitarianism (old style), provided that we understand, as Harsanyi does (*94/−6*), that further argument may be required to show that the traditional distinctions and the arguments based on them apply to my two-level theory. I do not believe that they do.

91/−5 My two-level act-cum-rule-utilitarianism *does* permit us to take account of the expectation effects of alternative moral codes or rules (i.e. prima-facie principles). That is an important consideration when we are selecting them.

92/20 The assessment of the utility loss under (3) made by rule- and act-utilitarians will be different only if they interpret (3) differently. The act-utilitarian takes 'if *A* were permitted to break his promise (sc. and so broke it)' in its natural sense to mean (roughly) 'if *A* broke his promise as a result of it not being thought wrong to do this'. The rule-utilitarian takes it to mean 'if there were a rule permitting *A* to break his promise'.

My own theory is an attempt to mediate between rule- and act-utilitarianism. How it does this can be explained in the light of my note on Frankena *51/−13*. Almost all our acts are to some degree influential in supporting or weakening the institutions in society of which our intuitive moral principles are constitutive or regulative. All acts are to some greater or lesser degree educative, in that they form the characters of those who do them, and of others; and (a related point) they help to form the expectations of people as to what others will do. This is especially true of obviously educative acts like bringing up children; but it is also true of any acts which influence the expectations or characters of people. These consequences of our acts have to be taken into account at the critical level even by an act-utilitarian. They will lead us to rule out certain *acts* (e.g. of promise-breaking) whose consequences, if their institution-weakening features were ignored, might be thought beneficial on balance. The weakening of the institutions tilts the balance.

A wise critical moral thinker will therefore make all his recommendations depend partly on these institution-affecting consequences. But the most important of his recommendations will concern moral education itself. This includes the cultivation of moral dispositions which will guide people at the intuitive level. The distinctive feature of a two-level theory like mine is that it makes critical thinking select these dispositions, which are to be cultivated in education, on the score of the utility of the *acts* of cultivating them. It is an act-utilitarianism which pays particular attention to acts of cultivating rules, and is thus a kind of rule-utilitarianism too.

It must be admitted that this argument depends on empirical assumptions; but it is a virtue of utilitarianism in general, including rule-utilitarianism, that it bids us attend to the empirical facts of the real world. See *MT* 167 f., H 1977, 1979*a*, 1984*g*:115, and on Richards *126/−16*. If it were the case that situations frequently arose in which to break a promise would be for the best, even taking into account its institution-weakening effect, then we should have seriously to reconsider the principle which prohibits promise-breaking. The principle, as most people interpret it, has in fact already been qualified, because of such considerations, to allow us to break some trivial promises when the effects of keeping them would be very bad. This can be accepted both by a rule-utilitarian like Harsanyi and by a two-level utilitarian like me.

If, on the other hand, such cases are rare, then the two views may diverge. He will say that in such cases we ought to keep the promise, just because the rule demands it (unless we decide permanently to alter the rule in the light of that case). I shall say that an omniscient and wholly impartial being might with confidence say that he ought to break it; but that a human being would be wise to keep it, in view of his inability to be sure that promise-breaking would be for the best in this case, and of his liability to self-deception and special pleading. The empirical facts on which I rely are, first, the obvious fact that we do suffer from this human weakness and ignorance, and secondly, that we have preserved our respect for the principle requiring promise-keeping through countless generations, and have therefore, presumably, found it best on the whole to cultivate it in our acts. We have just seen that the rare exceptions are allowed for in the principle as interpreted by most people. The durability of the institution is some evidence that acts of cultivating and sustaining it by observing its principles have been thought to maximize utility. But of course if the world were otherwise it might not be so.

92/−3 My own two-level system is able to be as unpermissive in its choice of prima-facie principles for intuitive thinking as critical thinking can justify, which may be as unpermissive as Harsanyi would wish.

93/15 It is unfair to J. S. Mill, Sidgwick, and Moore to say that they attach little importance to moral rights and obligations. They have a utilitarian way of accounting for and justifying them, which anticipates my two-level theory; and I too treat rights and obligations as of dominant importance *at the intuitive level*. On 'special obligations' (*94/7* ff.) see H 1979*b*.

93/−13 It is simply false that the moral calculus of an act-utilitarian society would be unable to take account of these expectation effects. It would take account of them in so far as they were the effects of acts, including acts of cultivating and reinforcing dispositions to respect or disregard these rights and obligations. Harsanyi in effect recognizes this in *95/12*. As we have seen, nearly all acts do this to some degree.

95/12 I agree that Harsanyi's and my methods will lead to the same moral decisions in case (1). In case (2), the expectation effects of the moral rule or code will be a factor in our choice of actions to the extent that actions have institution-weakening or institution-strengthening effects; and I hold, as a matter of empirical fact, that this is nearly always the case. At any rate, it is the case often enough for us to have stuck firmly to these rules, and to be glad that we have. This is the cause of Harsanyi's having, like the rest of us, those powerful intuitions which his version of rule-utilitarianism is intended to buttress. But I think that my two-level system is just as able to buttress them, provided that they can be justified, as the sound ones can, by critical thinking.

96/8 A sound critical thinker will not take any more liberties with other people's property than Harsanyi would, if he is conscious of the great improbability in the real world, given human fallibility, of increasing utility by doing so. See Moore 1903:162, cited in H 1972a:11.

96/−18 I have made clear in *MT* 142 how in general I would counter this kind of move; see especially the 'Roman circus' example. It is true of the 'Nazis and Jews' example too that it becomes ineffective against my view as soon as realism is insisted on. It goes without saying that, in Germany as it was, the holocaust did not increase utility. This was so for a number of reasons, even if we leave out of account the sufferings of the Jews. An important reason (often ignored in these philosophical discussions) is that, in order to carry through such an effective massacre, the whole apparatus of totalitarian dictatorship, with its suppression of freedoms, especially freedom of information, was a precondition; and that was certainly not optimific. It would obviously have been better for almost everybody if the Nazis had been ousted and the Jews spared.

Another reason is that in the actual case those whose desires not to have Jews around were strong enough to make them want to kill all Jews were relatively few. In order to make them numerous enough, and their desires strong enough, and their victims few enough, to justify Harsanyi's use of this example against me, he would have to adjust the case in a way bordering on fantasy. The nearest actual cause I can think of is the treatment of homosexuals in the time of Oscar Wilde; but most of us now agree that the recent liberalizing of the law increased utility, and it was actually urged on utilitarian grounds. Although no doubt there were a few people who were terribly shocked, they got over their shock, and the social disaster which Lord Devlin's arguments would have led one to predict (1959) did not occur.

A third reason is that in all actual cases there will be a better alternative to the policy which Harsanyi seeks to father on the act-utilitarian: namely to push our institutions in the direction of the abandonment of harmful pleasures and desires, and hope that those who now indulge in them will soon change their ways. This has happened in many instances in history, of which Germany is one of the most recent. In the fairly short run this can usually be accomplished given the will.

97/2 On the distinction between external and personal preferences see on Gibbard *64/−8* ff. The distinction as made in the citations that Harsanyi gives from Dworkin is not entirely serviceable, though it is important. I prefer Gibbard's way of making the distinction in different words. Dworkin's formulation is of no use to Harsanyi, because, if we are prepared to take as many liberties as Harsanyi does in imagining cases, then we can construct intuitive counter-examples to utilitarian social-utility functions by bringing in only personal preferences, without appealing to any external ones. It is therefore not true, as he claims it is (*97/−16*), that the exclusion of external preferences would resolve his problem. For we can *conceive* of a small society in which the Nazis have an intense desire not to *look* at hooked noses, and this is a personal preference. Such desires might not be fanatical in a strict sense, because they might not be universalized: those who had them might not mind *other people* having to look at Jews. But they would be enough to defeat Harsanyi's move, if enough people had them.

As I said when discussing Gibbard's views, I have hesitated whether or not to make things easier for myself by excluding external preferences. My reason for being averse to doing so has nothing to do with my present dispute with Harsanyi. It arises, rather, from the facts that my basic theory seems to require me to include *all* preferences, and that to exclude them would still leave me with difficulties stemming from the possibility of fanatacism and 'autofanaticism' (see *MT* 105), whose resolution demands a move which resolves the external-preference difficulty too. Here I need to point out only that it remains open to me, so far as Harsanyi's arguments go, to exclude external preferences with as much alacrity as he does.

The present problem can be removed, in my view, by insisting on the distinction between the levels of moral thinking. Malevolent and undesirably censorious preferences (*97/−1* ff.) can be excluded by having *intuitive* principles which deny them any weight; and in the same way benevolent preferences can be given appropriate extra weight. This will enable our actual everyday moral thinking to conform to the intuitions that Harsanyi and most of us now have. But this will be achieved, although in *critical* thinking all preferences have equal weight strength for stength (see *MT* 140 ff.). Harsanyi himself is in the same predicament, and could if he wished take a similar way out of it; for he needs to make only his 'rules' discriminate against malevolent desires. The utilitarian reasoning whereby he selects these rules would still come out with such rules, even if *within the reasoning-process* there was no discrimination between good and evil desires. This is because, in the world as it is, among people as they are, to discriminate against malevolent and other evil desires in our choice of moral rules has obvious utility.

98/12 ff. It seems to me that we are *not* giving the same weight to everybody's interests if we ignore the interest that parents have in the well-being of their children. Clearly orphans have as much claim on us, in respect of their personal preferences, as other otherwise similar children. But if Harsanyi had to choose between saving an orphan from drowning and saving the child of loving parents, would he not think he ought to save the latter, *ceteris paribus*?

8. Comments on Nagel

101/1 It could be that because I want to find solutions to the problems of ethics I have convinced myself that my solution works. But it could as well be that because Nagel believes that 'one should trust problems over solutions, intuition over arguments, and pluralistic discord over systematic harmony' (1979:x), he has convinced himself that it does not work. My view, in any case, is not that there is, in any substantial sense, 'a foundation for moral argument that lies beyond the reach of moral disagreement', only that, as Nagel goes on to say, 'when people disagree . . . they must mean the same thing by the terms they use to express their differences' (see *MT* 69). I think that argument, based on the logic of these common concepts, can produce agreement out of disagreement. On 'foundations' see also on Williams *193/−1*. I do not 'leave the existence and intractability of actual moral disagreements unexplained'; my theory offers explanations of them, and ways in which they might be resolved. They are explained by disagreements about the facts, lack of understanding of the concepts used, lack of perseverance in exploring both these sources of disagreement, confusion, prejudice, and other obstacles which, like these, can in principle be surmounted. But I am not claiming that moral thinking is *easy*; any theory which makes it seem so must be wrong. See on Brandt *33/19 s.f.* So Nagel is right about the intractability in practice of moral disagreements.

102/8 Nagel here attributes to me a change of view on two points (logical constraints and universalizability). On such alleged changes of mind see my Introduction, pp. 197 ff., and on Singer *147/−5*.

102/23 It is not clear to me what Nagel means here by 'at the level of the principle itself'. Of course I agree that there can be 'disagreements within morality about the stringency and proper interpretation of moral impartiality'. See *MT* 135 ff. It is the business of critical thinking to adjudicate between these conflicting views, any of which may be couched in terms of a universal principle. 'Impartiality' can have different interpretations, *one* of which is that imposed by the (formal) thesis of universalizability. I do not see that Nagel has here put his finger on any difference between us.

This formal universalizability, correctly stated by Nagel in *102/−12*, is the only kind I require for my argument. See on Singer *147/−5*; and for the distinction between universality and generality, see on Hudson *12/−14*. What I require in addition is not a strengthening of universalizability. What Gibbard (*60/9*) calls 'strong universalizability' (a formal, logical thesis) is strong enough for me, and is what I have always embraced. But, as Nagel I am sure realizes, I never claimed that *by itself* universalizability yields a more than formal impartiality (i.e. an impartiality in the content or substance of moral judgements). What I need in addition is what Gibbard calls (*60/−13*) the Condition Reflection Principle, argued for in *MT*, ch. 5, which is independent of universalizability (see *MT* 108).

102/−4 What kind of egoism? There are many kinds. Some of them logically cannot be expressed without the use of singular terms; others of them can be, but would not be accepted by someone who put himself in the shoes of his victims. For example, if we say 'Everyone ought to look out only for himself', that is logically (formally) speaking universal; the question is whether we would accept this universal prescription, if we saw how it would affect ourselves if we were in the position of the weak who would go to the wall. See *FR* 105 f., 171, 218; *MT* 109.

I have not abandoned the view that some 'appalling' prescriptions can be universalized without internal logical inconsistency. They can be 'consistently stated' (*104/−11*), but will be rejected by someone who thinks critically and considers their application to his own position as victim in hypothetical cases, unless his desire to have them fulfilled is impossibly strong. But in that case he is not a counterexample to my theory. See *MT* 181 f. and on Singer *149/−18*.

103/17 On my view, my universal preference does not depend *only* on what I want to happen to myself if I occupy the various positions, though it has to be consistent with this. It must be remembered also that I may, on reflection, in considering what my universal preference is to be, *change* my preference for what should happen in some of the particular cases falling under the principle, including even those in which I am affected favourably or adversely. I may do this because in order to get a universal preference I have to take the rough with the smooth. This is involved in the 'balancing' (below).

103/−12 Nagel here says that he will confine the discussion to the critical level. But he later uses arguments which collapse once the levels are distinguished. See on *107/8, 108/−15, 109/5,* and *110/−8* below.

103/−10 It is important that Nagel here, like many others, puts the boundary between form and substance in the wrong place. That moral judgements in critical thinking should give equal consideration to everyone is a formal principle as I use it (though this, as I have stressed, is consistent with my view that other arguments are needed to justify substantial impartiality in our everyday intuitive judgements). In consequence, utilitarianism too is a formal doctrine. From universalizability, prescriptivity, and the Conditional Reflection Principle in conjunction, though not from universalizability by itself, it follows that in moral thinking we have to give equal weight to the preferences of those affected whoever they are; and from this, in conjunction with the assumption that we give positive weight to *our own* preferences, utilitarianism directly follows. For this argument see H 1972*c*:171. This, however, does not determine what, in substance, we should do. To put in the substance, whether partial or impartial, we have to ask what the preferences actually are, or would be, regarding the consequences of adopting one or another principle to live by. So formulated, utilitarianism itself is not a substantial moral thesis but a formal, logical one, like the thesis of universalizability to which it is so closely related, and like the Kantian Categorical Imperative; but like these it can guide our reasoning, in combination with substantial information about preferences, towards the adoption of substantial principles.

104/1 It may clarify matters if I say that I accept (1), as I think Nagel does (see *102/−12*); that I, unlike him, accept (2); but that (3) and (4) are stronger than I claim or need to claim. I also accept (5), but that is outside the scope of Nagel's discussion. (3) is too strong, because of the inclusion of the word 'only' (see on *103/17* above and H 1984*f*). (4) is likewise too strong if 'depends on' means 'depends only on', for the same reason. I shall, like Nagel, concentrate on (2); but from what I have just said it is evident that his whole reconstruction of my argument needs itself to be reconstructed.

104/−15 This too is a serious misconception. See Griffin 1982 and Hudson *13/−1*. Utilitarians like Griffin and myself do not have to talk about 'the quantity of a value which is the same

for all agents'. People value or desire many different things;
what, according to utilitarians, has to be maximized is the
satisfaction of these desires, not the production of some *one*
thing which we all desire.

104/−9 ff. Here, it seems to me, Nagel starts to use words in a
way that loses contact with my own view. I do not use
'prescribe' and 'universally' in such a way that to prescribe
universally implies a claim 'that everyone has a reason to act
in accordance with my prescription'. Nor do I think that
moral judgements, which on my view are universalizable
prescriptions, imply any such claim. *LM* 31 and 197 were
badly phrased if they gave that impression. I was implying
merely that moral judgements, in their central prescriptive
uses, entail prescriptions, on the part of the speaker, that those
to whom a moral judgement applies should do what it
requires. I can certainly say to someone 'You ought to do it'
without implying that *he* has a reason or motive (yet) for doing
it. The moral judgement provides a reason only in the sense
that to *accept* it is to accept that there is a (moral) reason. If the
person addressed agrees with me, 'he must acknowledge a
reason to act in that way', as Nagel says below. He will have
acquired a reason, in the shape of the moral principle which
he will thereby have implicitly accepted. Because a moral
judgement is a universalizable prescription, to accept it is to
accept some principle, though not necessarily the same
principle as the speaker had in mind; and the principle
provides the moral reason. But in making a moral judgement
the speaker does not claim that either before or after
acceptance the person addressed necessarily has a *prudential*
reason for acting accordingly.

It is therefore unclear to me what Nagel is claiming in
105/6 ff. We must not confuse the true statement that to make
a moral judgement is to claim that anybody who accepts it
will have acquired a reason, with the false statement that to
make a moral judgement is to claim that everyone, whether or
not he accepts it, already has a (perhaps unrecognized) reason
to act accordingly. The second statement is even more
obviously false if for 'reason' we substitute 'motivation', as
Nagel in places does.

'The connection with motivation that should be preserved

by any account of moral prescription' (*105/23*) is a connection
with the motivation of the speaker. As an 'internalist' I hold
that to utter sincerely a moral or any other prescription is to
be (morally or otherwise) motivated. But why does Nagel
suppose (if that is what he supposes) that in addition it is to
think that others are similarly motivated?

105/−8 Throughout my work I have emphasized that I do *not*
'interpret moral judgements as imperatives in a fairly literal
sense'. See e.g. *LM* 2, 180 f. They are a different sort of
prescriptions, but resemble imperatives in belonging to this
same genus, and therefore can display *some* of the characteristics of imperatives. I believe that Kant thought the same,
and that Nagel misinterprets him in what follows. Surely
Kant thought that moral 'imperatives' are an expression of
the Will, which is Practical Reason (see *MT* 6 n.). In his
footnote, Nagel should have written not 'content' but 'form',
and similarly in *106/19* below; see above on *103/−10*.

107/8 See above. Such a moral view *is* arrived at 'from
something more fundamental', viz. critical thinking. Two
paragraphs further on Nagel anticipates this reply, and says
'Perhaps Hare is right.' In H 1979*b* and *MT* 135 ff. I discuss
at length how critical thinking, which is itself impartial, can
conclude that partial principles ought to be adopted for use at
the intuitive level, which is where we need them.

107/18 This indeed raises a serious question, but one which
has to be dealt with seriously and not just used as ammunition.
I mention it, but do not adequately discuss it, in *MT* 199, 201.
It seems to me that, if the affluent person does not desire to
give the donation, he does not really, in critical thinking, think
that he ought. Perhaps he just has guilty feelings, or opinions
about what is generally thought. See *LM* 167. Such feelings
are normally, and should be, the accompaniments of *intuitive*
principles, and these we can have without acting on them. See
MT 59 f.

107/−5 Nagel's eccentric use of 'prescribe' has led him into
paradox: can one really and sincerely prescribe something
universally, *ceteris paribus*, which one does not desire should
universally, *ceteris paribus*, be done?

108/7 My logical claim embodies no moral view. See above. It is simply a question of how we are going to use the word 'prescribe'. People are apt to accuse me of smuggling in moral views in the guise of logical theses; but I have never seen any of these accusations substantiated, least of all by Nagel here.

It is important here not to confuse the two questions distinguished in another context on *MT* 178, viz. (1) Is my theory correct?, and (2) If it is correct, what follows from it? See my Introduction, p. 203.

108/−15 'In the actual world, it is clear that, if no one gave priority to his own children' in his intuitive thinking, the consequences for children in general would be disastrous. But this has no bearing on how we should do our *critical* thinking, except that it has to take account of this obvious fact. See H 1979*b* and *MT* 135 ff.

108/−2 'Can be correct' is a misinterpretation; it should be 'can be rationally defended'. See on *102/−4* above. The 'appalling' principles there mentioned can be consistently stated without offence to the logic of the moral concepts. But they cannot (in the absence of impossibly strong desires) be *defended* without appeal to irrational intuitions. The purpose of a theory of moral reasoning is to lead us to those principles that can be defended without such an appeal. See also on Richards *115/−8* and *MT* 179.

109/5 'A less demanding morality with agent-relative permissions to favour yourself and those close to you' is 'likely to work even better', even *qua* moral system, if what we are speaking of is a set of prima-facie intuitive principles for ordinary use. But that is just what I say in other words in *MT* 135 ff. However, this has no direct bearing on critical thinking, about which Nagel purports to be speaking.

109/11 See *MT* 184 for my actual view. The amoralist does not have to 'refrain from using the moral vocabulary', but is barred from all but judgements of indifference. And I cannot see how Nagel's 'farther out' amoralist (below) differs from mine. Mine too 'has no views about how everyone should behave, or what reasons for action [i.e. principles] everyone should recognize', except that it simply does not matter morally.

110/4 On 'objective standards' see on Griffin *74/−15* ff. and on Singer *151/12* and also Parfit 1984:4 ff. It seems to me that Nagel here ignores a lot that I have said about 'objectivism', e.g. H. 1976*b* and *MT*, ch. 12. Though (4) is of course 'not a moral tautology' (and does not even represent my own view— see above), it is nearer to my view than any theory which seeks to establish an 'objective list' of goods without examining people's preferences. Unless based on what people prefer or would prefer, such a list can only be compiled, and in particular can only be *closed*, by appeals to unsupported, wholly irrational intuitions of the speaker.

110/−8 See above. Nagel here ignores my two-level move, which effectively counters this sort of objection. I think it highly probable that a sound critical thinker, using only additive and aggregative maximization of preference-satisfactions as his guide, would come up with intuitive principles for everyday use which would accord with Nagel's. That, at least, is where my own critical thinking leads me, or thereabouts (I cannot promise that my political views exactly correspond with his). But why does Nagel think that these good intuitive principles have to be inserted into the canons of *critical* thinking? They will come out in the bottom line even if they are not inserted higher up, given the conditions of the actual world. If Nagel had understood this, he would not have said what he says in the next three paragraphs.

111/2 See on Richards *118/8*.

111/−12 Nagel has 'shown' this only by appeal to his own view about what a moral prescription has to be—a view which I find most implausible. See above. Otherwise his arguments are mere suggestions that I might not be right.

112/18 In his final paragraph Nagel seems to be asking for a refutation of amoralism. It would be nice if he could give us one that works. But it will not do to *assume*, as he seems prepared to, that morality is 'a set of claims about how everyone has reason to behave'. Not, at any rate, if 'reason' means 'prudential reason'. I argue in *MT*, ch. 11 that there *are* prudential reasons for becoming a morally motivated person; but to write into the definition of morality a requirement that everyone has to be morally motivated, as Nagel seems to want to do, is to beg the entire question, in just the way he has accused me of doing. The pot, not the kettle, is 'packing a strong motivational assumption into the conditions for using moral language'.

9. Comments on Richards

113/1 Professor Richards's tributes to me at the beginning and end of his paper are kinder than I deserve. He is also more than merely fair when he calls his own remarks 'perhaps tendentiously intuitive' (*127/4*). But it is indeed the intuitive character of many of his moves that I shall be complaining of.

115/–8 There are no 'anti-utilitarian constraints internal to critical morality itself'. Richards will later seek to introduce them; but he can do so only by importing into the canons of critical thinking his own substantial moral intuitions, in a way that I warned against in *MT* 11 ff. Unlike Richards and many others, I think it an abandonment of rationality, and viciously circular, to introduce, into a system of reasoning whose main purpose is to scrutinize and justify, or else reject, moral convictions that we have, canons unsupported by anything except those same moral convictions, dignified under the name of 'ideals of critical reason' (*116/1*). That was why I abjured, in setting up my method of critical thinking, any support but that provided by logic based on the meanings of the moral words, to which anybody must agree who is using the words in the same senses. See on Nagel *108/–2*.

116/9 The expression here is inexact or at least unclear. See on Gibbard *59/4*.

116/21 I never argued that the Nazi's principles would be *established* by his sincerity. Rather, I thought myself faced with a difficulty in showing that they could be *refuted* by a liberal thinker. Richards perhaps confuses this issue by using in *116/–8* the ambiguous verb 'legitimate', which might mean 'say without fear of refutation', or might mean 'establish so that *other people* have to accept them'. There are many things we can say without fear of refutation, but which we cannot compel others to agree with. So I can accept what these critics argued.

The 'criterion' referred to in the next sentence was not mine, and I was not guilty of confusion. Warnock's point, if I have understood it, was that from the statement that someone sincerely says that something ought to be done one cannot derive the conclusion that it ought to be done. Nobody would think that I disagree who had not himself confused my position with that commonly called 'old-fashioned subjectivism', namely the view that what we ought to do depends on what we think we ought to do, or that in moral matters 'thinking makes it so'. I have never held this view, and find its repeated attribution to me very strange. See *MT* 208 f. and refs.

116/−12 This conception is already tolerably clear in *FR* 172, 182 f., where the 'impure fanatic' of *MT* 170 f. is described but not so named. Richards fails here to establish a difference between the views expressed in *FR* and *MT*; and so he cannot claim that *MT* is closer to his own view. See my Introduction, pp. 198 f.

117/12 Here Richards is kind enough to assimilate my view to one that he finds more acceptable, with its 'rational aims reasonably universalized' and its 'ideals of critical reason'. It is therefore not surprising that he finds a tension between these and my actual view.

117/−7 I find nothing even implicitly Kantian in this perspective. Modern intuitionists, ever since Prichard, have been too ready to attribute their own views to Kant, with increasingly inadequate documentation. Kant, after all, was a convinced rationalist, and would surely have rejected appeals to unsupported intuitions, such as are needed in order to select the above-mentioned 'narrower range of goods' or to specify our 'rational powers as persons', if these are going to incapsulate substantial moral presuppositions.

118/8 For this alleged 'blunder' (which Nagel too imputes to me, *111/2*), see H 1984g:106 f. and on Vendler *182/−5*. Would the people who repeat this allegation of Rawls (1971:27) say that an impartial arbitrator is failing to take seriously the difference between persons if he administers even-handed justice by treating the equal interests of two different parties as *ceteris paribus* of equal weight, just as in our prudential judgements we so treat our own interests? Does such an arbitrator not know that he is dealing with two different persons (can he not count)? Rather, he is, like the utilitarian, trying to do *justice* between the parties, showing them equal concern and respect.

118/−6 Richards is correct in finding this affinity between ideal-observer theories and my own utilitarianism (see *MT* 44 and refs.). Since God is the paradigm ideal observer, the 'blunder' is committed by most forms of Christian ethics. God too knows that we are different people, but he loves us all equally. See H 1986*g*.

119/10 The basic difference between ethics and prudence is that moral judgements have to be impartial (as universalizability, when joined with prescriptivity and the Conditional Reflection Principle, demands), whereas prudential judgements are not. Where do I 'elide' this difference? It is the foundation of my system.

119/13 I do defend *something like* what Richards calls a 'metaethics of the ideal observer', in the person of the 'archangel'. I even say that 'Provided that we do not give it a "subjectivist" or "relativist" interpretation, there is no harm in saying that the right or best way for us to live or act either in general or on a particular occasion is what the archangel would pronounce to be so if he addressed himself to the question' (*MT* 46). See on Frankena *48/19*, who cites this passage in *45/−5*. I do not, however, *define* 'right' in this way, but rather in terms of universal prescriptions. In this narrow sense I am not, as Richards rightly sees, an ideal-observer theorist in metaethics.

119/−6 To treat persons as equals is to show them equal concern; and this is to treat their *equal* interests or preferences as of equal weight. It is not to treat *any* interest of any person as of equal weight to that of any other person, however great or small. Otherwise we should have, in order to treat persons equally, to give the same weight to one person's dying in torment as to another's scratching his finger. Is this what Richards wants us to do? So far as I can see, the most promising way of avoiding it is to give equal weight to equal preferences of people.

120/17 ff. Note the slide in this passage from 'rational' to 'reasonable', and thence to 'universally applicable principles expressive of their common powers and the circumstances of interpersonal life'; and thence to 'the formation, expression and revision of the basic values of conscience which give shape and order to all the other pursuits in persons' lives', and thus to 'equal liberty lexically prior to arguments of utilitarian aggregation' (*121/9*). By this 'natural elaboration of constructivist metaethics' (*121/14*), Richards arrives at a substantial moral position which has not been argued for.

121/−16 What is this 'real sense' in which 'the argument does not take persons or [the] personal point of view seriously'? My whole method of argument is based on thinking what it would be like to be in other people's shoes. It is Rawls who fails to take them seriously, by forcing on them a list of 'primary goods' or 'common goods' (*121/−9* below), culled from his own intuitions—goods which some of them may not in all circumstances prize as much as he does.

121/−13 The rhetorical expression 'containers of preferences' presumably means, when put into ordinary English, 'people who have preferences, i.e. prefer one thing to another'. Does Richards think *that* morally irrelevant? If Tom cuts Jane's finger off, is it not a moral consideration that she would prefer to keep her finger? Or is she just a 'container of preferences'?

122/11 We do in fact often accept sacrifices of one person in order to realize the greater total good of others. In the War I accepted a duty to get myself killed if that were necessary to the cause we were fighting for (the ending of Nazism); and I should have been condemned if I had not been ready to do this. We do, indeed, accept prima-facie principles forbidding certain sacrifices of one person to others; but these principles have a justification in utilitarian critical thinking, because their acceptance-utility is high. In order to secure respect for these principles, we do not need wholly irrational short cuts in the argument.

123/1 It is characteristically fair-minded of Richards to allow that my adoption of a two-level system might answer the objections he has made. I address below the two 'intractable difficulties' which he has with the system.

123/17 What is 'elitist' about critical morality? See on Scanlon *131/−10* and on Williams *185/1, 188/−17.*

123/−7 What is supposed to be the difference between 'issues of principle' and 'utilitarian strategies'? My view is that a wise utilitarian will cultivate, until they become second nature, principles and dispositions such as intuitionists like to appeal to, as Richards does here. In *124/5* Richards treats as a concession what is an integral part of my theory. There is little difference at this point between the two views, except that the utilitarian can say *why* we should cultivate the dispositions, and the intuitionist cannot (see *MT* 137). I see no reason at all why 'these practices would surely erode' (*123/−9*), or why utilitarianism and a defensible conventional morality would be 'unstably connected'.

Aristotle understood better the relation between critical thinking and the moral dispositions (see *EN* 1103a3, discussed in *MT* 46). They are rational because they are what reason would bid us cultivate, cling to, and not depart from without the greatest repugnance. Richards obscures this by using the term 'conventional morality' in a very weak sense (as I did myself in *LM* 77, 125); but that is not the sort of thing we are here speaking of.

I know by critical thinking why it is right, for example, to have a horror of lying; but this reinforces, rather than impairs, my tendency, if ever I am tempted to tell a lie, to pull myself up and say 'Mind out! If you start telling lies, you'll never stop, and look what will come of that.' This kind of self-discipline is barred to the intuitionist, who can give no reason for the principle. Such objections are made by those who lack an understanding of how the good man keeps himself to his principles. He has no need to keep his principles, or his moral thinking, to himself (*123/−5*). See on Harsanyi, esp. *92/20* and on Williams *189/−20.*

125/−1 The abandonment of the requirement of a culpable mind might (conceivably) make the administration of criminal trials (let us not call it 'criminal justice') more certain and effective. But the question is rather whether it would have a greater acceptance-utility than our present practice. Richards has missed the point, unless he thinks that the only utility that matters is that of making criminal trials more certain and effective. If he thinks that, he must be in favour of an efficient police state. Actually, there are many utilities and disutilities to be considered, of which the utility of effective policing is only one. The main point, of which I am sure Professor Hart is seized, is that justice in the commonly understood sense, in which the abandonment of *mens rea* as a requirement would be unjust, has enormous utility. This applies both to justice in the laws themselves, and to justice in their administration. For this reason the law does not often dispense with *mens rea*— though sometimes, for sufficient utilitarian reasons, it does something rather like this, as in cases of strict liability. Utilitarianism can thus justify, as a very firm prima-facie principle, our actual practice of demanding *mens rea*. This type of justification is much stronger than appeals to intuition. I am surprised if Richards thinks, as he appears to, that the abandonment of the *mens rea* requirement, whether in general or in particular cases, would *in fact* conduce to maximal preference satisfaction. If this is his preferred example, it is a weak one.

126/−16 I must ask who is guilty of 'irresponsible inattention to fact': one who bases his argument on the obvious fact that justice has utility, or one who thinks that it needs to be shored up by intuitions which owe nothing to factual enquiry.

10. Comments on Scanlon

129/6 My aim too will be to explore my agreements and disagreements with Scanlon. I find few disagreements once the issues are clarified, and indeed detect palpable traces of utilitarianism in his position (e.g. *139/−8, 140/4, 143/5*). Like him I have been attracted by the two lines of thought, leading to a two-level view, that he mentions; and like him I find them compatible. One may come to such a view because of the 'perceived complexity of ordinary moral argument' (*129/−11*), and then, if one is a utilitarian, see that it also avoids the vulgar objections to the doctrine (*129/12*). My third ground for adopting a two-level view is that it explains the way in which philosophers have so readily accepted ethical theories with such obvious defects. See *MT*, ch. 4, and on Williams *186/−7*.

Like Scanlon, I think that intuitive and critical thinking can be 'quite continuous with one another' (*130/15*), in the sense that our thought will usually begin at the intuitive level, and proceed to the critical level as necessary. This is then 'the completion of the moral thought begun at the intuitive level' (ibid.). There is no 'division of labour' (*133/1*) except that which is implicit in the distinction between levels itself, and which Scanlon accepts. When in *130/18* he corrects himself, and says that, if critical and intuitive thinking yield different answers, the judgement given by [sc. rightly done] critical thinking 'is always the right answer', he comes even closer to my own view.

However, the use of the word 'right' in such a context opens a can of worms which becomes only too apparent with Scanlon's scare quotes (' "really" right') in *130/−5*. It is never wise to answer the question, 'what is *the* meaning of "right"?', because there are several. The central meaning I still think to be that explained, on my usual universal-prescriptivist lines, in *LM* 181 ff. But now that I have adopted a two-level view I see more clearly that there are also meanings corresponding to the first two meanings of 'ought' listed on *LM* 167 and distinguished from the third, central, use—though, I said, they often occur in a 'confused mixture'. At the intuitive level, where we are appealing to accepted standards and ingrained dispositions, the confusion is pardonable and even useful, though even there we have to remember that 'right' is still prescriptive, because the standards and the dispositions are being subscribed to by the speaker. So 'right' may mean 'prima facie or intuitively right' (see on *136/−12* and on Frankena *48/19*).

But we must still distinguish the question, 'What does "right" mean?', from two others: (1) 'What are the grounds for calling an act right?' (the answer to which lies in whatever substantial moral principle we then apply to the action); and (2) 'How do we determine whether an action is (in the central sense) right?' (the answer to which is, of course, 'by doing some critical thinking').

131/−10 See on Williams *185/1*, *188/−17*, who disavows this libel, as does Scanlon below.

133/7 It does not seem at first sight as if US constitutional
arrangements would be a good model for rational moral
thought. Though I defer to Scanlon's greater knowledge of the
law, especially US law, he has not convinced me that this is
so, for all the analogies that there certainly are between law
and morals.

There are two main reasons why laws, especially bills of
rights, are 'given a simple and general formulation' (*133/12*).
The first is the respectable one implied by Aristotle (*EN*
1137b14 ff.), that the law has to apply to a number of different
situations resembling one another only in their general
features, and therefore has to be couched in general terms
applicable to all of them. Too specific a law would, in many
contexts, be useless, though the law can be pretty specific
when it needs to be. The other reason is less respectable,
namely that 'ambiguity may also be politically useful'
(J. E. Hare 1984). In order to secure enough agreement on a
bill to ensure its passage, rather vague words are inserted into
it which the various parties can each interpret in their own
way and hope that the courts will do likewise. This in effect
deputes to the courts the task of determining precisely what
the law is to be. It is an obvious feature of US handling of
rights, but is becoming common in Europe too since we have
had a Convention on Human Rights and a Court to interpret
it (H 1986*a*). It happens, though less blatantly, in Britain too.

133/−12 For what is involved in applying laws, and the
analogy with morals, see *LM* 52 ff. Both moral principles and
laws are often vaguely formulated in the way just described.
This is sometimes because they contain value-words; but this
need not be so if the words, though descriptive, are loose
enough. These words have therefore to be 'interpreted'. It is
important to make clear, as I did in *LM*, what is then
happening. To use the example I borrowed from Hart, to
decide whether the occasional cricket ball landing in a public
street is a 'nuisance' might be thought to be to decide whether
it *really* falls under a classification whose boundaries were
already (intuitively?) known. If we take this view, we shall be
likely to say, as Scanlon in effect says, that the 'critical
thinking' involved in the interpretation of the law is a
discovery of what was in the law already. In some cases this

may be so. But in others what is being reached is what I called in *LM* a 'decision of principle': the law was *not* yet determinate and the judge has made it more so. He is not deciding that the cricket balls really are a nuisance; he is prescribing that they be treated by the law as a nuisance, incurring penalties. He may have grounds, good or bad, for so deciding; these will normally have to include the fact that the case is similar enough to others where the law has already been determined by statute or the courts; but they may also include moral reasons, reasons of public policy, or even the judge's own politics or prejudices.

There are some analogies between this and moral thinking, but they do not support Scanlon's view that his account of the relation between its two levels is radically different from mine. I too can allow that intuitive moral principles have to be rather general and are often vaguely expressed, so that they need application and interpretation. But it would be wrong to treat this process as always a *discovery* of what was in a principle already. It may be an extension or restriction or other qualification of the principle, disguised as an interpretation. It certainly involves, not just the application of a descriptive word, but a prescription for a class of cases for which previously there was no determinate prescription. See H 1986*c*.

This point is as good as conceded in *134/11* ff. It is misleading, therefore, to say, as Scanlon there does, that 'the object of our thought is the same—the same familiar but also complex and elusive idea'. The judge has *changed* the concept, and so may the critical moral thinker. What has been decided was not all in the law already.

134/−16 A 'division of labour' has therefore not been avoided, nor should it be. Ironically, the US Constitution, founded on the separation of powers, has succeeded in passing over some of the powers of the legislature to the judiciary; but within what the judiciary does there is still a division of function between merely applying the laws as made by the legislature, and making them more precise than the legislature made them. Similarly, we should not be deceived, by the fact that in moral thinking the same *word* ('lie', for example) has been used, into supposing that a principle has not been changed.

The person who says, 'That must be condemned as a lie, because it was a falsehood uttered with intent to deceive', is engaged in a quite different sort of activity from the person who says, 'False, yes, but it had a wholly innocent purpose, and so let us not call it a lie *tout court*, which would imply condemnation; let us call it a white lie and not condemn it.' The first is applying the principle which forbids lying, but the second is changing it, by altering the extension of the term 'lie', as used in that principle. Admittedly, because even application implies endorsement, there is some evaluation or prescription going on in the first person's statement (see H 1986*c* on F. C. S. Schiller's views); but the endorser is implicitly *not* changing; his activity is different from that of changing.

135/−3 ff. I agree that the conclusion is that they really are wrong. But the law has come to say this through a change in the principle, at least from a vague to a more determinate one. It is a central part of my theory that critical thinking can change intuitive principles.

136/−12 See on *129/6* above. We have now located yet another sense of 'determine what is right'. Critical thinking, by changing the principle in the light of 'the permissions and injunctions which it is reasonable to adopt', has brought it nearer to what is right in general (the new qualification makes it prescribe what is right in more cases than before) and, we hope, made it prescribe what is right in this particular case. This happens when critical thinking has been fully exercised. But, as Scanlon allows, there are other cases in which, owing to lack of time or capacity, we apply intuitive principles without doing any critical thinking. All this is in accord with my own views. There are different kinds of occasion, and I never said that the same procedure was best in all of them— only that my account of the two levels allows for appropriate handling of each.

137/−7 ff. I think it could be argued that my view and Scanlon's, if the latter were suitably clarified, must yield the same conclusions, giving in each case 'a utilitarian answer to the contractualist question' (*145/−15*). There is no room to do this fully here, but I shall be giving some hints. The basic point is that the consistent following of Scanlon's recipe here, without appeals to intuitions, like the consistent following of Rawls's, produces a utilitarian dish. I certainly think that my theory does not require me to dissent from much that he says in the next few pages.

138/15 The examples referred to from H 1976*a* need to be reconsidered in the light of Gibbard's paper. See especially on Gibbard *64/–8 ff*. In dealing with them in H 1976*a*, I relied heavily on the force of preferences other than those for experiences of the preferrer, e.g. preferences for what should happen after my death, and preferences for what others should do even if I do not know it. Dworkin's term 'external preferences' (1977:234) has somewhat the same meaning. I appealed to the first in dealing with the death-bed promise case, and to the second for the other three cases. If, in response to Gibbard's criticisms, I were to put such preferences out of court, then clearly I could not use the main argument I used in H 1976*a*.

I should therefore have to rely entirely on the other defences which are available. I mentioned one of these in H 1976*a*:129 which Scanlon cites: that of pleading that the cultivation of the principles against which the people in the examples err has a utilitiaran justification. To this we might add that, if the principles are cultivated, we shall have the feelings and intuitions to which the anti-utilitarians who use such examples appeal; and so they are not really counter-examples to utilitarianism, because the utilitarian wants there to be these feelings and gives reasons for cultivating them.

I can also defend myself by saying that in some of the examples (certainly the death-bed promise case and the car-pushing case) occasions on which utility would be maximized by breaking the principle are so rare as not to be a basis for the choice of intuitive principles or for altering people's moral education. Parfit, in a penetrating treatment of the voter example (1984:73 ff.), has shown on independent grounds that it does not prove what the anti-utilitarians think it proves. I would add to this argument another: nearly always in an election the overall voting figures matter a great deal politically. My constituency in Britain is such a safe seat that it is inconceivable that any but the Conservative candidate could win; but I vote all the same, to affect the national figures, which will be constantly quoted during the life of Parliament, and taken as a basis of policy.

I think that such defences might suffice me. But I have not yet been able to decide whether I have to abandon the 'chief answer' of H 1976*a*:130, which Scanlon terms 'more ambitious' (*138/−2*), and himself appears to favour (*139/−5*). I would like not to, because it fits in so well with my universal-prescriptivist ethical theory. This is part of the 'unfinished business' left in *MT* 104–6, which needs further thought. In this I have been greatly assisted by critics like Gibbard and Scanlon.

140/16 Death-bed promises differ from death-bed decrees in the acceptance-utility of principles requiring their observance, and in their effects, respectively, on the general respect for promises (which is valuable) and 'decrees' of private persons (which has no value). This may be enough to account for the difference between our intuitions in the two cases. Even if I do not rely on the acceptance-utility argument exclusively, I can use it as an auxiliary argument in some cases, as also in that which Scanlon cites in *140/−7*. There too I can appeal to the auxiliary argument; principles requiring compliance with the desires in question have negative acceptance-utility.

140/−10 The accusation of circularity is rebutted in H 1971*b*:132. I would add the arguments of *MT* 140 ff. about good and evil desires. See on Harsanyi *96/−18*.

141/18 Would we disapprove of the behaviour of dogs in mangers if their attitude had utility?

141/−14 See on Gibbard *64/−8* ff., and on *138/15* above. I reach the conclusion unhesitatingly because I have that intuitive principle, which might be pre-moral rather than moral (H 1971*b*:132). To justify morally the cultivation of the intuition, longer argument is needed, of either my own or Scanlon's kind. The question is, 'Which works?' See below on *144/16*.

142/13 Both these reasons appeal to acceptance-utility or the reverse, so I can share them with Scanlon. The same applies to the qualification 'without compelling reason' in the next

paragraph, at the end of which the word 'burdensome' gives
the game away. For fear of appealing to intuition, utility is
invoked.

143/−12 ff. I doubt whether there is a difference between
Scanlon and me here. How is 'comparison and balancing of
interests' to be done without some kind of at least rough
comparability, which will bring with it the possibility of
aggregation? Such balancing is discussed in Griffin's paper.
The argument *is* a utilitarian argument.

143/−7 The 'ineliminable element of judgement' is not objectionable if it is merely estimation of fact (see on Urmson
166/−16). So it can be 'involved in utilitarian decision-making'
too.

144/16 It is important to distinguish, as (e.g.) Rawls 1971:130
does not, different faults that a proposed moral principle may
have, and the different ways of dealing with them.

> (1) The principle may contain ineliminable singular
> terms, including references to particular times and
> places.

> (2) It may contain 'rigged' descriptions (Rawls's term)
> which, though universal, contingently pick out a par-
> ticular person or group. Rawls does not tell us how to
> distinguish those descriptions that are rigged from those
> which are not, and in fact it cannot be done on formal
> grounds alone.

In my own theory the first kind of faulty principles is ruled out
on formal grounds, because moral judgements have to be
universalizable; but the second requires a quite different
manœuvre, involving universalizability but other moves
besides, which is explained on *FR* 106 f. It is essentially the
same manœuvre as provides the nerve of my whole argument
for utilitarianism in *MT*, chs. 5 and 6.

Scanlon seems (*144/−15* ff.) to think that he can scotch both
kinds of faulty principle by the same manœuvre, which closely
resembles that called by Marcus Singer 'reiterability' (1961:81;
see H 1962). But at least in Singer's version it does not work,
because for *any* proposed moral principle alluding to some
universal feature of situations, another universal feature can

be arbitrarily substituted, thus making us reject all moral principles whatever. If Scanlon makes it work, it is by using the same basically utilitarian arguments as I do.

Thus I agree with Scanlon that what he calls (*145/2*) a 'unilateral' procedure for selecting moral principles would be reasonably objected to. What we need on my view, as on his, are principles to which we can all rationally subscribe as the *universal* principles which, putting ourselves into the shoes of all those affected, suit us best. See on Brandt *38/−9*. I think that this procedure will yield a unique set of universal principles acceptable to rational selectors. I question whether Scanlon has proposed a procedure which is both viable and different. See on Singer *157/9*.

146/−12 They are not the *only* considerations. There are also formal considerations (prescriptivity and universalizability at least). I wish to rule out from rational argument considerations which have no basis other than intuition. See on Richards *115/−8, 117/−7* and on Singer *150/1*.

11. Comments on Singer

147/1 I agree so much with nearly all the points that Singer has made, and he has expressed them so clearly and cogently, that I have little to add by way of comment on his own views. But he does raise some questions which call for further discussion. I am especially glad that he has mentioned the views of John Mackie, whose absence from this volume is the saddest thing about it.

147/−5 For some comments by me on Mackie's 'three stages of universalization', see H 1984*g*:113, *MT* 108. I need for my purposes only one kind of universalizability, which I expounded most recently (but without change of view from my earliest treatment of the related notion of supervenience) in H 1984*b*. This is the doctrine that moral judgements made about one situation, etc., have, on pain of logical inconsistency, to be made about any situation which is exactly similar in its universal non-moral properties. Singer's (i) corresponds to this single notion. His (ii) is achieved, not by introducing a different notion of universalizability, but by using the same notion, and adding the move made in *MT*, ch. 5, which does not depend on universalizability (see *MT* 108 and my Introduction, p. 200). His (iii) is a more difficult matter, Singer's discussion of which I shall take up shortly.

149/−18 This is not quite what I argue. What Singer means, I think, is 'to disregard the content of the ideals we may hold when deciding what weight to give them in critical thinking'. We have, of course, to have regard to their content for other purposes, for example in deciding whether to adopt intuitive principles encouraging or restraining their pursuit. If an ideal because of its content has high acceptance-utility, we shall encourage it; if low, discourage it.

However, if some deontologists held dear some principles which sound critical thinking would reject, this would not impugn my views about the logic of moral language. If these deontologists did more and better critical thinking, they too would reject these principles. Deontological and fanatical views of the most extreme sort can be *expressed* without offence to logic (see *FR* 219 and on Nagel *102/−4*). But the question is, will the views continue to be defended after their proponents have thought the matter through in the light of the requirement to universalize their prescriptions and of the facts about the impact of their proposals on other people? Most 'absolutists' who maintain principles that a utilitarian would reject agree that moral judgements have to be universalizable; but they think (not having thought enough) that they are prepared to universalize these principles through thick and thin. They are not differing from me about the concepts; they are just neglecting considerations which would affect their thinking if their minds were not closed to them.

150/1 Singer here deftly puts his finger on the essential point which, as he says, is common to Mackie and myself. If moral judgements either are non-descriptive as I maintain, or are descriptive but all false as Mackie thought, then the person who wishes to give extra weight to his moral ideals because of their content cannot buttress his position by appealing to their objective truth. It is in any case very strange to speak of the truth of ideals, as Singer supposes my opponent might. If this appeal to the objectivity of ideals cannot be made, the deontologist is left just unilaterally and irrationally affirming his ideals, which is no argument. The strength of my position is this: we are looking for moral principles which can be rationally defended; intuitionists cannot so defend any of theirs; utilitarians can defend many of the same principles, but will reject or qualify others. The ones that are rejected are left with no leg to stand on, because intuitionists have not provided any. See on Brandt *40/6*.

151/12 Mackie does not make clear here what he means by 'degrade an ideal which he endorses to the level of a mere preference'. But the next phrase may indicate that he is the victim of a common confusion about subjectivity, which elsewhere he has disavowed. The confusion can also arise in connection with a question which Griffin asks about the objectivity of values (*83/15*); but I will discuss it here, not for the first time. See *MT* 206 ff. and H 1976*b*.

Let us first be clear that when we speak of values we may have different things in mind. If we ask about 'a person's values', we are asking what things he tends to value; that is, about what states of mind he tends to be in with regard to outcomes of various sorts. In this sense values are clearly something subjective, since states of mind are; and so are ideals, in the sense in which we ask what are a person's ideals.

On the other hand, when people ask whether values or ideals are objective (or are 'built into the fabric of the world') they purport to be talking about something other than states of mind. In H 1985*a* I have questioned, as Griffin does, whether this question corresponds to any real distinction, as Mackie evidently thought it did. For what, I asked, as I had asked before (H 1960), is the difference between a world into the fabric of which these values are built, and a world from which they are absent, but in which people still have values and ideals in the subjective sense?

This distinction once made, we can ask of both sorts of values whether their existence *depends* on someone's valuing something (i.e. on someone's state of mind). If 'values' is being used in the first (subjective) sense, the answer is that it clearly does, and similarly with ideals. In the second sense, the question itself is quite opaque. For to ask it we have to assume that the values and ideals, of which we are asking whether they depend, etc., are things of which we can ask such a question, or *any* question.

I must confess that when Mackie here says 'This matters only because I care for it', I am not at all clear what the 'only' is supposed to exclude, or what contrast, it is supposed to mark. If Mackie believed in 'objective values', and could say what they were, then we might know what other reason he is suggesting that there might be for the thing mattering. But neither of these conditions is satisfied. In his scheme of things, which excludes 'objective values', there is nothing else left to be a reason why something matters except that it matters *to someone*; and this is another way of saying something subjective, viz. that he is concerned or cares for it. So I still cannot see what the 'only' is doing.

If, on the other hand, Mackie is merely contrasting two different subjective states of mind, one called 'caring for', and the other called 'wholeheartedly endorsing ideals' (or 'values'), then he does not seem to me to be disagreeing with my view. I have never said that all these subjective states are identical; only that they form a genus, for which I used the convenient Aristotelian word *orexis* (see *FR* 170 n.) In particular, some of them are universal preferences (in this wide sense of 'preference') and some singular. But this does not help Mackie, because merely being universal does not give a preference any edge. So, unless he can give some reason for dignifying one sort of *orexis* at the expense of others (and this he does not do), he has not lent any support to ideals against 'mere preferences'.

Suppose, however, that we leave Mackie aside and (as is perhaps more relevant in the context of Griffin's paper) confront a true-blue 'objectivist' who thinks that values and ideals are built into the fabric. He purports to say that values and ideals, in his 'objective' sense, unlike values and ideals of the 'subjective' sort, do not depend on states of mind, but that, on the contrary, the states of mind called valuing and having ideals depend, or should depend, on the existence of these objective values and ideals. In Griffin's expression, this 'objectivist' thinks that we value things because they are valuable; they are not valuable because we value them. It is hard to see what this could mean. Certainly we value things (as Griffin says) because they have the properties they have. Jack values the experience of being with Susan because the experience is like that; John has the ideal of becoming a painter like Gaugin because it would be like that to be like Gaugin. But it is simply not helpful to say that either of these people value those things because they are valuable. This seems to mean that they attribute to them value-giving properties because they have those properties. And being valuable is not one of the value-giving properties.

It may be asked, what makes the properties value-giving. The 'subjectivist' will answer, 'the fact that they are valued'. But this is wrong. For it is not self-contradictory to speak of someone valuing something which is valueless, and which therefore has no value-giving properties. The way out of this morass is never found by descriptivists, but is plain to prescriptivists like myself. To say that something has value is to express, oneself, an evaluation. So if I say that something has value but is not valued by someone, I am expressing a favourable evaluation which, I say, he does not agree with. When I express this evaluation, I am not stating something about my state of mind, so I am not stating a subjective fact (I am not stating *any* fact). Subjectivism about this kind of value-statement is therefore quite wrong, sharing the faults of descriptivism in general.

We may therefore say that the 'subjectivist' is right about values and ideals in the 'subjective' sense, but wrong about them in the 'objective'. But when we have explored this 'objective' sense in the hope of finding some illumination, it turns out that the 'objectivist' is wrong about them too. He first confuses the values with the value-giving properties, and supposes that because the latter are objective, so are the former; and then he mistakes an expression of an evaluation for a statement that something has a property. About values in the second, 'objective', sense, both the 'objectivist' and the 'subjectivist' are quite at sea, and anybody who, because he is a descriptivist, thinks that everyone must be one or the other, is bound to be in the same boat. But I do not accuse Singer of these confusions, and must apologize for having digressed from his paper.

153/3 The move against me which Singer here contemplates is disturbingly similar to one I have myself used against descriptivist opponents like Warnock (H 1968, 1972*e*). But there is a crucial difference. See *MT* 187.

156/−10 On this, see my reply to Mackie in H 1984*g*:115. Philosophers often argue that a dominant race can secure happiness for itself by adopting a narrowly constrained set of concepts which allows it to oppress a different race. But this belief would not survive a visit to South Africa, in the state in which it now is, produced by people who thought this. Some might argue that our duties to non-human animals present a more difficult case for me. But it seems to me (and I am sure that Singer would agree) that the maltreatment of such of them as are capable of suffering is not necessary for, nor even conducive to, human happiness. In other words, we could be happier if we changed our ways, and so would the animals. Singer and I might not agree on what this would still allow us to do to which animals; but that is too big a question for treatment here.

157/9 See H 1981*b*. We must note the similarity of the argument which Singer suggests here to that which he has deployed earlier, with my support, against the 'objectivist' deontologist and the fanatic. If to do our moral thinking rationally is to seek opinions for which one can give reasons, one must eschew those for which one cannot give reasons. However, as Singer sees, the argument will not work in this case. For the tribe that wishes to restrict the scope of universalizable moral judgements to its own members has a reason for so doing, namely its own lack of concern for anyone outside the tribe. This is not a moral reason, but it is a reason.

Singer's way out of the difficulty in the rest of his paper, which looks to me promising, bears some resemblance to that suggested by Scanlon, in my comments on whom I claim (*144/16*) that it is consistent with my own position. It is also very reminiscent of Parfit's contention (1984:126 ff.) that all the arguments which Self-interest can use against the 'Present-aim Theory' can be turned by Morality against Self-interest. In a similar way, and potentially with equal effect, Singer can argue that any argument which can be used by those who want to restrict the scope of morality to their own tribe can be used equally well against them by those who wish to restrict it still further and so exclude *them*; and that, if they resist the latter set of arguments, they cannot then use their original arguments against those who wish to extend the scope still further. Both Singer's and Parfit's arguments are attractive, and I wish them success.

12. Comments on Urmson

162/10 Urmson's tactic has been, first to oversimplify my theory outrageously, and then to accuse it of being 'breathtakingly simple'. Actually it is quite intricate. So when in *164/2* he says that 'Morality is more complex than Hare allows', he should have said 'Morality is more complex than Urmson allows Hare's account of it to be.' An example of this oversimplification follows immediately, where he speaks of 'such irrational procedures as "weighing" the principles' (*162/17*). When he comes later to cite the passage in which I write about this, he leaves out the crucial last two sentences of it (see on *166/3*). It is not my view that 'weighing' is necessarily irrational; it is so only if we have no idea of the difference between a right and a wrong way of doing it.

163/4 Urmson says that 'Hare offers' this trite picnic example. Actually it has been current for years. I expressly deprecated it as 'the kind of trivial example that used to be favoured by intuitionist philosophers', and quickly passed to 'more serious examples' (*MT* 26, 29). I did not dwell on it for long, and therefore did not consider (though I had done so in an earlier draft) expedients like asking my children to release me from my promise, or putting off the picnic until the next day (*163/15*). The example is easily altered, without departing from verisimilitude, so as to make such expedients unavailable.

163/18 Here it begins to be evident that, as part of the tactic of oversimplifying my view, Urmson is operating with a different and far narrower understanding of the word 'principle' than I am—as where he speaks in *164/6* of 'ready-made maxims of relative generality and manageable complexity'. He sensibly says himself (*164/11*), 'I doubt whether there is a very rigid use of the word "principle" in everyday life.' And in any case nothing in the argument between us ought to hang on the ordinary correct use of the word. It started (by way of a translation of the Aristotelian '*archē*') as a term of art, and has borne many meanings even in philosophy. I have used it to mean any properly universal prescription, and explain my use in H 1972*a*.

I think that Urmson's use is eccentric. I wonder how many people beside him confine the word to 'rules of conduct . . . to be followed (ordinarily) blindly', i.e. 'being unwilling to consider arguments to the contrary'. My own intuitive or prima-facie principles are a bit like this, though not usually so rigid; but they are only a particular class of principles. There are many principles that we have, but are perfectly willing to reconsider either on a particular occasion or for all our future conduct. I may have a principle not to betray my friends, but break it if a friend starts giving away nuclear secrets to the Russians. I may even, if I think it may happen again with other friends, substantially modify the principle. Examples of different sorts of principles (including Urmson's sort) are given in *FR* 42–6.

I do not think, however, that he means to be as rigid as he starts off by being; he later says, 'What I am calling a principle merely needs to be given unquestioning obedience in the ordinary circumstances which they were designed to deal with' (*164/−8*). This is very like my own treatment of prima-facie principles; so perhaps Urmson exaggerates the difference between us.

In *164/−2*, by his (surely incorrect) use of the word 'adage', Urmson betrays the over-narrowness of his use of 'principle'. What he calls 'adages', most people would call 'principles'. He has left a gap in his vocabulary that has to be filled (unhappily) by 'adage', which actually means, according to the *OED*, 'a maxim handed down from antiquity; a proverb'. The examples in the *OED* make it clear that an adage is a kind of *saying*. Urmson says in *165/11*. 'There are indeed conflicts of principle'; and I suppose there are conflicts of adages too, in the usual as opposed to his private sense of the word ('Many hands make light work' vs. 'Too many cooks spoil the broth'). But they are hardly the same kind of conflicts.

I take it that Urmson's intention is to put me into a

dilemma: either I am using the word 'principle' in his sense, in which case I am left saying a lot of very absurd things; or else I am not using it in his sense, in which case I am misusing it. My reply is that I have explained the way I am using it; that if this were a deviant use, it would not matter, because it is a term of art; but that in fact it is he that is misusing it, by applying it only to a very narrow range of cases, which are principles for sure, and are indeed covered by my own wider use, but are far from being the only kind of principles.

We may take as an example the principle 'Friends have some claim on one' (as Urmson puts it in *163/−16*). I could phrase it my way by saying that one should under certain conditions (which could be loosely specified) do for one's friends what they want. This is certainly a principle in one current sense, and if Urmson did not acknowledge it I should value his friendship less than I do. I would even say that friendship imposes *duties* (though not perhaps in the very rigid sense of 'duty' that Urmson appears to have acquired from his upbringing, which must have been of almost Kantian severity). I have a duty (though not an obligation in the narrow sense of *MT* 149) to be nice to my friends. When Urmson says, 'I might still decide to do this kindness to my friends, even though I have no duty' *(163/−4)*, he is treating his friends like strangers—and one may have a duty, though not such an exacting one, even to strangers.

165/−14 On the Warnock Committee, see H 1987*a*, 1987*d*. The Committee proceeded for the most part intuitively, as Urmson would no doubt wish, and gave only the sketchiest of reasons for its recommendations. The result was that where these were controversial the case for them lacked the support that the Committee could have given it, and there is a danger that more reactionary measures will be approved by Parliament. If the Committee had done some critical thinking, and so made its principles (in the ordinary sense) clear and defended them, it would have done more good.

166/3 The quotation from *MT* which follows is incomplete. It goes on, 'It [the judging or weighing process] is, further, not a one-level but a two-level procedure, without any explanation of what is supposed to happen at the second level. The procedure can, however, be made viable within an adequate two-level system.' My objection, then, is not to judging or weighing duties, but to pretending to do this without having a method for doing it (weighing without any scales, or without any understanding of what the figures on the dial mean, or of the difference between weighing correctly and incorrectly).

I do not object to rational weighing or judging, in which there is a way of telling whether it is done well or ill. Moral intuitions of the sort that Urmson wishes to invoke differ from all his other examples of judging, in that there is no such way beyond an appeal to consensus, unless something like my second-level critical thinking is brought in. In all the other examples, we may speak of judging or even of intuition, but there is a way of telling, at least *post eventum*, whether the judging has been rightly done, or whether the intuition was correct.

166/−16 Scientists use their judgement in deciding what hypotheses to test first; but they do not have to use judgement in deciding, after a crucial experiment, that either the experiment was in some way faulty or the hypothesis has to be rejected. There is a method here, accepted by nearly all scientists and by most philosophers of science except the avowed anti-rationalists. Juries use their judgement in deciding whether, for example, a witness is telling the truth. But this is an example of (factual) intuitive thinking whose existence I have never denied. It can be rational because there is a way of determining, perhaps later, whether a witness *was* telling the truth. So we can build up an idea of whether the intuitive thinking we were doing was methodologically sound. The same applies to weather forecasts. In all these cases, there is, at least in principle, some other method than intuition of checking the correctness of the intuition. What makes moral intuitions, when unsupported by critical thinking, irrational is that there is no such method.

The same applies to my judgement of my Australian friends' state of mind, and to the other examples given in *166/9* ff. I shall know later whether the new carpet was the best investment, and whether I got more money in the end, in real terms, by going for growth or income. As to the peasant in New Guinea, I have to use my judgement on whether Oxfam or the Church Missionary Society will do more for him; but in principle, when they have done their best, I can know how successful they have been, unless this depends on judgements of moral or other value. If that turns out to be the case, I shall have to employ critical moral or other evaluative thinking. Even for these evaluations, I cannot for ever rely on my unsupported intuitions.

It is indeed difficult to become philosophically clear on the nature of the weighing or judging that we do. But in my account of critical thinking I have tried harder to achieve this than have the intuitionists, who for the most part seem content to leave us in darkness.

167/−12 Plato's point about nodding does not help Urmson. The philosophers whom I am attacking (and whom he too does not admire) are not claiming merely that an act can be wrong in one respect but right in another. With this I can agree, at any rate so far as the intuitive level of thinking goes. That is to say, it can be contrary to one intuitive principle which should not be abandoned, and yet in accordance with, or required by, another; or it may be contrary in one respect, but conformable in another, to a single sound principle. They are claiming something much stronger: that it can be both right, full stop, and wrong, full stop. Plato did not say that something can be both moving, full stop, and stationary, full stop.

168/−3 Here is another example of Urmson's oversimplification of my views. Where do I say that the *only* distinction to be made is between those who accept fewer or more principles to guide their moral life? I certainly make other distinctions in this area, and in this part of *MT*.

169/−9 That I 'fail to allow for whole ranges of moral life which are not concerned with fulfilment of duty and obligation' is a slander that others beside Urmson have propagated. I must ask to be pardoned if I digress in order to rebut it. Since I started doing moral philosophy, though I have occasionally talked about duty and obligation, I have on the whole concentrated on other words. In *LM* I discussed principally the words 'good', 'right', and 'ought' as used in both moral and non-moral contexts. They seemed to me, and still do, to be the simplest concepts to start on; an understanding of their character puts us in a position to understand the others.

I also noted, but did not discuss at length, secondarily evaluative words like 'tidy' and 'industrious' (*LM* 121), to which some of my opponents want us to confine our attention (see H 1986c). 'Kind' and 'neighbourly', like 'cruel' and 'courageous', belong to this class. I was well aware of their existence; but I thought it most helpful at that stage to confine my attention to the simplest examples of value-words, in order to get clear about their workings. How wise I was becomes clear, when we see how little of use to practical issues has come from the examination of these secondarily evaluative words by their *conoscenti*. The reason is that they already incapsulate entrenched values, and so beg the important questions. Their character can be readily explained once we understand that of the simpler words which we are told to ignore.

After that, in my subsequent books, I concentrated in the main on 'ought', again because I think it the most fundamental concept in moral thinking, and probably the simplest apart from 'must'. This by no means implies a neglect of other words and other types of moral thinking. These are amply allowed for in my developed theory. In particular, the 'good dispositions', such as kindness, affection, courage, and the like, are easily understood as dispositions to act and feel in ways which, if we were to try to frame explicit precepts about them, we should specify in principles (i.e. universal prescriptions) like the one mentioned earlier, 'One should be nice to one's friends.' To understand the logic of our thought about these, it is helpful to formulate them in language. There is absolutely no conflict between a 'virtues' account of morality and a 'principles' account, or between either and an account which lays stress on human relations of love and affection. What we are after in all cases (cf. Aristotle *EN* 1106b16, 24) is a way of thinking, feeling, and acting which it is best that we cultivate. This can be described either as a set of virtues, or as the internalization (as psychologists may say) of a body of principles, or simply as becoming that sort of person. I still think that the best way of *characterizing* such a 'morally good life' would be by a set of precepts or prescriptions specifying just how a person who lived it should seek to think, feel, and behave.

So, when Urmson says (*168/21*), 'There are various types of action which we might call kind, considerate, chivalrous, charitable, neighbourly, sporting, decent, or acts of self-denial and self-abnegation; actions, so described are in many circumstances neither duties nor obligations; to fail to do them would not be positively wrong (though perhaps, unneighbourly, unkind, etc.), nor are they dictated by what I call principle', he opens a wide but quite imaginary gulf between virtue and duty, and reveals how over-narrowly he is using 'duty' and 'principle'. An act is wrong *because* it is unkind; we have a duty to be kind; the principle (in my sense) that we should be kind to others (which is almost impossible unless we have the appropriate feelings towards them) is a principle expressing a disposition which we all ought to cultivate in ourselves and others, i.e. a virtue.

13. Comments on Vendler

171/1 It may be helpful if I begin by giving my own view of the relation, in general, between Vendler's ideas and mine. Since I published *MT* he has given us a very interesting and stimulating book (1984). In this he carries further the theses he put forward in the paper to which I appealed for support in *MT* 119–21. It is therefore necessary for me to decide how much of what he now says I have to take over for my own argumentative purposes. I greatly admire the boldness with which Vendler has challenged orthodoxy in his spectacular revival of the Kantian 'Transcendental Self'. But I shall refrain from committing myself to this doctrine, not because I am sure that it is wrong, but because I do not need to stick my neck out so far. I have suffered too much from mis-understandings of my own views to expose myself willingingly to those of which Vendler will certainly be a victim.

I shall therefore err on the side of caution. The argument in which I enlisted Vendler's support was a limited one I had been having with Christopher Taylor (1965). It concerned whether it is logically possible to perform the operation which I had claimed was a constituent of moral thinking, and which is called, metaphorically, 'putting myself in somebody else's shoes'. Taylor had maintained that if I try to put myself in the shoes of another, and the shoes are understood as including all his characteristics and those of his situation, I am trying to cease to be myself, which is logically impossible. This is because who I am is determined by *my* characteristics (or a central core of them), and therefore if I lost those it would no longer be me.

To this I replied, following my understanding of Vendler, that we have to distinguish between the two hypotheses 'If I were Jones . . .' and 'If Hare were Jones . . .'. I conceded at least for the sake of argument that the latter assumes a logical impossibility, on one interpretation (though there is another, I said, on which it does not). But the former, I claimed, assumes nothing logically impossible; for, although it may be that 'Hare' has to be introduced into our language via a specification of some characteristics which Hare has, this is not true of 'I'. Though I may have an essence qua Hare, I have none qua I, and therefore there is nothing in logic to stop my imagining that I were Jones with all his charcteristics. I went on to make the related point, also due to Vendler, that the word 'I' has no *descriptive* content. Vendler in his present essay says that 'I' is an indexical, though I did not myself use that word.

I still think that this limited move enables me to answer Taylor. It is a merely linguistic move, and does not necessarily bring with it the more ambitious metaphysical claims that attract Vendler. It is sufficient for my argument if we can (as we certainly can) meaningfully say 'If I were Jones . . .', 'Imagine being Jones', and 'Imagine what it would be like for you if you were Jones.' The latter in particular does not commit me to imagining that Hare is Jones (which is perhaps impossible).

I am therefore inclined to avail myself only of the main linguistic points that Vendler makes, and no more. It is possible that if he could be old-fashioned enough to resume his former style and put *all* his claims in linguistic dress, I might be able to accept them. But, although he says that his Transcendental Self is not a *thing* (see on *175/18* ff. below), he will certainly be misinterpreted as claiming this, and I do not want any of the misinterpretations to attach to me. My relation to Vendler is therefore a bit like my relation to David Lewis (*MT* 115); I accept some of his linguistic points but do not commit myself to his metaphysics. The question which has to be considered in what follows is, then, to what extent I have to accept Vendler's grander claims in order to support myself in my argument with Taylor, and carry through my project of explaining moral thinking.

173/15 I take it that if God can represent to himself what it is like to have a human body, archangels could without offence to logic be supposed to have this power. For, as Vendler says, the Archangel is just an idea; and the question is, whether the idea is coherent. I am no theologian; but I know that there is a tension in Christian theology between the doctrine that, as the first of the Thirty-nine Articles puts it, God is without body, parts, or passions, and the doctrine (so vividly set out in the poem of Blake that I quoted in *MT* 99 and in this volume on Brandt *39/13*) that God can suffer with those who suffer. But I shall not pursue the matter here, since it is, as Vendler says, a digression. I am sure that even humans can sometimes summon up the necessary sympathy to do some critical moral thinking; and therefore it makes sense to me, for expository purposes, to conceive of this power being superhumanly extended.

So I think that in *173/−2* Vendler goes too far. I agree that no human can *fully* know what it is like to be another organism; but Vendler has not convinced me that it is incoherent to suppose the Archangel endowed with the perfection of a power which we have imperfectly.

175/18 ff. I agree that indexicality is not a source of qualitative differences anywhere. And I am no more committed than Vendler is to saying that the other I is a *thing*. I do not want to posit the sort of self that Hume rejected, any more than the sort that Descartes believed in; Vendler puts this point well in *176/5* ff. But I do think that the other I is distinct from this I; for I care whether this I suffers, but may not care whether that I suffers. That is, I accept different *prescriptions* about the two Is. See on Richards *118/8* and *MT* 99.

176/−4 I do not understand why Vendler says 'But' here. I

am not committed to the view that 'indexicality' is all there is to the meaning of 'I'. At least it has, in addition, the feature which in *MT* 96 f. I call 'prescriptivity'; and this makes a difference to my position *vis-à-vis* Vendler. For, as we have just seen, I do distinguish in my *concerns* between possible states of myself and possible states of other people. Vendler himself makes a somewhat similar point at the end of his essay: although my moral obligations would attach to anybody who has the same universal properties, it is I who have to fulfil them. I do not think that in fact we differ on the point I have just made.

176/—1 The stove differs from me in not having concerns. It is sometimes said that stoves, mountains, and trees are outside the scope of morality (we cannot have duties to them) because we cannot put ourselves in their positions. I think that this is badly expressed. We can put ourselves in their positions, but, since when we do this we have no sentience and therefore no concerns, it simply does not matter to us what happens to us if we turn into such things, any more than it matters to us if we are going to be put on the rack after we are dead. So moral arguments relying on the move 'Are you prepared to prescribe that it should be done to you if you were a tree?' get no grip (see H 1987*b*).

177/13 Vendler is here supposing that I want 'the purity of the self-referential indexical' to do more than help me in my argument against Taylor. But it is a much larger question how it could help me in any attempt to imagine being another individual. It merely removes one obstacle to that; the others may remain. However, Vendler has made abundantly clear that it makes sense to say 'Imagine being Jones'; and all I needed for my purposes in *MT* 119 ff. was this linguistic point.

178/6 It is not clear that anything else has to be said to make my limited point. I never claimed that the consistency of 'I might be in Smith's precise situation', said by Jones, *follows* from the indexicality of 'I'. I said merely that, if we understand that 'I' behaves differently from 'Jones' in this context, we shall not think this statement self-contradictory in the way that, perhaps, 'Jones might be in Smith's precise situation' could well be thought to be self-contradictory. One of the differences is that 'I' is indexical. As Vendler says, we certainly have to explain in addition (though not for the purpose of my argument with Taylor) what it is for an individual to be in the I-position; and I am satisfied that Vendler has shed some light on this. But that was not my ambition in *MT* 119 ff. I said something about it in *MT* 98 f., but not enough.

178/23 Vendler has persuaded me that it was foolhardly of me to use, without caution or qualification, common expressions like 'Put yourself in his shoes', 'individuals occupying roles', and the like. They do indeed suggest that selves are *things* that can be slotted into *places*. However, we certainly do use such ways of speaking, and seem to mean something by them. The question is whether my account of moral thinking can be carried through without using them. Or alternatively whether an innocuous explanation can be given of their meaning. Vendler thinks that the former is the case.

179/6 There are various stronger and weaker interpretations of Leibniz's principle of the identity of indiscernibles. I hold that it is true in some of its weaker versions, but false in some of its stronger. For example it is true that no two numerically different things can share all their properties, including those specifiable only by the use of singular terms; but it is false that no two numerically different things can share all their universal properties. The discussion in Strawson 1959:119 ff. still seems to me powerful. Such a weaker version is compatible with my account of moral thinking, and in the present example A and B can share all their universal properties while being different individuals.

179/10 The view that Vendler here cites from me seems to me compatible with his own. When I said, 'If you and I changed places, the world would be no different in its universal properties', I was not intending to claim that you and I are 'bare particulars'. Vendler himself thinks that it makes sense to suppose that I were Napoleon, though not that Hare were Napoleon; and the former was all I was suggesting in that perhaps unfortunately phrased passage. If I were Napoleon the world would not be changed in its universal properties. It certainly does not follow (as Vendler rightly says) that I and

Napoleon have no properties. We both have properties
(different ones from each other); what is being suggested is
that I might have the properties which Napoleon actually
had. 'Changing places' then means not literally 'changing
spatial locations' (which suggests something that only *things*—
indeed only the class of things which have spatial locations—
can do, namely move in such a way that one comes to occupy
the place that the other previously occupied, and vice versa),
but rather 'exchanging all their universal properties' (to
achieve which, nothing would have to move spatially).

179/18 I wish I had kept off the 'possible worlds' terminology.
It often sheds more darkness than light, and in that context
was not necessary. It is a good maxim, in order to remain
within 'the bounds of sense', to translate all sentences
containing this term into sentences containing the words
'can', 'may', 'might', and the like. So 'There is a possible
world in which I am Napoleon' means no more than 'I might
be Napoleon'; and so, imagination shows me, I might be. The
world in which I was Napoleon would be a different world
than this, though not in its universal properties. It would
certainly be very different *for me*.

179/−4 'Brought into the "now" position' seems to me as
objectionable, by Vendler's canons, as anything I have said.
As he says himself, 'Our natural concepts are not designed to
carry such a burden; they are stretched to the breaking point,
yet we have nothing better to replace them' (1984:104). But
we must in the end try to do better, and I think he has shown
me a way in which I can.

181/8 'I bring him into the "I"-position as it were.' The last
three words seem to be an apology for taking a liberty with
language—one no less than I have taken. I do not literally
have a *position* into which Castro can be brought. If I had, then
perhaps I could change positions with him. But although
these locutions are out of order, we perhaps understand what
we are trying to mean by them. We mean that I can imagine
having Castro's universal properties, and losing my own, and
at the same time having the same *concern* for the person who
has those properties as I now have for the person who has my
actual properties.

181/11 I agree to this; more is meant by 'the "I" being an empty frame of awareness, indifferent to content', than that 'I' is a bare self-referential indexical. Part of the more, I would claim, is that the 'awareness' includes concern for my own experiences. Perhaps this is all I need for my account of moral thinking.

181/20 Where do I say that the claim that 'I' is a pure subject can be derived from the claim that the word 'I' is a (nearly) pure indexical? I say in *MT* 120 that the point that I have no essence and the point that 'the bringing into use of the expression "I" involves the ascription of no essential properties' are related, though not identical, points. But I nowhere use the expression 'pure subject'; that is Vendler's.

182/11 So far from 'shying away', I have no objection to viewing 'imagining being in the same qualitative conditions as another person' as the same as 'imagining being that person'; and I am grateful to Vendler for giving me the opportunity of saying this. However, it must be added that the exercise includes imagining having the concerns that that person has.

182/16 This aposiopesis and relapse into metaphor is entirely pardonable. I am not a what or a such except in the sense that I do (actually) have properties, and might have had others.

182/−5 I am not sure that there is a disagreement. So far as can be said in universal terms, there is only one situation. And whatever can be said morally about that situation has to be said about it whoever has the properties of the people in it. But *in the moral argument* we have to appeal to the *concern* which those people have for themselves in that situation; and we have to say that the car-man's concern for the car-man and the cycle-man's concern for the cycle-man have both to be taken into account. In so doing, we are taking into account the concerns of two different people, both of whom refer to themselves as 'I'. So in that sense there are two Is and not one. But I do not think that Vendler wishes to deny this; he says that there are 'two persons involved'. We do not need (at least for the purposes of moral thinking) to speak of a Transcendental I of which there is only one. I accept from Vendler the suggestion that it is not necessary for me to speak of my changing places in any literal sense, even in the imagination.

But I do have to imagine taking on the properties of a different person, and with them his concerns.

14. Comments on Williams

185/1 It was good of Williams to give my ideas so much attention in his writings. But for reasons of space I shall have in what follows to concentrate mainly on what he has said about me in the present volume. That his criticisms elsewhere can be answered I am sure; but I assume that the ones he has brought forward here are those he considers the most important. This is borne out by the fact that the only criticism of utilitarianism in the introduction to Sen and Williams 1982 which does not succumb to my two-level defence and other moves in *MT* is that voiced on p. 16 of that book and amplified in this volume. This criticism is answered in my note on *189/−20* below.

I am especially grateful for what he has done here to distinguish the objections he wishes to make peculiarly to my views from those which elsewhere he has levelled at utilitarians in general. Some of these, as he says, pass me by. I do not like to be tarred with too broad a brush. In particular, I am glad that he does not think that I am, in the words of his splendid slogan, a 'Government House utilitarian' (*188/−11*). From the fact that Scanlon (*131/−10*) actually cites Williams for this allegation, it looks as if some of the tar has stuck. But the record is quite clear; see Scanlon's next paragraph, *MT* 45, and, for disavowals of Government House Platonism and paternalism in moral education, H 1964, 1973, 1974, 1982*b*.

186/7 The objection that Williams makes to the World Agent model in 1985:88 seems to me ill taken. If a single agent can have conflicting preferences, there can be no objection in principle to my having conflicting sympathetic preferences when I am thinking morally about a choice affecting others. This, far from showing that I am '(to put it mildly) in bad shape', shows that I am giving due weight to the preferences of others as morality bids me do.

Moreover, Williams's (*c*) in *185/−2* is altogether too sweeping: even if I fully represent (*MT*, ch. 5) and universalize (*MT*, ch. 6), which are different requirements, I do not have to identify with *everyone's* preferences, as perhaps God does, but only with the preferences of those affected by actions I am thinking about.

186/—7 It was indeed one purpose of my two-level theory to save these appearances, thus removing the objection to utilitarianism that it yields counter-intuitive prescriptions. Another was to remove objections to my theory about the nature of the moral concepts, by showing that, if moral thinking takes place at more than one level, it is likely that rival views will have, to those who think only about (or at) the intuitive level, a certain attraction and plausibility, which disappear once we have the whole picture. This should help to allay the doubt Williams expresses in the next two paragraphs about the role of (*b*). See *MT* 65 ff., 80, and on *191/—6* below.

187/n.3 On this objection of Mackie's, see H 1984*g*. On my 'very demanding conception', see on Nagel *101/1*, and on Brandt *33/19 s.f.*, which gives my answer to Williams 1985:90. Morality *is* demanding. See also H 1984*f* for the relations between different preferences which can be had simultaneously. I never thought that 'impartial concern for others' preferences' would give *one* of the preferences of *one* of these people a veto on all other preferences of my own or other people. This would not be impartial. To appreciate fully a preference which is not now present, I have to imagine myself having it in another person's, or my own future, shoes; and then, if I fully succeed in doing this, I shall form a preference now for that future state which is equal in strength to what it would then be. But of course it has to compete with other preferences, and this may account for its *relative* weakness in relation to my other present preferences. Yet, in spite of what Williams says, if I do not feel the preference with the intensity which the person in the situation feels it, I have not fully represented his situation to myself. That humans cannot often do this is obvious but irrelevant. See *MT* 98 f.

188/11 I have never denied that language can embody illusions. If there is no God, the word 'blasphemy' embodies one (*FR* 89). The most I have claimed is that these illusions can be eradicated by a careful attention to what we mean and to the facts. That is one reason why attention to language is so much more powerful a tool in moral philosophy than Williams here suggests.

188/−17 On 'Government House utilitarianism' see on *185/1* above.

189/−20 The question of when one should think intuitively and when critically is certainly of philosophical *interest*; what I said on *MT* 49 was that there was 'no philosophical answer to the question; it depends on what powers of thought and character each one of us, for the time being, thinks he posesses.' But I cannot understand why Williams makes such heavy weather, in the succeeding passage, *192/4* ff. and elsewhere, of the combination of critical with intuitive thinking. My own experience of moral thinking (which may be different from Williams's) yields plenty of evidence of their compatibility. In the last chapter of his book (1985) he calls morality a 'peculiar institution'; and his conception of it may indeed be so.

Williams also misunderstands my military analogy. The point about the general in *MT* 52 was not that he combines tactical with strategic thought. That should not be difficult, and is not analogous to the combination of intuitive with critical thinking. I had in mind, rather, that a general who has the overall aim of victory may at one and the same time think of tactical *or* strategic principles (economy of forces, concentration of force, offensive action, etc.) *and* look at the details of the decision facing him, in the light of his overall aim.

Take, for example, the 'Principle of War' known to teachers of tactics as 'the Principle of Offensive Action'. An instructor at the Staff College might say, 'You should have a bang at the enemy whenever you get the chance, rather than sitting on your backsides.' This excellent intuititive or prima-facie tactical principle can be justified by critical military thinking. Even if no tactical gains are made, it stops the enemy relaxing, so that he cannot carry out necessary maintenance and supply, or even take a rest, because he never knows what you will do next. Thus the principle has, in military terms, a high acceptance-utility.

Suppose, then, that a commander is wondering on a particular occasion whether to attack the enemy or not. The principle bids him do so; but that might conflict with other principles or just lead to unacceptable loss. I can see no difficulty in his combining these detailed conflicting considerations with a firm grasp of and adherence to the good prima-facie principle. He knows it is a good principle; he may have it so much in his bones that he disobeys it with great reluctance—he would love to have a bang at the enemy. But in the circumstances, after some critical thinking, he may decide that discretion is the better part of valour; and, if it really was the better part, nobody is going to accuse him afterwards of not believing in the good principle, although his subordinates, if they share his offensive spirit, may, like him, have fretted at the time. And if for a military we substitute a moral principle, similar things can be said.

So it is manifestly false that thoughts combining intuitive with critical thinking are 'not stable under reflection' (*190/15*). See on Richards *123/—7*, and on *192/16* below. Does Williams suppose that when, at Salamanca, the Duke of Wellington refrained from attacking Marmont for many weeks, and just marched and countermarched parallel to him, he was succumbing to a lack of offensive spirit (Longford 1969:280 ff.)?

190/—12 The 'rules of thumb' position is, as Williams says, certainly not mine. See on Frankena *49/11* ff.

191/12 I find this confusing. I have supposed that an archangel can do perfectly what we humans can do only imperfectly. But all the same the critical thinking that we do is, so far as it goes, archangelic in form, only subject to our human limitations. See on Vendler *173/15*, and on *187/n.3* above.

191/—6 I have indeed proceeded 'downwards from the top of the system', in that I thought out what the properties of the moral concepts were before I tried to use them to construct a system of moral reasoning. I was genuinely surprised when, in *FR*, the resulting system turned out to be a utilitarian one, but delighted when the two-level move enabled me in *MT* not only to square its precepts with our common intuitions, but to defend my theory of the moral concepts itself against much-canvassed objections. See on *186/—7* above. I have done my best in *MT* to provide the 'further argument' that Williams says is needed. My method has this in common with 'reflective equilibrium', that I regard it as a support for my views if I can thus square them with common intuitions. But the reason for this is different from Rawls's, better knit and more complex: see H 1971*b*:117 ff., *MT* 12 ff., 65 ff., 80, and H 1986*b*.

There is indeed 'no guarantee that the appearances deserve to be saved' (*192/3*). But there is a presumption that they do. If I am right about the moral concepts, then it can be predicted that people will on the whole hold certain moral opinions. If they do hold them, the theory has survived that test. True, the opinions are the outcome, not only of the use of the concepts, but of factual beliefs (which may be mistaken) and thought processes (which may have gone astray through muddle or bias), as well as of the inclinations of the parties affected (which may differ from one time to another). However, all these disturbing factors can in principle be allowed for, so that it is normally possible to use actual moral opinions as a test of ethical theory. And if we assume that people are on the whole more wise than foolish (because they learn by bitter experience) we can even draw comfort from the fact that their moral opinions tally with those which critical thinking, in accordance with our theory, would recommend. This does not stop theory being sometimes used to criticize common opinions, if it can draw attention to the disturbing factors I have mentioned. For an example, see H 1985*b*.

192/16 I agree with Parfit's account, and regard it as answering this objection. I do not understand the objection expressed in the last sentence of this paragraph. If the theories are good ones, everyone should accept them in the spirit of the Duke of Wellington. How many people *will* accept them is another question; I think that many people already do think in the way that I am trying to clarify, and that more would (perhaps even enough to save mankind from self-destruction) if moral philosophy were better done and better understood.

193/−1 The expressions 'foundations' and 'foundationalism' play a big part in the criticisms that follow; but Williams (in spite of what he says in his 1985:30–70) has not made clear to me how he is using them in relation to my views. What is it to be a 'foundationalist'? We naturally think of Descartes, especially in view of Williams's important work on him, and his reference in *196/7*. But in *LM* 32, 38 f. I explicitly dissociated myself from the Cartesian method. My situation is different, because, in the end, Descartes rested on an assumption of the truth of certain *substantive* theses because they were 'clear and distinct', whereas I rest, not on this, but on a clear understanding, which all parties to an argument can share, of the *words* they are using.

The same goes for the difference between me and the intuitionists. They are much more open to this attack, since they do indeed appeal to principles thought to be self-evident. But is it 'foundationalism' to try to find a secure method of moral reasoning, which is what I am doing? Such a method, to be secure, has to be based on an understanding of what we are up to when we are thinking morally; and this, I argue, can be achieved by a thorough examination of the concepts we are using in our thought. If *this* is an improper ambition, what is there left for the moral philosopher to do? See on Nagel *101/1*.

The sense in which 'foundations' are now out of fashion (which in itself is no fault in them) is not that in which I have been seeking them. I have been doing what philosophical logicians have always done, namely try to improve our thinking by carefully examining the words and concepts we use in it. However, it is important that the concepts are not 'merely "ours" ' (*195/−10*), but that we share them with those with whom we argue, even if their moral opinions are very different from ours. This is not so with the 'foundations' provided by the intuitionists. That is the 'methodological reason . . . independent of the substantial point on which he and they disagree' that Williams asks for in *195/−2*.

I do not say that the opinions of intuitionists are always 'mere prejudice' (*194/14*); only that they sometimes are, and that the intuitionists themselves have no way of telling whether they are. A better moral philosophy than theirs might show most of their opinions to be justifiable. In one sense, this would be to provide a foundation for them; but Williams ought not to object to this, unless he thought (which I am sure he does not) that it is wrong to try to justify or argue for one's moral opinions.

194/18 Biographically speaking Williams's use of 'present view', 'now believes', and 'moved to believing' (*195/6*) is misleading. I always believed that (ii) and (iv) would turn out to be true; and, by Jove!, they have, in the innocuous sense of 'foundations' just explained. As one develops philosophically, what was an 'open question' (*195/8*) can get answered, in this case affirmatively. I cannot put my finger on Williams's reasons for answering it negatively. So I do have 'an assurance that these two things, the external view of what morality is, and the internal representation of it in moral practice, will necessarily fit together' (*195/15*).

REFERENCES AND BIBLIOGRAPHY

1. Writings of R. M. Hare

References in the text of the form (H 1955a: 295) are to this part of the bibliography, the second figure being the page. References to *The Language of Morals* (1952), *Freedom and Reason* (1963a), and *Moral Thinking* (1981a) take the form of the letters '*LM*', '*FR*', and '*MT*', respectively, followed by the page. A complete bibliography up to 1971 is printed in H 1971a, and from 1971 to 1980 in H 1981a. For completeness, all works published since 1981 are listed.

1952   *The Language of Morals* (Oxford U.P.). Translations: Italian, *Il linguaggio della morale* (Astrolabio-Ubaldini, 1968); German, *Die Sprache der Moral* (Suhrkamp, 1972); Spanish, *El Lenguaje de la Moral* (Mexico U.P., 1975). Also Chinese and Japanese.

1955a   'Universalisability', *Aristotelian Society* 55. Repr. in H 1972b.

1955b   'Ethics and Politics' (two articles and letters), *Listener* (Oct.). First article repr. in H 1972d. Spanish trans. in *Revista Universidad de San Carlos* 33 (1955).

1957   'Geach: Good and Evil', *Analysis* 17. Repr. in Foot (1967) and in H 1972b.

1960   ' "Rien n'a d'importance": l'anéantissement des valeurs est il pensable?', in *La Philosophie Analytique*, ed. with foreword by L. Beck; also discussion of other papers (Minuit). English version in H 1972d.

1962   Review of *Generalization in Ethics*, by M. Singer, *Ph. Q.* 12.

1963a   *Freedom and Reason* (Oxford U.P.). Translations: Italian, *Libertà e ragione* (Il Saggiatore, 1971); German, *Freiheit und Vernunft* (Patmos, 1973; Suhrkamp, 1983). Also Japanese.

1963b   'Descriptivism', *British Academy* 49. Repr. in Hudson (1969) and in H 1972b. Spanish trans. in *Etica y Analysis* 1, ed. E. Rabossi and F. Salmeron (U. Aut. de Mexico).

1964   'Adolescents into Adults', in *Aims in Education*, ed. T. C. B. Hollins (Manchester U.P.).

1968   Review of *Contemporary Moral Philosophy*, by G. J. Warnock, *Mind* 77.

1971*a*   *Practical Inferences* (London, Macmillan), containing bibliography of writings of R. M. Hare to 1971.

1971*b*   *Essays on Philosophical Method* (London, Macmillan): article 'The Argument from Received Opinion'.

1972*a*   'Principles', *Aristotelian Society* 73.

1972*b*   *Essays on the Moral Concepts* (London, Macmillan): article 'Wrongness and Harm'.

1972*c*   'Rules of War and Moral Reasoning', *Ph. and Pub. Aff.* 1. Repr. in *War and Moral Responsibility*, ed. M. Cohen *et al.* (Princeton U.P., 1974).

1972*d*   *Applications of Moral Philosophy* (London, Macmillan). Also Japanese.

1972*e*   Review of *The Object of Morality*, by G. J. Warnock, *Ratio* 14 (English and German edns.).

1973   'Language and Moral Education', in *New Essays in the Philosophy of Education*, ed. G. Langford and D. J. O'Connor (Routledge). Repr. in 1979*d*.

1974   'Platonism in Moral Education: Two Varieties', *Monist* 58.

1975*a*   'Autonomy as an Educational Ideal', in *Philosophers Discuss Education*, ed. S. C. Brown (London, Macmillan).

1975*b*   'Abortion and the Golden Rule', *Ph. and Pub. Aff.* 4. Repr. in *Philosophy and Sex*, ed. R. Baker and F. Elliston (Prometheus, 1975).

1976*a*   'Ethical Theory and Utilitarianism', in Lewis (1976). Repr. in Sen and Williams (1982).

1976*b*   'Some Confusions about Subjectivity', in *Freedom and Morality*, ed. J. Bricke (Lindley Lectures, U. of Kansas).

1977   'Justice and Equality', *Etyka* 14 (Warsaw, in Polish with English and Russian summaries). English version (revised) in *Justice and Economic Distribution*, ed. J. Arthur and W. Shaw (Prentice-Hall, 1978). Discussion in *Dialectics and Humanism* 6 (Warsaw, 1979, in English).

1979*a*   'What is Wrong with Slavery?', *Ph. and Pub. Aff.* 8. Repr. in *Readings in Applied Ethics*, ed. P. Singer (Oxford U.P., 1986).

1979*b*   'Utilitarianism and the Vicarious Affects', in *The Philosophy of Nicholas Rescher*, ed. E. Sosa (Reidel).

1979*c*   'What Makes Choices Rational?', *Rev. Met.* 32. German trans., *Conceptus* 15 (1981).

1979*d*   Repr. of H 1973 with criticism by G. J. Warnock and reply, in *The Domain of Moral Education*, ed. D. B. Cochrane *et al.* (Paulist P. and Ont. Inst. for St. in Education).

1981*a*   *Moral Thinking: Its Levels, Method and Point,* containing bibliography of writings of R. M. Hare, 1971–80 (Oxford U.P.).

1981*b*　Review of *The Expanding Circle*, by P. Singer, *New Republic* (7 Feb.).

1982*a*　*Plato*, in Past Masters series (Oxford U.P.). Translation: Spanish, *Platon* (Alianza, 1988). Also Chinese.

1982*b*　'Utilitarianism and Double Standards: A Reply to Dr. Annas', *Oxford Rev. of Edn.* 8.

1982*c*　'Moral Philosophy: Some Waymarks' (in Hebrew), in *New Trends in Philosophy*, ed. A. Kasher and S. Lappin (Yachdav).

1983　'Philosophical Introduction', in *Psychiatric Ethics*, ed. S. Bloch and P. Chodoff (Oxford U.P.).

1984*a*　'Do Agents have to be Moralists?', in *Gewirth's Ethical Rationalism*, ed. E. Regis, Jr. (U. of Chicago P.).

1984*b*　'Supervenience', *Aristotelian Society*, supp. 58.

1984*c*　'Utility and Rights: Comment on David Lyons' Paper', *Nomos* 24, *Ethics, Economics and the Law*.

1984*d*　'Arguing about Rights', *Emory Law J.* 33.

1984*e*　'Liberty and Equality: How Politics Masquerades as Philosophy', *Social Philosophy and Policy* 2.

1984*f*　'Some Reasoning about Preferences: A Response to Essays by Persson, Feldman and Schueler', *Ethics* 95.

1984*g*　'Rights, Utility and Universalization: A Reply to John Mackie', in *Utility and Rights*, ed. R. Frey (U. of Minnesota P.).

1985*a*　'Ontology in Ethics', in *Morality and Objectivity* (essays in memory of John Mackie), ed. T. Honderich (Routledge).

1985*b*　'Philosophy and Practice: Some Issues about War and Peace', in *Philosophy and Practice*, ed. A. P. Griffiths (R. Inst. of Ph. Lectures 19, supp. to *Philosophy* 59, Cambridge U.P.).

1985*c*　'Little Human Guinea-pigs?', in *Ethical Issues in Modern Medicine*, ed. M. Lockwood (Oxford U.P.).

1985*d*　'The Ethics of Clinical Experimentation on Human Children', in *Logic, Methodology and Philosophy of Science* 7, Proc. of 7th Int. Congress of Logic, M. and Ph. of Sc., Salzburg, 1983, ed. R. B. Marcus *et al.* (N. Holland). 1985*c* and 1985*d* do not overlap.

1985*e*　'How to Decide Moral Questons Rationally' (in Italian), in *Etica e diritto: le vie della giustificazione razionale*, ed. E. Lecaldano (Laterza). English version forthcoming in *Critica* (Mexico).

1985*f*   Comment on 'Manipulative Advertising', by T. Beauchamp, *Business and Professional Ethics Journal* 3.

1986*a*   'A Kantian Utilitarian Approach', in *Moral Rights in the Workplace*, ed. G. Ezorsky (SUNYP); excerpt from longer paper 'The Rights of Employees: The European Court of Human Rights and the Case of Young, James and Webster' (forthcoming).

1986*b*   'Why Do Applied Ethics?', in *New Directions in Ethics*, ed. R. M. Fox and J. P. de Marco (Routledge). Repr. forthcoming in *Applied Ethics and Ethical Theory*, ed. F. Shehadi and D. M. Rosenthal (U. of Utah P., 1988).

1986*c*   'A *Reductio ad Absurdum* of Descriptivism', in *Philosophy in Britain Today*, ed. S. Shanker (Croom Helm).

1986*d*   'Health', *J. Med. Eth.* 12.

1986*e*   'Liberty, Equality and Fraternity in South Africa?', *S. Afr. J. of Ph.* 5. Also in *Ph. Forum* 8 (1986).

1986*f*   'Punishment and Retributive Justice', in *Phil. Topics* 14, *Value Theory*, ed. J. Adler and R. N. Lee (U. of Arkansas P.).

1986*g*   'Universalizability' and 'Utilitarianism', in *New Dictionary of Christian Ethics*, ed. J. Childress and J. Macquarrie (SCM), also published as *Westminister Dictionary of Christian Ethics*, ed. J. Childress and J. Macquarrie (Westminster).

1987*a*   'An Ambiguity in Warnock', *Bioethics* 1.

1987*b*   'Moral Reasoning about the Environment', *J. App. Ph.* 4.

1987*c*   Review of *The Philosophy of Rights and Wrong*, by B. Mayo, *Ph. Q.* 37.

1987*d*   '*In Vitro* Fertilization and the Warnock Report', in *The Ethics of Human Design*, ed. R. Chadwick (Croom Helm).

1987*e*   'Why Moral Language?', in *Metaphysics and Morality: Essays in Honour of J. J. C. Smart*, ed. P. Pettit *et al.* (Blackwell).

1988*a*   'Embryo Experimentation: Public Policy in a Pluralist Society', *Bioethics News*.

1988*b*   'Philosophy and the Teaching of Medical Ethics', *Med. Ed.*

1988*c*   'A Kantian Approach to Abortion', in *Right Conduct: Theories and Applications*, 2nd edn., ed. M D. Bayles and K. Henley (Random H.).

1988*d*   'Philosophy of Language in Ethics' (in English), in *Sprachphilosophie*, ed. M. Dascal *et al.* (de Gruyter).

1988*e*   'Some Sub-atomic Particles of Logic', (forthcoming).

The date 1988 is conjectural. The following volumes of essays are in preparation, and will contain reprints of many of the above papers which were not reprinted in 1971*a*, 1971*b*, 1972*b*, and 1972*d*, as well as unpublished papers.

Essays in Ethical Theory.
Essays on Political Morality.
Essays on Religion and Education.
Essays on Bioethics.

2. Other Writings

References in the text of the form (Anscombe, 1958: 17) are to this part of the bibliography, the second figure being the page.

ANSCOMBE, G. E. M. (1958), 'Modern Moral Philosophy', *Philosophy* 33. Repr. in Hudson (1969).

ARENDT, H. (1973), *The Origins of Totalitarianism* (Harcourt Brace Jovanovich).

ARISTOTLE, *De Interpretatione* and *Nicomachean Ethics* (refs. to Bekker's pages and columns given in margins of most edns. and translations).

ARROW, K. J. (1963), 'Utility and Expectation in Economic Behaviour', in *Psychology: A Study of a Science*, ed. S. Koch, vol. 6 (McGraw-Hill, 1963).

—— (1977), 'Extended Sympathy and the Possibility of Social Choice', *Am. Econ. Rev. Papers and Proc.* 67.

—— (1978), 'Extended Sympathy and the Possibility of Social Choice', *Philosophia* 7.

AUSTIN, J. L. (1962), *How To Do Things With Words* (Oxford U.P.).

BAIER, K. (1958), *The Moral Point of View* (Cornell U.P.).

BEARDSMORE, R. W. (1969), *Moral Reasoning* (Routledge).

BRANDT, R. B. (1970), 'Some Merits of One Form of Rule Utilitarianism', in *Readings in Contemporary Ethical Theory*, ed. K. Pahel and M. Schiller (Prentice Hall).

—— (1979), *A Theory of the Good and the Right* (Oxford U.P.).

—— (1982), 'Two Concepts of Utility', in *The Limits of Utilitarianism*, ed. H. B. Miller and W. H. Williams (U. of Minnesota P.).

CARLYLE, T. (1892), Letter to Froude, *Longman's Magazine*, quoted in *General Theory of Value*, by R. B. Perry (Harvard U.P., 1954).

DAVIDSON, D. (1986), 'Judging Interpersonal Interests', in *The Foundations of Social Choice Theory*, ed. J. Elster and A. Hyllard (Cambridge U.P.).

DEVLIN, Lord (1959), 'The Enforcement of Morals', *British Academy* 45.

DWORKIN, R. M. (1977), *Taking Rights Seriously* (Harvard U.P.).

FOOT, P. (1958), 'Moral Beliefs', *Aristotelian Society* 59. Repr. in Foot (1967).

—— ed. (1967), *Theories of Ethics* (Oxford U.P.).

GEACH, P. T. (1956), 'Good and Evil', *Analysis* 17. Repr. in Foot (1967).
—— (1977), *The Virtues* (Cambridge U.P.).
GEWIRTH, A. (1978), *Reason and Morality* (U. of Chicago P.).
GRIFFIN, J. (1982), 'Modern Utilitarianism', *Review Internationale de Philosophie* 141.
—— (1986), *Well-being* (Oxford U.P.).
HALLETT, G. (1977), *Companion to Wittgenstein's Philosophical Investigations* (Cornell U.P.).
HAMPSHIRE, Sir Stuart (1971), 'Ethics: A Defence of Aristotle', in his *Freedom of Mind and Other Essays* (Princeton U.P.).
—— (1978), 'Morality and Pessimism', in his *Public and Private Morality* (Cambridge U.P.).
HARE, J. E. (1984), 'Philosophy in the Legislative Process', *Int. J. of Applied Ph.* 2.
HARSANYI, J. C. (1976), *Essays on Ethics, Social Behavior, and Scientific Explanation* (Reidel).
—— (1977), *Rational Behavior and Bargaining Equilibrium in Games and Social Situations* (Cambridge U.P.).
—— (1983), 'Basic Moral Decisions and Alternative Concepts of Rationality', *Soc. Th. and Prac.* 9.
HART, H. L. A. (1968), 'Prolegomenon to the Principles of Punishment', in his *Punishment and Responsibility* (Oxford U.P.).
—— (1983), 'Between Utility and Rights', in his *Essays in Jurisprudence and Philosophy* (Oxford U.P.).
HUDSON, W. D., ed. (1969), *The Is-Ought Question* (London, Macmillan).
—— (1974), *New Studies in Ethics* (2 vols.; London, Macmillan).
HUDSON, W. D. (1977), 'Learning to be Rational', *Proc. of the Phil. of Ed. Soc. of Gr. Brit.* 11.
—— (1980) *A Century of Moral Philosophy* (Lutterworth).
—— (1983) *Modern Moral Philosophy*, 2nd edn. (St Martin's).
KANT, I. (1785), *Grundlegung zur Metaphysik der Sitten*, translated as *Foundations of the Metaphysics of Morals* by Lewis White Beck (Bobbs-Merrill, 1959).
—— (1963), *Lectures in Ethics*, translated by L. Infield (Harper & Row).
KRIPKE, S. (1980), *Naming and Necessity* (Harvard U.P.).
KUHN, T. S. (1965), 'Reflections on My Critics', in Lakatos and Musgrave (1970).
LAKATOS, I. and MUSGRAVE, A., ed. (1970), *Criticism and the Growth of Knowledge* (Cambridge U.P.).
LAYARD, P. R. G. and WALTERS, A. A. (1978), *Micro-economic Theory* (McGraw-Hill).

LEWIS, H. D., ed. (1976), *Contemporary British Philosophy* 4 (Allen and Unwin).

LONGFORD, E. (1969), *Wellington: The Years of the Sword* (Weidenfeld and Nicholson).

MACINTYRE, A. C. (1957), 'What Morality Is Not', *Philosophy* 32.

—— (1981), *After Virtue* (Duckworth and U. of Notre Dame P.).

MACKIE, J. L. (1977), *Ethics: Inventing Right and Wrong* (Penguin).

MILL, J. S. (1861), *Utilitarianism*, ed. O. Piest (Bobbs-Merrill, 1957).

MOORE, G. E. (1903), *Principia Ethica* (Cambridge U.P.).

NAGEL, T. (1974), 'What Is It Like To Be a Bat?', *Phil. Rev.* 83. Repr. in Nagel (1979).

—— (1979), *Mortal Questions* (Cambridge U.P.).

—— (1982), Review of *Moral Thinking*, by R. M. Hare, *London Rev. of Books*, 1/15.

NORMAN, R. (1971), *Reasons for Actions* (Blackwell).

NOZICK, R. (1974), *Anarchy, State and Utopia* (Basic Books).

PARFIT, D. (1984), *Reasons and Persons* (Oxford U.P.).

PHILLIPS, D. Z. and MOUNCE, H. O. (1965), 'On Morality's Having a Point', *Philosophy* 40. Repr. in Hudson (1969).

POPPER, Sir Karl (1959), *The Logic of Scientific Discovery* (Hutchinson).

—— (1965), 'Normal Science and Its Dangers', in Lakatos and Musgrave (1970).

PRICHARD, H. A. (1949), *Moral Obligation* (Oxford U.P.).

RAWLS, J. (1971), *A Theory of Justice* (Harvard U.P. and Oxford U.P.).

—— (1980), 'Kantian Constructivism in Moral Theory', *J. Phil.* 77.

—— (1982), 'Social Unity and Primary Goods', in Sen and Williams (1982).

RESCHER, N. (1975), *Unselfishness* (U. of Pittsburgh P.).

RICHARDS, D. A. J. (1971), *A Theory of Reasons for Action* (Oxford U.P.).

—— (1977), *The Moral Criticism of Law* (Dickenson-Wadsworth).

—— (1981), 'Rights and Autonomy', *Ethics* 92.

—— (1982), *Sex, Drugs, Death and the Law: An Essay on Human Rights and Overcriminalization* (Rawman & Littlefield).

—— (1986), *Toleration and the Constitution* (Oxford U.P.).

ROBINSON, H. M. (1982), 'Is Hare a Naturalist?', *Phil. Rev.* 91.

ROSS, Sir David (1930), *The Right and the Good* (Oxford U.P.).

—— (1939), *Foundations of Ethics* (Oxford U.P.).

SCANLON, T. M. (1975), 'Preference and Urgency', *J. Phil.* 72.

—— (1982), 'Contractualism and Utilitarianism', in Sen and Williams (1982).

SEARLE, J. (1964), 'How to Derive "Ought" from "Is" ', *Phil. Rev.* 73. Repr. in Hudson (1969).

—— (1969), *Speech Acts* (Cambridge U.P.).

SEN, A. K. (1973), *On Economic Inequality* (Oxford U.P.).

—— and WILLIAMS, B. A. O. (1982), *Utilitarianism and Beyond* (Cambridge U.P.).

SIDGWICK, H. (1874), *The Methods of Ethics* (refs. to 7th edn., 1907; London, Macmillan).

SINGER, M. (1961), *Generalization in Ethics* (Knopf).

SINGER, P. (1979), *Practical Ethics* (Cambridge U.P.).

—— (1981), *The Expanding Circle: Ethics and Sociobiology* (Farrar, Straus, and Giroux, and Oxford U.P.).

STEVENSON, C. L. (1944), *Ethics and Language* (Yale U.P.).

STRAWSON, Sir Peter (1959), *Individuals* (Methuen).

TAYLOR, C. (1982), 'The Diversity of Goods', in Sen and Williams (1982).

TAYLOR, C. C. W. (1965), Review of *Freedom and Reason*, by R. M. Hare, *Mind* 74.

VENDLER, Z. (1977), 'A Note to the Paralogisms', in *Contemporary Aspects of Philosophy*, ed. G. Ryle (Oriel).

—— (1984), *The Matter of Minds* (Oxford U.P.).

WARNOCK, G. J. (1967), *Contemporary Moral Philosophy* (London, Macmillan).

—— (1971*a*), Review of *Modern Moral Philosophy*, by W. D. Hudson, *Ph. Q.* 21.

—— (1971*b*), *The Object of Morality* (Methuen).

—— (1974), 'Contemporary Moral Philosophy', in 2nd vol. of Hudson (1974).

WEBSTER, N. (1919), *New International Dictionary of the English Language*, ed. W. T. Harris and F. S. Allen (Merriam).

WWILLIAMS, B. A. O. (1972), *Morality: an Introduction to Ethics* (Harper & Row and Cambridge U.P.).

—— (1973), in *Utilitarianism: For and Against*, by J. J. C. Smart and B. A. O. Williams (Cambridge U.P.).

—— (1985), *Ethics and the Limits of Philosophy* (Harvard U.P.).

WINCH, P. (1960), 'Nature and Convention', *Aristotelian Society* 60. Repr. in Winch (1972).

—— (1965), 'The Universalizability of Moral Judgments', *Monist* 49. Repr. in Winch (1972).

—— (1972), *Ethics and Action* (Routledge).

WITTGENSTEIN, L. (1958), *The Blue Book* (Blackwell).

—— (1974*a*), *Philosophical Grammar* (Blackwell).

—— (1974*b*), *Philosophical Investigations* (New York, Macmillan, and Blackwell).

INDEX

situational ethics 44
Socrates 81–2, 87–8, 147, 195, 235, 238
Stevenson, C. L. 9–10, 147, 150
Strawson, Sir Peter 284
style of response (in this volume) v, 200
subjective (-ism, -ity) 73–4, 83–4, 172–3, 237, 239, 256–7, 270–2
supererogatatory acts 162, 167–9
supervenience 211, 268
sympathy theorem 64–70

Taylor, C. 212
Taylor, C. C. W. 280–4
telos of man 17–18, 214–15
transcendental self 280–1, 286

universalizability 4, 11–15, 28, 31, 36, 39, 41, 44–8, 51, 57–72, 90, 102–12, 114–24, 136, 138–9, 147–59, 161, 171–82, 185, 202–4, 208–9, 211, 214, 217–20, 229–31, 233–4, 246, 248–52, 257–8, 261, 266–9, 271, 273, 275, 279, 287
  strong 60, 63–5, 67–72, 230, 233, 248
  weak 59, 60, 63–4, 230
Urmson, J. O. 7, 161–9, 267, 274–80
utilitarian (-ism) 3, 5, 12–13, 22, 27–8, 32–3, 40, 45, 51, 57, 63–4, 69–71, 74–5, 83, 89–99, 103–12, 114–19, 122–30, 137, 139–40, 143, 147–59, 169, 182, 186, 188, 190–2, 194, 199, 203, 208, 212, 219, 221, 224, 227, 231–5,

243–7, 250–1, 257–60, 264–5, 267–70, 287–8, 290
  act-utilitarianism 3, 5–6, 27–8, 30–2, 35–7, 39–41, 44, 46–55, 89–96, 139–41, 145, 217, 221, 224–7, 242–6
  Ideal utilitarianism 40
  rule-utilitarianism 3, 45, 48, 50–3, 55–6, 89–99, 129, 139–41, 226–7, 242–3, 245
  utility 73, 107, 228, 243–5, 247, 266–7
    acceptance 22, 50–2, 138–9, 226, 258–9, 266, 269, 289
    cardinal 98 n.
    marginal 37, 219, 232
    social 89–94, 96–8

Vendler, Z. 4–5, 171–83, 219, 256, 280–7, 290
verification theory of meaning 10
virtues 279–80

Walters, A. A. 87 n.
wants *see* preferences
Warnock Commission 165, 276
Warnock, G. J. 11, 15, 116, 120, 211, 256, 273
well-being 33, 36, 39, 73–5, 77, 79, 82–8, 111, 220
Wilde, O. 245
Williams, B. A. O. 6–7, 13, 21, 131, 185–96, 201, 208, 223, 248, 259, 261, 287–93
Winch, P. 12, 18
Wittgenstein, L. 4, 11, 19, 205
Wolff, J. 137 n.
World Agent model 186, 287